Nicholas Hammond

Fragmentary Voices

Memory and Education at Port-Royal

Biblio 17 – 152

gn𝕍 Gunter Narr Verlag Tübingen
2004

Bibliografische Information der Deutschen Bibliothek

Die Deutsche Bibliothek verzeichnet diese Publikation in der Deutschen
Nationalbibliografie; detaillierte bibliografische Daten sind im Internet über
<http://dnb.ddb.de> abrufbar.

Biblio 17

Suppléments aux *Papers on French Seventeenth Century Literature*
Directeur de la publication: Wolfgang Leiner
Secrétaire de rédaction: Nathalie Gerber
Romanisches Seminar – Wilhelmstraße 50 – D-72074 Tübingen

© 2004 · Gunter Narr Verlag Tübingen
P.O. Box 2567 · D-72015 Tübingen

Gedruckt auf chlorfrei gebleichtem und säurefreiem Werkdruckpapier.

Internet: http://www.narr.de · E-Mail: info@narr.de

ISSN 1434-6397
ISBN 3-8233-6055-8

BIBLIO 17

Collection fondée en 1981
Directeur Wolfgang Leiner

152 **BIBLIO 17**

Nicholas Hammond

Fragmentary Voices
Memory and Education at Port-Royal

I dedicate this book to the memory of my father,

Michael Hammond (1928-2003)

ACKNOWLEDGEMENTS

This book has been a long time coming, and I have many people and organizations to thank for their moral, intellectual, practical and financial help: Michael Hawcroft, Richard Parish, Emma Gilby, Joe Harris, Anne Chassagnol, Delphine Denis, Philippe Sellier, Gérard Ferreyrolles, David Wetsel, Patrick Dandrey, Pierre Force, James Helgeson, Stephen Bold, Peter Bayley, Judy Sproxton, Sarah Kay, Tarquin Ukarnis, Jeremy Robbins, John Leigh, Neil Kenny, Wolfgang Leiner, Alex Kudrin, Michael Moriarty, Henry Phillips, Amy Wygant, Terence Cave, Russell Goulbourne, Heather Jarman, Gonville and Caius College, Cambridge, the Department of French Studies, Cambridge, the Arts and Humanities Research Board, and the librarians at the Bibliothèque de la Société de Port-Royal.

CONTENTS

INTRODUCTION

This book is concerned with the conscious shaping of memory within the community known as Port-Royal and the contribution which its members thought that memory could make to the new ideas which they held of education. Increasingly marginalized by both political and religious authorities, this small society of nuns, together with its associated group of *solitaires* (men who had retreated from prestigious positions within the secular world and who now led lives of austere simplicity), was gradually dispersed, culminating, upon the order of Louis XIV, in the complete destruction of their community during the early years of the eighteenth century.

Port-Royal might be seen, within the wider history of seventeenth-century France, to operate only on the margins. Yet, in such an authoritarian age, the margins are precisely where we need to look in order to understand better the inner workings of a world where such communities were considered dangerous or subversive enough to merit demolition, for Port-Royal was no ordinary establishment. Quite apart from the many prominent theologians who dominated both religious and political controversies over the course of the century, such as the abbé de Saint-Cyran (Jean Du Vergier de Hauranne), Antoine Arnauld and Pierre Nicole, this community was also to a large extent responsible for producing two of the greatest writers of the age, Blaise Pascal and Jean Racine.

Although these writers have often been studied within the context of Port-Royal, it is my aim to consider them from the particular perspective of memory and education, a perspective which has not been fully explored and which may help us to view them, and the age as a whole, afresh. I hope to maintain a balance between texts which are well known and writings which have remained up until now on the periphery. Unpublished accounts and transcriptions of conversations never intended for publication will therefore rub shoulders with some of the great canonical texts of the seventeenth century. The fragmentary voices of my title highlight both the Port-Royal writers' awareness of the incomplete status of their works and the very important role played by conversation in their conception of education.

Although each section can be read in isolation, the effect of the succeeding chapters of this book is intended to be cumulative, for the findings of the first two chapters should contribute to the interpretation of memory and education in the works of Pascal and Racine just as the final two chapters might help to enrich our understanding of the earlier analysis of a community and educational establishment where memory was so important.

Both the impending and eventual destruction of Port-Royal resulted in a profusion of memoirs which were haunted by the need to remember this society, where the concept of memory, in its very fragility, attained a peculiar significance. This will be the subject of the first chapter, where not only the established memoirs of the period but also some previously obscure narratives will be considered. The chapter will end with a brief examination of ancient and seventeenth-century writings on memory which were both read by, and permeated the works of, figures associated with Port-Royal. Some recent theoretical studies of memory will be introduced also in this section.

Chapter 2 will be devoted to the theory and practice of education at the petites écoles of Port-Royal. Formed to a large extent in opposition to the Jesuit colleges, the Port-Royal schools developed their own approach to the role of memorization in the pedagogical process, a fact which is reflected not only in the theoretical writings of Coustel and Nicole and reports of daily life at the schools but also in the fascinating collection of conversations (known as the *Recueil de choses diverses*) which were held between many former Port-Royal teachers and pupils. The chapter will end with a consideration of the close correspondence between memory and prayer both at the schools and at Port-Royal more generally.

Pascal and his sister Jacqueline's interest in and input into education at Port-Royal have often been overlooked. By viewing Pascal from the perspective of memory and education in chapter 3, I shall be interpreting his most celebrated works, the *Lettres provinciales* and the *Pensées*, in a new light. In addition to these famous texts, some of his lesser known writings, such as his letters, the *Discours sur la condition des grands* and the *Entretien avec M. de Sacy*, will be examined. Pascal's reading of other writers (including St Augustine, Epictetus and Montaigne) will be shown to be significant. More than that, I will argue that memory provides a crucial key to interpreting Pascal and to understanding the fragmentation of the *Pensées*.

Although the ideas contained in Racine's theatre have often been compared to the Augustinian theories of Port-Royal, leading, in my view, to unsubstantiated and overly speculative readings, less has been written on the actual evidence provided by the notes made by Racine while he was a student at Port-Royal, some of which have never been published. In chapter 4, I shall examine these notes and a number of Racine's earlier plays from the particular perspective of memory and education, culminating in the two plays which both coincide with Racine's reconciliation with Port-Royal and were written expressly for a pedagogical purpose, *Esther* and *Athalie*. The chapter will end with a discussion of the one work (surprisingly neglected by many scholars) which Racine wrote on Port-Royal itself, the *Abrégé de l'histoire de Port-Royal*.

In the conclusion, I shall point briefly to some other seventeenth-century texts where memory and education play a role and I shall consider the ways in which memory and education encapsulate the experience of Port-Royal and the many texts associated with it.

Since I started research for this book, memory has become an increasingly fashionable subject, with a profusion of books on the topic appearing in recent years. As will be clear from both footnotes and books listed in the bibliography, I have made full use of many of these studies. However, it is my intention to consider theories of memory predominantly in conjunction with the practical concerns of pedagogy and not in splendid isolation. I hope that my discussion of memory and education will lead the reader not only to consider anew the many wonderful seventeenth-century texts discussed in this book but also to examine the excellent recent works on memory.[*]

---

[*] I shall follow the original spelling of seventeenth and eighteenth-century editions, except in those modern editions where the spelling has been modernized.

CHAPTER 1

FROM MEMOIRS TO MEMORY

I. History and Memoirs

The seventeenth century is an age invariably associated with the memoir. Not only around 1660 were memoirs particularly "à la mode", as Emmanuèle Lesne puts it,[1] but towards the end of the century and in the eighteenth century, there remained the compulsion to commemorate the events and the people of the previous era through both memoirs and histories.

At the very head of the State, the King was being memorialized by numerous historiographers and artists.[2] Even Louis XIV himself was writing his memoirs, ostensibly for the instruction of the Dauphin. Yet immediately the appearance of such an intimate memoir, from father to son, is shown to be misleading, for it was both never completed and largely written by others, such as Périgny, Colbert, Chapelain and Pellisson, thereby compromising both its intimate status and its position as a memoir rather than hagiography or history.[3]

This brief example, albeit at the highest level of temporal power in France, is symptomatic of many of the memoirs and histories of the age, for both genres not only are inherently ambiguous but also are complicated by each other. Memoirs have always been placed in direct opposition to History. Pierre Nora's declaration that "tous les Mémoires sont d'abord des

---

[1] Emmanuèle Lesne, *La Poétique des Mémoires (1650-1685)* (Paris: Champion, 1996), p. 15.

[2] See P. Burke, *The Fabrication of Louis XIV* (New Haven: Yale University Press, 1992).

[3] For an excellent analysis of the problematic status of Louis's *Mémoires*, see Kathryn Hoffmann, *Society of Pleasures: interdisciplinary readings in pleasure and power during the reign of Louis XIV* (New York: St Martin's Press, 1997), chapter 1. See also C.Jouhaud, *Les Pouvoirs de la Littérature: histoire d'un paradoxe* (Paris: Gallimard, 2000), pp. 152-161; L.Marin, *Le Portrait du Roi* (Paris: Minuit, 1981).

anti-histoires"[4] is not far removed from the seventeenth-century attitude. Certainly memoirs were deemed to be inferior to public histories, as borne out by the dictionary definitions. Whereas "le mémoire" in the singular is defined by both the Académie and Furetière dictionaries as "écrit pour instruire, pour faire ressouvenir de quelque chose", thus implicitly accentuating its personal status, "Mémoires" in the plural is defined by the Académie as "relation de faits, ou d'événements particuliers pour servir à l'Histoire" and by Furetière as "des livres d'historiens écrits par ceux qui ont eu part aux affaires ou qui en ont été témoins oculaires, ou qui contiennent leur vie ou leurs principales actions", thereby explicitly equating them with and even subordinating them to public history.[5] Dictionary definitions of "Histoire", on the other hand, would seem to exclude the idea of personal or even false histories, in that only public history, deemed to be true, is evoked. Richelet describes "Histoire" as "une narration continuée de choses vraies, grandes, et publiques, écrite avec esprit, avec éloquence et avec jugement pour l'instruction des particuliers et des Princes, et pour le bien de la société civile", while Furetière sees it as "cette narration véritable suivie et enchaînée de plusieurs événements mémorables qui sont arrivés en une ou plusieurs nations".

The questions surrounding the problematic status of both history and memoirs in the seventeenth century are ones which have been comprehensively researched, and it is clearly beyond the scope of this study to rehearse all the arguments. However, some of the major issues surrounding both, which will help to throw light on the particular example of Port-Royal, need brief elucidation.

The notion of what constitutes History in the seventeenth century has been dominated by a number of different aspects, such as the diversity of areas explored by historians of the time, the relationship between history and the novel, and the emergence of a more critical approach to the various

---

[4] P. Nora, 'Les Mémoires d'Etat', in *Les Lieux de Mémoire.II. La Nation* (Paris: Gallimard, 1986), p. 369.

[5] Jean Mesnard observes that "si le mémoire, au singulier, se définit par son sujet, il n'y a de mémoires, au pluriel, que de quelqu'un", in 'Les Mémoires comme genre', *Le Genre des Mémoires: essai de définition*, ed. M.Bertaud and F.-X. Cuche (Paris: Klincksieck, 1995), p. 364.

ideologies surrounding History.[6] Certainly there was no shortage of different Histories. As the abbé Goujet, himself an ecclesiastical historian and a historian of Port-Royal, writes in the eighteenth century,

> Dans le XVIIe siècle [...], l'étude de l'Histoire fut si commune que chaque nation, chaque province, et presque chaque église et chaque monastère, voulurent avoir un Historien particulier: et de là, que d'écrits en ce genre n'a-t-on pas faits! On formeroit aujourd'hui une bibliothèque très-nombreuse si on vouloit les recueillir tous, et la vie de plusieurs hommes ne suffiroit pas pour les lire.[7]

Perhaps the most fundamental opposition can be found between the essentially secular histories and the religious histories which proliferated at the time. To quote Bernard Chédozeau,

> Ce qui naît et s'impose en France entre les dernières années du concile de Trente et la fin du XVIIe siècle est une solide Histoire religieuse catholique, très nouvelle et de formes variées, dont les finalités universalistes, à fondements religieux, dans certains cas à visées sotériologiques et ecclésiocentriques, seront récusées en France par les machiavéliens, les libertins et les gallicans au cours d'un conflit majeur qui verra renaître et s'affirmer une Histoire de France rationaliste, nationaliste et laïque, mais se voulant elle aussi à valeurs universelles.[8]

The evident aim of many of the secular nationalist histories was to legitimize and bolster the power of the ruling monarch, often listing the rights of the king in contradistinction to the rights of the Pope. As a result, these works were largely encomiastic in character, carefully restricted by royal censors. Those historians who were deemed to have strayed from the official line were duly punished. In spite of, or perhaps even because of, the immense popular success of Mézeray's *Histoire de France* (which had

---

[6] For an eloquent synthesis of some of the major issues, see B. Chédozeau, 'Situation de l'Histoire en France au XVIIe Siècle', in *Chroniques de Port-Royal* 46 (1997), pp. 7-14. See also C. Jouhaud, *Les Pouvoirs de la littérature*, as well as the articles 'Historiens et historiographes', by B. Grosperrin, and 'Historiographie', by Ch.-O. Carbonell, in *Dictionnaire du Grand Siècle* (Paris: Fayard, 1990), ed. F. Bluche.

[7] Abbé Goujet, *Discours sur le renouvellement des études*, in C. Fleury, *Discours sur l'Histoire Ecclésiastique* (Paris: J-T. Hérissant, 1763), p. 503.

[8] B. Chédozeau, 'Les jésuites et l'histoire au XVIIe siècle', in *L'Histoire au XVIIe siècle*, *Littératures Classiques* 30 (1997), p. 9.

been reprinted six times by 1712 and appeared in an abridged version in 1667), its author was eventually disgraced for daring to criticize royal policies of taxation.[9] Moreover, in Lesne's words, "la liste impressionnante des historiographes royaux au dix-septième siècle est à l'image des difficultés que l'histoire rencontre pour trouver sa réalisation".[10] Many historians or commentators of history from the time, such as Mézeray, Sully, Le Moyne and Rapin,[11] testify to the difficulties of writing a successful history, perhaps no more cogently expressed than in Rapin's assertion that "on doit trembler quand on se mêle d'écrire l'Histoire où il est si difficile de réussir".[12] Claude Fleury, who wrote a number of works on History, distinguishes between two principal ways in which the historian of his time can write, the one consisting of long quotations from original passages, with commentary in between, and the other dominated by a continuous and elegant style. He deems both of these methods to be flawed. As far as the first method is concerned, Fleury writes that

> on se trompe si l'on prétend que cette méthode laisse au lecteur la liberté entière de juger. Le choix des faits et des passages dépend toujours de l'auteur: souvent il supprime ce qui est contraire à ses préjugés: et quant aux passages qu'il rapporte, souvent il les détourne ou les affoiblit par les réflexions et les dissertations que cette méthode attire nécessairement.[13]

The second method, on the other hand, can lead to fabrication of the truth: "quand l'auteur a l'esprit brillant et l'imagination fertile, il a peine à se contenir dans les bornes étroites de la vérité",[14] Fleury tells us.

---

[9] F. E. Mézeray, *Histoire de France depuis Pharamond jusqu'à maintenant* (Paris: Mathieu Guillemot, 1643). See F. E. Beasley, *Revising Memory: women's fiction and memoirs in seventeenth-century France* (New Brunswick and London: Rutgers University Press, 1990), pp. 13-15, for an account of Mézeray's disgrace.

[10] *La Poétique des Mémoires*, pp. 28-9.

[11] Sully, *Mémoires des sages et royales oeconomies d'estat domestiques, politiques et militaires d'Henri le Grand* (no place: imprimés au chateau, 1638); P. Le Moyne, *De l'Histoire* (Paris: Thomas Jolly, 1670); R. Rapin, *Instructions pour l'Histoire* (Paris: Sébastien Mabre-Cramoisy, 1677).

[12] *Avertissement, Instructions pour l'Histoire*.

[13] C. Fleury, *Discours sur l'Histoire Ecclésiastique* (Paris: J-T. Hérissant, 1763), p. 21.

[14] *Ibid.*, p. 21.

The basis of Fleury's anxiety in writing a history seems to lie in the control exerted by a historian of the present over events of the past. Indeed, historians, whether they acknowledge it or not, are just as concerned with writing in the present as writing of the past. They are caught between what Roland Barthes calls "le temps de l'énonciation et le temps de la matière énoncée".[15] As Michel de Certeau puts it, "l'histoire n'est pas une critique épistémologique. Elle reste un récit. Elle raconte son propre travail *et*, simultanément, le travail lisible dans un passé".[16]

Seventeenth-century religious histories, on the other hand, often used the Bible as their sole source for both chronology and geography, leading often to anachronisms and to the omission of lands (such as China) not mentioned by the Bible, lacunae which became increasingly apparent to critics of these histories during the century. [17] Even within the Catholic Church, there was a marked division between Jesuit histories (by figures like Petau, Labbe and Briet), where to a large extent the sacred and profane commingled, allowing greater room for human endeavour and freedom, and the more rigorist works of Augustinian historians (such as Arnauld d'Andilly, Antoine Le Maistre, Sacy, Lancelot, Du Fossé, Hermant and Tillemont), whose initial impetus was hagiographical and who attempted to subsume all history into a providentialist plan: "il s'agit de trouver dans l'histoire, et presque malgré l'histoire, des morceaux d'éternité", as Jean-Louis Quantin sees it.[18]

In a work like Bossuet's *Discours sur l'histoire universelle*, published in 1681, providentialist history and political expedient overlap in a particular way, in that it was written ostensibly for the education of the Dauphin. As a result, not only do "les princes y apparaissent comme les

---

[15] R. Barthes, 'Le discours de l'histoire', in *Le Bruissement de la Langue: Essais critiques IV* (Paris: Seuil, 1984), p. 164, originally published in *Information sur les sciences sociales*.

[16] M. de Certeau, *L'Ecriture de l'histoire* (Paris: Gallimard, 1975), p. 56.

[17] See Chédozeau, 'Situation de l'Histoire', pp. 8-9, 11-12, for an analysis of these aspects.

[18] J-L. Quantin, 'Port-Royal et l'histoire', in *L'Histoire au XVIIe siècle, Littératures Classiques* 30, p. 28. For a fuller analysis of the differences between Jesuit and Jansenist histories, see the articles by Chédozeau and Quantin, *art. cit.*, in *L'Histoire au XVIIe siècle*.

instruments de la volonté divine",[19] but its pedagogical purpose and
dedicatee change the way in which it functions as History. To quote
Barthes again,

> Dans le discours historique, les signes de destination sont
> communément absents: on en trouvera seulement lorsque l'Histoire se
> donne comme une leçon; c'est le cas de l'*Histoire universelle* de
> Bossuet, discours adressé nommément par le précepteur au prince, son
> élève; encore ce schéma n'est-il possible, d'une certaine manière, que
> dans la mesure où le discours de Bossuet est censé reproduire
> homologiquement le discours que Dieu lui-même tient aux hommes,
> sous forme précisément de l'Histoire qu'il leur donne: c'est parce que
> l'Histoire des hommes est l'Écriture de Dieu que Bossuet, médiateur
> de cette écriture, peut établir un rapport de destination entre le jeune
> prince et lui.[20]

We shall come across the teaching of history and its implications in the
next chapter and the influence of the *Histoire universelle* on Racine in
chapter 4.

The question of 'destination' raised by Barthes's analysis of history
is indeed an important one with respect to memoirs, for, unlike with
history, memoirs give the appearance of intimacy, despite the fact that they
are usually intended for publication and public consumption. As
Emmanuèle Lesne sees it, "leurs stratégies d'énonciation sont variées:
absence d'allocution, dissimulation de la destination, allocution strictement
préfacielle, autodestination feinte, superposition de destinataires anonymes
et de destinataires familiers. En aucun cas les Mémoires ne peuvent annuler
le destinataire".[21] The very fact that memoirs have no single fixed point of
address and that their subject matter, being more personal, cannot easily be
regulated gives them greater freedom than many official histories; but at
the same time they allow a greater diversity which becomes more difficult
to define.[22]

---

[19] Denis Lopez, 'Discours pour le prince: Bossuet et l'histoire', in *L'Histoire au XVIIe*
siècle, Littératures Classiques 30, p. 175.

[20] R. Barthes, 'Le discours de l'histoire', p. 167.

[21] E. Lesne, 'Les Mémoires et leurs destinataires', in *Le Genre des Mémoires, essai de*
définition, p. 43. See also Lesne, *La Poétique des Mémoires*, pp. 297-328.

[22] *Cf.* Lesne, 'Les Mémoires et leurs destinataires', p. 33. It is interesting to note at this
stage that Histories in turn began to be shaped differently during the seventeenth

I have chosen Port-Royal, and the extraordinary writers associated with it, as the principal subject of this book, because many of the paradoxes which we have met already in the writing of histories and memoirs are intensified by the particular situation in which the Port-Royal community found itself in the latter part of the seventeenth century, as demonstrated in the memoirs which they left of their lives there.

II. Memoirs at Port-Royal

In his own memoir, Louis XIV lists among his various achievements the following feat:

> Je m'appliquai à détruire le jansénisme, et à dissiper les communautés où se fomentait cet esprit de nouveauté.[23]

The choice of the words "esprit de nouveauté" unwittingly presages a renewal which the very act of destruction engendered, for when in 1709, on the king's orders, the abbey at Port-Royal des Champs was demolished, a "laboratoire de mémoires", as Pascale Mengotti-Thouvenin calls it,[24] was set up.

For this reason, it is fitting that the first half of this first chapter should be concerned in many ways with the post-history of Port-Royal and the second half with some aspects of its pre-history, for with the publication in the eighteenth century of the vast majority of memoirs relating to Port-Royal as it existed in the seventeenth century, an attempt was made to reconstruct and commemorate an edifice which had been dismantled. In other words, it is impossible not to consider the seventeenth-century Port-Royal from its later perspective, knowing as we do of its

---

century as a direct result of the influence of memoirs. See M.Fumaroli's remarkable piece, 'Les Mémoires au carrefour des genres en prose': "le caractère hybride des Mémoires révèle ainsi sa fécondité, non seulement en créant les conditions d'une manière neuve d'écrire l'Histoire, tout à fait différente de celle des Anciens, mais en favorisant la mutation des genres en prose", *La Diplomatie de l'esprit, de Montaigne à La Fontaine* (Paris: Hermann, 1998), pp. 200-1.

[23] Louis XIV, *Mémoires*, ed. J. Longnon (Paris: Tallandier, 1978), p. 75.

[24] P. Mengotti-Thouvenin, 'Port-Royal, laboratoire de mémoires', in *Port-Royal et les Mémoires, Chroniques de Port-Royal* 48 (1999), pp. 15-55. See also C.Maire, *De la Cause de Dieu à la cause de la nation: le jansénisme au XVIIIᵉ siècle* (Paris: Gallimard, 1998): "le jansénisme se met alors à vivre de sa propre mémoire", p. 474.

destruction and of the legacy left by its major figures.[25] Moreover, the fact
that two major writers associated in different ways with Port-Royal, Pascal
and Racine (the subject of chapters 3 and 4 respectively), have been
subsumed into a wider literary history inevitably will redefine the way in
which we read the entity that is Port-Royal. Terence Cave's comments
about collective memory seem pertinent here:

> Il est évident que le souvenir collectif – 'l'histoire' – comporte un
> résidu encore plus lacunaire des événements réellement vécus; à plus
> forte raison, donc, cette 'face d'ombre' dont parle Sartre, peut sembler
> impénétrable, irrécupérable quand on se donne la tâche de déchiffrer
> les traces d'un passé lointain.[26]

Whereas our reconstruction of that past can only be partial, it is nonetheless
worth acknowledging the fact that those living that history can never
foresee exactly the aftermath of their lives.

Yet, in many ways, the case of Port-Royal is unique, for those in
charge were all too well aware of the possible destruction of their
establishment and of the concurrent need to preserve the memory of their
work. Even before the persecution against Port-Royal began, one can find
strong evidence of their wish to commemorate their lives there. Catherine
Maire has written in her important work on Jansenism in the eighteenth
century of "cette inclination commémorative inhérente à la mystique
eucharistique de Port-Royal du 'saint sacrement'".[27] And indeed, in the
very Constitutions of the monastery, it is written that "cet ordre devoit
avoir pour objet de sa dévotion le Saint Sacrement comme un autre
mémorial vivant qu'il a plu à Jésus-Christ d'établir".[28] The persecution
which they then began to face took on deeper significance as a result of the
importance which they attached to eucharistic commemoration. As Maire
elaborates, "la persécution fonde la mémoire de Port-Royal, parce qu'elle

---

[25] Terence Cave's comments on Montaigne in his *Pré-histoires: textes troublés au seuil
de la modernité* (Geneva: Droz, 1999) can readily be applied to Port-Royal in this
context: "pour nous qui sommes sa postérité, et en partie sa création, Montaigne est la
personnification même d'une conscience en veilleuse prête à se livrer à l'histoire", p.
18.

[26] T. Cave, *Pré-histoires*, p. 19. His reference to Sartre comes from *L'Idiot de la famille*.

[27] Maire, pp. 473-4.

[28] *Les Constitutions du Monastere de Port-Royal du S. Sacrement* (Mons: aux dépens de
la Compagnie, 1665), p. 2.

permet à la potentialité héroïque présente dans sa mystique eucharistique de s'accomplir".[29]

The troubles faced by those attached to Port-Royal cannot be underestimated. For much of the latter half of the seventeenth century, they found themselves constantly threatened with extinction. To take just a few examples between 1660 and 1664, one of the most volatile periods, the Port-Royal schools (which will be the subject of the next chapter) were definitively closed in 1660; the postulants and novice nuns were expelled from Port-Royal in 1661, followed soon afterwards by the spiritual directors; and after an uneasy period when many nuns were coerced to sign the *formulaire*, a document which effectively refuted the very basis of their order,[30] in 1664 the Mothers and various other nuns were removed. As a result, from as early as 1650 the almost neurotic compulsion to gather together all material which had a bearing on the History of Port-Royal (as we shall see, almost all memoirs were accompanied by the phrase "pour servir à l'Histoire de Port-Royal") indicates not only the desire to maintain the memory of their community but also a strong awareness of its possible destruction.[31]

On another level, this destruction, or fragmentation, of the Port-Royal community is in many ways mirrored in the diverse documents which were kept in the hope that all fragments might one day be formed into a full and complete History. As Francis Mariner puts it, "en absence d'une Histoire définitive et autorisée, il y aura forcément des histoires, reflets caractéristiques des différentes époques et des différentes optiques de ses lecteurs".[32] As we shall see, both in the way that eighteenth-century editors truncated the memoirs of figures like Fontaine and Du Fossé, in so doing trying to make them more cohesive, and in the attempt by the Port-

---

[29] Maire, p. 476. Maire quotes also from a letter written by Lancelot to Sacy on 1st January 1665 in which he prophesies that "la ruine de Port-Royal est sa gloire", p. 476.

[30] The nuns had to sign the *formulaire* which declared adherence to the Bull *Cum Occasione* (1653) by Pope Innocent X, which condemned five propositions allegedly drawn from Jansenius's *Augustinus*, four as heretical, one as false.

[31] See also Maire, p. 183, for a discussion of the way in which Port-Royal became emblematic of a wider political battle in the eighteenth century.

[32] F. Mariner, *Histoires et autobiographies spirituelles: les Mémoires de Fontaine, Lancelot et Du Fossé* (Tübingen: Biblio 17, 1998), p. 12.

Royal editors to make a work like Pascal's *Pensées* more complete, we find a continual tension between the desire for completion and a fragmentariness which is inherent to Port-Royal itself.

a) Early historiographical projects

The first historiographical material was gathered between 1630 and 1640, mostly in order to record the reforms made to the Abbey in 1609 by its young abbess Angélique Arnauld in her *Relation* (1638).[33] The existence of the *Relation* depended also on a paradox not dissimilar to the destruction/rebuilding paradox described above. Louis Marin, in a brilliant discussion of Angélique Arnauld, calls the presence of this historiographical piece a "double justification", the first coming from the tradition of the Church, and the second emanating from the fact that "la demande de récit dont est traversée la communauté [of Port-Royal] à l'égard de sa fondatrice ne se formule et n'a le droit de se formuler que dans la présence de la mort de la Mère dont elles désirent le récit; présence de la mort qui […] n'est pas le pur et simple *hic et nunc* de l'événement de la mort, mais son imminence, son extrême proximité".[34]

However, the first systematic attempt to document material for the purpose of constructing a History of Port-Royal began in 1651-2 with the work of Angélique Arnauld's nephew, Antoine le Maistre, and his cousin, Angélique de Saint-Jean Arnauld d'Andilly. All their documents, and a number of subsequent accounts, were eventually published in 1742 in three volumes known as the *Mémoires d'Utrecht* (after their place of publication).[35] While Le Maistre wrote down the conversations which he held with his aunt between 1651 and 1654, Angélique de Saint-Jean gathered the testimony, both oral and written, of many of the nuns, the most valuable written evidence coming, according to Angélique, from her aunt Anne-Eugénie de l'Incarnation Arnauld, who "étoit extrêmement

---

[33] For a detailed analysis of the different memoirs relating to Port-Royal, see J. Lesaulnier, 'Les manuscrits port-royalistes et jansénistes', in *XVIIe Siècle* 192 (1996), pp. 461-476, and P. Mengotti-Thouvenin, 'Port-Royal, laboratoire de mémoires'.

[34] Louis Marin, *Pascal et Port-Royal* (Paris: PUF, 1997), p. 394.

[35] The full published title is *Mémoires pour servir à l'Histoire de Port-Royal, et à la vie de la Reverende Mere Marie Angelique de Sainte Magdeleine Arnauld Reformatrice de ce Monastere* (Utrecht: Aux dépens de la Compagnie, 1742) 3 volumes. I shall refer to it as the *Mémoires d'Utrecht*.

exacte, et l'on se pouvoit absolument fier à sa sincerité et à sa memoire".[36]
It is significant too that the 1650s were the years that the project to commit
the collective memory of Port-Royal to writing took shape, for it was
precisely at this time that the two writers who will be discussed in chapters
3 and 4 were first becoming acquainted with Port-Royal: the young Jean
Racine was a pupil at the Port-Royal petites écoles, and Pascal's links with
the community were being cemented, both by the entry of his younger
sister Jacqueline into Port-Royal as a nun in 1651 and by what is known as
his second conversion in 1654, when he submitted himself to his spiritual
director Singlin and paid a number of visits to Port-Royal des Champs.

In the *avertissement* to the *Mémoires d'Utrecht*, the editors claim
that their purpose in publishing the collection was "pour conserver à la
posterité la memoire des grands exemples de vertu qui ont paru dans cette
Maison" (pp. i-ii) and that the nuns themselves "n'ecrivoient point pour le
public, mais uniquement afin de conserver entre elles la memoire du bien
que Dieu avoit fait dans leur Monastere" (pp. iii-iv). However, the text
itself and the chronology of progress made on the memoirs indicate that the
nuns intended their work to be neither simply for themselves nor, despite
the hagiographical tone of most of the texts, a record of virtue alone, as can
be seen in the account of what happened after the deaths of Le Maître and
Angélique de Saint-Jean:

> Après la mort de M. de Maître, (arrivée en 1658.) tous nos desseins et
> nos esperances pour cette Histoire étant ensevelis avec lui, nous ne
> fîmes presque plus rien. Mais aussi-tôt après la mort de la Mere
> Angelique, (qui arriva en 1661.) le tems étant venu, où l'Ecriture
> permet de louer les Saints, et toutes les Sœurs desirant qu'on ne laissât
> pas effacer une memoire aussi precieuse que le doit être dans cette
> Maison celle d'une personne qui a été l'organe de toutes les graces
> que Dieu lui a faites, et de tout le bien spirituel et temporel qu'il y a
> mis, la Mere Agnès (sa sœur) ordonna que toutes les Sœurs écrivissent
> chacune à part ce qu'elles auroient pu savoir de particulier, afin que
> cela servît de Memoires lorsqu'il plairoit à Dieu de donner à
> quelqu'un la pensée d'en composer une Histoire toute entiere, et c'est
> ce qui fut fait; et l'on a conservé toutes ces Relations. (p. 5)

Given the fact of the upheavals at Port-Royal in the early 1660s and the
evidence here that they were writing their memoirs for "quelqu'un" (clearly
not someone of their own present membership) who would eventually

---

[36] *Mémoires d'Utrecht*, vol. 1, p. 3.

construct a complete History, the need to record their lives takes on an added urgency not acknowledged in the *avertissement*.

There are many individual examples of nuns' testimonies which often shift from a position of self-abasement and recognition of their value to the larger historiographical project. One of the most eloquent examples of this in the *Mémoires d'Utrecht* comes from the pen of Jacqueline Pascal. In a letter dated 10 June 1653 and addressed to Mère Angélique, she claims that her purpose in writing such a document is

> de vous en laisser un petit memorial, qui conserve à la faveur du silence et du secret que nous garderons entre nous, la memoire de ce qui s'est passé, laquelle nous serions autrement contraintes de laisser perir; et ce sera le monument de ma reconnoissance, et le fidele temoin du souvenir qui me reste de la grace que j'ai reçue, puisque je ne puis rien de plus.[37]

In this passage, on the one hand, she hints at the private nature of her testimony, a comment which is supported by her closing remark that she hopes to "conserver la memoire des obligations que j'ai à nos Meres, et les instructions si profitables que j'ai reçues en cette rencontre";[38] this combination of memory and instruction is one which, as we shall see in the course of this book, was very important at Port-Royal. On the other hand, the fact that she sees her contribution as a "monument" implies something more lasting and even public. This assertion is borne out by the comparison which she makes of her letter to a "relique" which will form part of a larger whole:

> C'est particulierement pour conserver le peu qui m'en est resté, que je vous le mets en main par cette Lettre, comme une relique qui ne laisse pas d'être bien precieuse, quoiqu'elle ne soit qu'une petite parcelle d'un grand tout.[39]

Even the most humble of nuns was aware of the wider significance of their efforts to memorialize Port-Royal.[40]

---

[37] *Ibid.*, vol. 3, p. 55.

[38] *Ibid.*, p. 94.

[39] *Ibid.*, p. 69.

[40] The various fragments of Port-Royal's history which proliferated at the time were knowingly viewed as parts of an eventual reconstructed whole, as can be seen also in

b) The *Journal de l'Abbaye de Port-Royal*: the case of the dying nun

The next stage in the historiographical process involved a more systematic record of the nuns' and confessors' daily lives, with a journal being kept of visits to the abbey and other notable events. Yet, the *Journal de l'Abbaye de Port-Royal*, various manuscript copies of which exist in different libraries,[41] is not a cosy collection of fond memories. On the contrary, with the airing of various fragmentary voices, the entries bear witness to a community in imminent danger of disintegrating. Detailed reports are given, often by the nuns involved, of their interrogation by various authorities who attempted to make the nuns sign the *formulaire*, in so doing effectively declaring Jansenius, Saint-Cyran and all who adhered to their beliefs to be heretical.[42] In the journal from 1661, for example,[43] all the nuns at Port-Royal and Port-Royal des Champs, including Agnès de Sainte Thècle Racine, Jean Racine's aunt, who would later become abbess, and Jacqueline Pascal, at that time mistress of the novices, record their interviews.

I have chosen to focus on an extract from the journal of 1664, for not only does it encapsulate the perilous situation in which the nuns found themselves but also it vividly rehearses some of the major problematics associated with writing their History. The extract consists of the closing moments of an interview, held on February 12 of that year, between an interrogator M. de Longval and a dying nun, whom he has been trying to persuade to sign the *formulaire*:

> M. de Longval: Pourquoi ne suivez-vous pas le plus grand nombre. Vous avez l'exemple de tant de personnes vertueuses et de toutes les

---

the *avertissement* to what is known as the *Recueil d'Utrecht* (as opposed to the *Mémoires d'Utrecht*): "Si le public agrée ce petit Recueil, on pourra le continuer, et en donner une suite. Par ce moyen on conservera à la posterité dans un certain ordre plusieurs Pieces fugitives dont une main habile pourra dans la suite faire usage, en composant une Histoire générale de Port-Royal", *Recueil de plusieurs pieces pour servir à l'histoire de Port-Royal* (Utrecht: aux dépens de la Compagnie, 1740).

[41] See Lesaulnier, 'Les manuscrits port-royalistes et jansénistes', pp. 467-8.

[42] The wording of the *formulaire* included the following proposition: "je condamne, de cœur et de bouche, la doctrine des cinq propositions de Cornelius Jansénius, contenues dans son livre *Augustinus*".

[43] Manuscript P. R. 37, Bibliothèque de la Société de Port-Royal.

communautez qui ont signé. Cela vous devroit crever les yeux et vous
porter à obeir sans discernement à ce qu'on vous demande. Vous
voyez un grand Roy qui le veut. Toute l'Eglise qui le fait. Les
Evesques qui l'ont ordonné partout. Vous devez cela à tout le monde.
La Malade: Je ne dois rien à personne au prejudice de ce que je dois à
Dieu.
M. de Longval: Hé bien puisque vous étes absolument determinée à ne
rien faire et que vous voulez demeurer dans votre desobeissance, je
vous declare de la part de Dieu, et comme vous tenant sa place que
vous n'étes pas en état de salut. Il vous donne aujourdhuy par mon
entremise un moyen d'y rentrer et vous le refusez. Vous verrez après
votre mort, mais il ne sera plus tems d'y remedier, qu'il vous aura
offert aujourdhuy ses plus grandes graces, qui sont la reconciliation et
la reception des SS et que vous les aurez meprisées, en aimant mieux
demeurer dans votre endurcissement, c'est pourquoi il n'y aura plus
de salut pour vous. Je vous le dis encore un coup de la part de Dieu.
<u>Vous serez damnée comme tous les diables</u>.[44] Je vous cite au
jugement de Dieu où je seray votre juge, et je vous y condamneray.[45]

The text is dominated by competing rhetorics: on the one hand, M. de
Longval progressively uses more threatening (and masculine) means to
terrify the dying nun into submission, investing his argument first with
royal power ("un grand Roy"), then with the might of the Church ("Toute
l'Eglise" and "les Evesques"), followed by a sequence of clauses which
stress his priestly role as God's spokesman ("comme vous tenant sa place",
"par mon entremise", "de la part de Dieu"), before assuming quasi-divine
authority himself in the final sentence (with "je" repeated three times); on
the other hand, the rhetoric of Port-Royal itself plays a part, for the direct
quotation of Longval's words (however truthful that transcription may be)
allows him in effect to condemn himself through his own mouth (a
technique which was used so effectively only a few years earlier by Pascal
in his *Lettres provinciales*). Moreover, the role which hagiography plays in
many of the memoirs from the same time must allow for a plotting of
narrative, in the same way that the term "Relation" is often used to describe
accounts of people or events.[46] Yet overall, the very fact that Longval is

---

[44] This sentence is underlined in the manuscript.

[45] *Le Journal de l'Abbaye de Port-Royal*, manuscript P. R. 64, Bibliothèque de la Société
de Port-Royal.

[46] See, for example, in the *Mémoires d'Utrecht, Relation de l'origine et de la querelle du
chapelet secret du Très Saint Sacrement*, vol. 1, p. 456, *Recueil de relations ou
mémoires de la sœur Anne-Eugénie Arnauld*, vol. 3, pp. 360-1.

able to call upon such an array of powerful examples to support his argument only serves to accentuate the vulnerability, isolation and ultimate courage of the dying nun.

In many ways, this tale is emblematic of the situation of Port-Royal as a whole, a community aware of its possibly imminent death and denied absolution by the Church authorities and finally the King himself. Moreover, the written account mirrors the difficulties which they faced in writing their History, for we have not only a documented account of a conversation which took place between two participants in this History but also a harrowingly vivid memoir which goes beyond the realm of objective reporting.

In *L'Ecriture de l'histoire*, Certeau makes the distinction between two problematic tendencies in historiographical research: the first is exemplified by the use which the historian makes of a series of documents to elaborate various models relevant to "sa situation épistémologique présente dans l'ensemble des recherches caractéristiques de la société où il travaille";[47] the second focuses on the relationship between the historian and a lived life, effectively ressuscitating the past; in Certeau's words, this tendency "veut restaurer un oublié".[48] Using a number of examples from the seventeenth century, Certeau posits his historiographical method as more effective, because through it the interplay between life and death when writing any history can be acknowledged, privileging what he calls "un tiers absent". As he puts it,

> Le discours sur le passé a pour statut d'être le discours du mort. L'objet qui y circule n'est que l'absent, alors que son sens est d'être un langage entre le narrateur et ses lecteurs, c'est-à-dire entre des présents. La chose communiquée opère la communication d'un groupe avec lui-même par ce *renvoi à un tiers absent* qu'est son passé.[49]

Yet, in the case of the Port-Royal community, I would argue that their belief that they were in the process of constructing their own History through documents such as the tale of the dying nun blurs the boundaries between life and death, making the *tiers absent* more present than absent.

---

[47] M. de Certeau, *L'Ecriture de l'histoire*, p. 47.

[48] *Ibid.*, p. 47.

[49] *Ibid.*, p. 60.

To a large extent, for us as later readers and even for those eighteenth-century readers who would have read the first printed Port-Royal Memoirs, Certeau's model is relevant, but when, like the nun, a community is knowingly dying and seeking some kind of absolution, the text of their History becomes all the more an attempt to defy or even to transcend that impending death. Certeau's later words unwittingly take on added intensity when applied to the Port-Royal historiographical effort:

> Le discours ne cesse de s'articuler sur la mort qu'il postule mais que la pratique historique contredit. Car parler des morts, c'est également dénier la mort et quasi la défier.[50]

The constant reference by all participants in the project to their contribution to an eventual larger History in effect amounts to a rebuilding process embarked upon before the original building has been demolished.

c) Port-Royal *Mémoires*: of memory and conversation

The next significant phase in the Port-Royal historiographical project came with the composition of numerous memoirs by men associated with Port-Royal. Although all these memoirs were first published in the eighteenth century (with the exception of the Pontis *Mémoires* which first appeared in print in 1676), they were all written in the seventeenth and were circulated amongst Port-Royal groups. In order of composition, we have Pontis's *Mémoires*, as recounted to Du Fossé (1657), followed by the *Mémoires* of Robert Arnauld d'Andilly (1666-7), Lancelot's *Mémoires touchant la vie de M. de Saint-Cyran* (1663-71), and then the *Mémoires* of abbé Antoine Arnauld (1677) and of Godefroy Hermant (1670-8), Hamon's *Relation de plusieurs circonstances de la vie de M. Hamon* (c. 1680), followed by the various *Mémoires* of Brienne le jeune (1683-4), Fontaine (1696-1700) and Du Fossé (1697-8). In addition to these, Racine's *Abrégé de l'Histoire de Port-Royal* was composed about 1697, and the abbé Goujet's *Mémoires pour servir à l'histoire de Port-Royal*, which consist almost entirely of documents by other seventeenth-century Port-Royal figures, were assembled around 1730.[51]

---

[50] *Ibid.*, p. 61.

[51] See E. Lesne's introduction to *Port-Royal et les Mémoires*, p. 10, for a useful list of the major works.

The fact that, of the various memoirs mentioned above, those by Lancelot, Hermant, Fontaine, Du Fossé, Racine and Goujet all contain in their titles references to "l'histoire de Port-Royal" indicates the historiographical impetus which the later editors wished to give to these works. Even those memoir-writers who do not explicitly allude to Port-Royal in their titles, while disavowing their own personal role as historians, are nonetheless clear in their reiteration of the need for a history of Port-Royal. Robert Arnauld d'Andilly, for example, writing in the charged years of 1666-7, cannot avoid attacking the Jesuits and anticipating the future history of a place to which he had retired:

> Etant arrivé dans cette sainte solitude que j'avois choisie pour ma retraite, j'y ai passé près de vingt années, et le repos dont j'y joüissois étoit trop grand, pour durer toûjours. Mais le fantôme du Jansenisme, à qui rien n'est impénetrable, qui court toutes les Provinces, qui passe et repasse si souvent les Alpes, et qui ne se lasse point de troubler l'Eglise, ne manqua pas de le traverser. Ce n'est pas ici le lieu de rapporter en particulier tous les maux qu'il a causés. De plus habiles que moi ont commencé, et pourront continuer à en écrire l'histoire: mais plus elle est véritable, plus la posterité aura de peine à la croire; tant il est difficile de se persuader que les J.*** ayent pû par leurs cabales et leur artifices faire joüer tant de ressorts, et élever de si grandes machines sur un fondement imaginaire.[52]

Similarly, Arnauld d'Andilly's son, abbé Antoine Arnauld, writes in his memoirs about Port-Royal, stressing that "cette histoire est trop importante et a trop fait de bruit, pour douter qu'elle ne soit écrite quelque jour par quelque plume exacte et éloquente, digne de la transmettre à la postérité",[53] before adding hastily, "mais j'oublie que je n'écris que des Mémoires".[54]

Abbé Arnauld's seeming forgetfulness of the purpose of his work is symptomatic of an uncertainty which is constantly expressed by the Port-Royal memorialists about the status of the self within the text. The Augustinian inspiration of all these memoirs means that a certain amount of

---

[52] R. Arnauld d'Andilly, *Memoires de Messire Robert Arnauld d'Andilly écrits par lui-même* (Hamburg: Van den Hoeck, 1734), Part II, pp. 134-5.

[53] A. Arnauld, abbé de Chaumes, *Mémoires de M. l'Abbé Arnauld, contenant quelques qnecdotes de la Cour de France depuis MDCXXXIV jusqu'à MDCLXXV* (Amsterdam: Jean Néaulme, 1756), pp. 100.

[54] *Ibid.*, p. 102.

introspection is to be expected. Indeed, St Augustine's *Confessions*, which (as I shall discuss in this and subsequent chapters) was a seminal text at Port-Royal, is the starting point for many of the memoirs.[55] Not only did Robert Arnauld d'Andilly produce a very influential translation of the *Confessions*, but also Jean Hamon's memoir explicitly states in its title that it is "sur le modele des Confessions de S. Augustin". Yet, by talking about oneself, the anxiety exists that the self and its worldly concerns might receive attention to the detriment of more spiritual preoccupations. For this reason, we find in the memoirs the uneasy coexistence of rhetorics of self-promotion (which is an inevitable part of autobiographical writing) and self-negation. Moreover, the very fact that one might be seeking the publication of one's memoirs can lead to the accusation of self-aggrandisement, so a number of strategies are employed to neutralize this criticism. Robert Arnauld d'Andilly, for example, claims repeatedly that he is writing only for his children and grand-children, "pour les exciter à la vertu par des exemples domestiques, et leur inspirer le mépris de ces faux biens dont la plupart des hommes sont si idolâtres".[56] The abbé Arnauld writes of his memoirs that "je n'ai point l'intention de les rendre publics",[57] adding that "ce ne sont que des Mémoires de certaines circonstances de ma vie, ou de choses qui ont fait une assez forte impression dans mon esprit, pour m'en pouvoir ressouvenir".[58]

All these concerns are perhaps best encapsulated in the only Port-Royal-related memoir to appear in the seventeenth century, which itself was widely imitated by other memoir-writers: *Memoires du Sieur Pontis*.[59]

---

[55] For a more sustained analysis of the role which the *Confessions* played in the writings of Port-Royal memoir writers, see P. Courcelle, *Les Confessions de saint Augustin dans la tradition littéraire: antécédents et postérité* (Paris: Etudes Augustiniennes, 1963), chapters 7 and 8. See also F. Mariner, *Histoires et autobiographies spirituelles: les Mémoires de Fontaine, Lancelot et Du Fossé*, pp. 97-105.

[56] R. Arnauld d'Andilly, *Memoires*, Part I, pp. 1-2. *Cf.* Part I, pp. 155-6 and Part II, pp. 154-5.

[57] Abbé Arnauld, *Mémoires*, p. vi.

[58] *Ibid.*, pp. vii-viii.

[59] See, for example, the *avertissement* to abbé Arnauld's *Mémoires*, in which he writes of Pontis, "j'avouerai ingénûment qu'ayant lu ses Mémoires avec plaisir, j'en ai conçu la pensée de faire ceux-ci", p. v. Marc Fumaroli observes that these memoirs "marquent exactement le point de fusion entre les Mémoires aristocratiques du seizième et du dix-septième siècle commençant et l'autobiographie d'inspiration augustinienne

Pontis had led a distinguished military career before retiring to Port-Royal in 1653 (when he was aged around 75). Pierre Thomas Du Fossé, who would later compose his own memoirs, wrote the work, based on conversations which he had with Pontis in 1657 and 1658, when Du Fossé was still a young man, and not long finished in his studies at the Port-Royal schools. The work was first published in 1676. As a talented pupil who in many ways was primed by the Port-Royal schools to write future lives of saints and histories, actively encouraged by his teacher Sacy, Du Fossé's work can be viewed in some respects as a pedagogical exercise, especially when, as we shall see in the next chapter, conversation was so important to education at Port-Royal.[60] In a paragraph which Pierre Nicole added to the *avertissement* in the 1678 edition, it is stressed not only that the memoirs emanated directly from conversation ("il se contentoit de s'entretenir avec son ami, sans s'informer s'il écrivoit en son particulier quelque chose de ce qu'il lui avoit dit") but also that Pontis "n'a eu aucune part dans la publication de ces Memoires, et [...] on ne peut l'accuser en cela d'aucune ostentation".[61] Facing the problem of who is to assume the narrative voice, Du Fossé finds himself torn between his role as a historian and the more intimate and story-like realm of the memoir-writer. As Nicole writes:

> Il croit aussi devoir avertir, que les ayant d'abord composez d'une autre maniere qu'ils ne sont, c'est-à-dire, n'y faisant point parler Monsieur de Pontis, mais parlant de lui, et rapportant comme un Historien tous les évenemens qui y sont, il trouva que la repetition trop frequente du Sieur de Pontis, qu'il falloit nommer une infinité de fois, rompoit toute la suite de l'histoire. Il jugea d'ailleurs qu'elle auroit tout un autre poids étant dans la bouche même de celui qu'elle regardoit et qui en faisoit le principal sujet. Ainsi il n'eut pas beaucoup de peine à se résoudre de changer cette premiere maniere

---

cultivée à Port-Royal", in *La Diplomatie de l'esprit*, p. 206. For a somewhat perfunctory discussion of Pontis's *Mémoires*, see A.Villard, 'Les *Mémoires du Sieur de Pontis* (1676) au plus près de la parole', in *Port-Royal et les Mémoires*, pp. 57-77. For a more sustained analysis, see E. Lesne, *La Poétique des Mémoires*.

[60] See F. Mariner, *Histoires et autobiographies spirituelles*, pp. 49-50.

[61] P. T. Du Fossé, *Memoires du Sieur Pontis, qui a servi dans les Armées cinquante-six ans, sous les Rois Henry IV, Louis XIII et Louis XIV* (Paris: Compagnie des Libraires Associez, 1715, first published 1676 and 1678), 2 volumes, *avertissement*. Conversation with a friend also acts as the cipher for Pontis's conversion, recounted towards the end of the *Memoires*: "comme Dieu avoit déja parlé à mon cœur [...], il se servit de cet entretien pour me toucher encore davantage, et je me confirmai peu-à-peu dans la résolution de quitter tout-à-fait le monde", vol. 2, p. 528.

dont il l'avoit composée, et de faire parler le sieur de Pontis lui-même au lieu de parler de lui. Mais comme d'abord on avoit toute liberté de loüer ce qui paroissoit de grand et de loüable dans sa conduite, quelque soin que l'on eût pris de retrancher ces éloges, il en étoit encore resté que l'on a ôtez en cette Edition, parce qu'on ne parle jamais avec trop de modestie de soy-même. Ce défaut ne doit donc nullement être attribué au Sieur de Pontis, comme étant infiniment opposé au caractere de son esprit, qui a été assez connu de tous ses amis.[62]

The combination of the movement from oral to written communication and the fact that the "je" of the central text is both the narrator and hero whereas the author and narrator are not the same person lend the narrative an instability which brings to the fore some of the major problems associated with the role of "je" in memoir-writing at Port-Royal. Each writer has to negotiate a role both for him/herself as the narrator of his/her own testimony or story and for the potential reader of the memoir.

Nicolas Fontaine, like Jean Hamon before him, tries to resolve the problem by situating himself firmly in an Augustinian context. Not only does he imitate the style of the *Confessions* by using the interrogative form frequently but also, like Augustine, the "je" of the text is addressed to the supreme reader, God. As Fontaine tells us, "je ne prétens point faire ici l'auteur", adding that "c'est pour moi uniquement que je travaille". [63] Yet, whereas for Augustine the *Confessions* act as the means for intense self-exploration, Fontaine devotes most of his writing to remembering others, fulfilling the function above all of a witness.[64] The first few pages would seem to contradict Fontaine's assertion that he is writing only for himself, for he recognizes the need for the memory of the remarkable people associated with Port-Royal to be preserved. Memory and the fear of forgetfulness are the all-important *points de départ* in the writing down of his *Mémoires*:

---

[62] *Ibid.* See E. Lesne, *La Poétique des Mémoires*, p. 350, and F. Mariner, *Histoires et autobiographies spirituelles*, pp. 52-60, for rich readings of this passage.

[63] Nicolas Fontaine, *Mémoires ou histoire des Solitaires de Port-Royal*, ed. P. Thouvenin (Paris: Honoré Champion, 2001), p. 234. All page references will be to this edition. *Cf.*p. 858: "Je vois bien que je m'étends beaucoup, mais c'est pour moi que j'écris ceci".

[64] *Cf.* Fumaroli, who states that "l'exercice de mémoire, ici comme chez Augustin, est devenu exercice spirituel", *La Diplomatie de l'esprit*, p. 206.

> La crainte que j'ai de tomber dans l'oubli des grâces que Dieu m'a
> faites, et dans l'ingratitude qui le suit ordinairement, me force de
> repasser dans ma mémoire ce que j'ai vu dans des personnes d'une
> éminente piété, avec lesquelles il m'a fait la grace de passer une bonne
> partie de ma vie. (p. 233)

The importance of safeguarding the memory of those attached to Port-
Royal implies future readers who themselves will be the recipients of that
memory. Fontaine associates the memory of his friends with conversing
with them:

> Il me semble que je parle avec eux et qu'ils s'entretiennent avec moi,
> que je les vois, que je contemple leur visage, que je m'occupe de leurs
> gestes, et que dans ce doux souvenir, ou je ne suis plus ici, mais où ils
> étaient, ou qu'ils sont ici avec moi. (p. 234)[65]

Like conversation, which is necessarily reciprocal, Fontaine hopes that the
act of remembering may be similarly reciprocal, as he states at a later stage
of the text: "je mets ma joie et ma gloire à me souvenir d'eux afin que je
devienne digne qu'ils se ressouviennent de moi" (p. 544).

Although Fontaine does not follow Augustine (who, as we shall see at
the end of this chapter, devotes Book X of the *Confessions* to a
consideration of the workings of memory) in explicitly searching for God
within the memory itself,[66] nonetheless memory assumes a primordial
importance in the text, for, in addressing his words to God, the act of
remembering (and conversing) becomes for Fontaine equivalent to an act
of confession: "Je prends plaisir, mon Dieu, à m'entretenir devant vous de
tout ce qui me vient dans la mémoire touchant votre Serviteur" (p. 253).
The phrase "je prends plaisir", associated with memory, is one which is
repeated during the course of the *Mémoires*, such as when he states, "je
prends plaisir de me souvenir de tout ce détail pour m'imprimer à moi-

---

[65] This idea of conversing with dead friends is a common topos, perhaps most famously
found in Montaigne's account of his friendship with La Boetie. See U.Langer, *Perfect
friendship: studies in literature and moral philosophy from Boccaccio to Corneille*
(Geneva: Droz, 1994).

[66] See Mariner, pp. 110-1 for an analysis of this. *Cf.* F. Charbonneau, 'Le théâtre
d'ombres de Nicolas Fontaine: augustinisme, platonisme, mémoire', in *Port-Royal et
les Mémoires*: "le texte de Fontaine ne formule jamais de façon théorique le lien entre
mémoire et recherche de Dieu, mais l'énonce indirectement, au travers des effusions",
p. 175.

même dans l'esprit combien il faut de conseils dans les affaires de Dieu pour n'y rien faire à la légère" (p. 245). In Francis Mariner's words, for Fontaine "l'écriture, l'acte ou le fait d'écrire provoque une extase, une absence de soi à soi qui facilite la tâche de remémoration".[67] Moreover, instead of musing on the deficiencies of memory, as Augustine does, Fontaine sees the writing process as a way of emptying a mind which is not lacking but rather is too full of memories, thereby avoiding future forgetfulness, whether by himself or by others: "Je ne travaille qu'au soulagement de ma mémoire, et pour éviter l'oubli, marquant fidèlement, mais succinctement les choses que j'ai vues" (p. 234). By moving from conversation to the written word, Fontaine is commemorating the lives of those at Port-Royal; the fact that he is careful to be both "fidèle" and "succinct" again suggests a readership beyond the eyes of God alone, readers who need to know the truth and whose attention needs to be held.[68]

It is interesting that truthfulness and brevity should be the two features accentuated by Fontaine, for his eighteenth-century editors were somewhat disconcerted not only by the lack both of chronology and at times of historical veracity but also by the digressive nature of the memoirs and a somewhat diffuse style.[69] As a result, they tried to make the work homogeneous by cutting and reordering it. Yet, as in the *Confessions*, where chronology is not strictly observed, Fontaine's digressive style could be more deliberate than it may at first seem. At regular intervals, he knowingly uses phrases like "je reviens", "je m'égare", "je m'étends", "je m'éloigne" and "j'anticipe". For a text in which the act of remembering is so important, it is not beyond the bounds of possibility that Fontaine is imitating the digressions of the memory within his written style. As he himself writes, "je ne sais où ma mémoire m'emporte mais je la suis avec plaisir" (p. 722). We shall see in chapter 3 how Pascal theorizes memory in relation to digression and fragmentation. Perhaps not surprisingly given the systematic fragmentation of Port-Royal itself, both the form and the subject matter of the writing of those attached to Port-Royal remain dominated by the notion of fragmentariness.

---

[67] F. Mariner, *Histoires et autobiographies spirituelles*, p. 113.

[68] In this respect, Catherine Maire's assertion in her otherwise excellent study that Fontaine and others "n'écrivaient pas pour être publiés", p. 483, would seem to miss the point.

[69] See Mariner, pp. 122-7, for a more detailed analysis of this.

By the end of Fontaine's memoir, his continuing attempt to preserve the memory of Port-Royal would seem to have succeeded, for the prevailing "je" of the text has been replaced by an inclusive "nous", and the threat of forgetfulness has been overcome:

> Etant d'ailleurs aussi solitaires que nous étions à Port-Royal et ne perdant pas beaucoup de ce côté-là, nous gagnons peut-être de l'autre en conservant en nous ce feu toujours nouveau pour un lieu qui ne s'efface point de notre mémoire, et que ni l'éloignement des lieux, non plus que la longueur du temps ne nous fera jamais oublier. Le souvenir de ce que nous y avons vu et des vertus dont nous y avons été témoins ne partira jamais de notre esprit. (p. 990)[70]

Hamon is the most explicit of all the Port-Royal memoir-writers in modeling his text on the *Confessions*, and yet rarely do his words amount to sustained self-exploration in the Augustinian mode. Instead, he tends to efface himself in describing the piety of the Port-Royal nuns. Nonetheless, albeit on a superficial level, memory again plays an important part. On the one hand, he mimics Augustine's description of his childhood with phrases punctuated by verbs associated with memory, like "je me souviens, qu'étant tout petit, j'avois un grand desir d'être aimé et estimé de mes Maîtres",[71] and "je me souviens qu'étant enfant je vis tomber une maison".[72] On the other, his memory of Port-Royal is directly associated by him with God: "je prens plaisir à me rappeler le souvenir de ces choses, parce qu'elles me portent à louer Dieu".[73]

Unlike both Fontaine and Hamon, Lancelot and Du Fossé attempt to sidestep the problematic "je" by casting themselves as historians, thereby both moving away from a specifically autobiographical mode and explicitly acknowledging future readers. Lancelot writes, for example, that "ce n'est pas à moi à me rendre juge entre de si grands hommes, la posterité en jugera mieux que personne. Je raconte les faits comme un historien qui doit

---

[70] *Ibid.*, vol. 2, pp. 581-2. I would argue, therefore, that the "je" plays a more complex role in the text than Fumaroli's statement that "le 'je' des Mémoires d'inspiration augustinienne n'affirme que son néant face à la plénitude divine", *La Diplomatie de l'esprit*, p. 209.

[71] J.Hamon, *Relation de plusieurs circonstances de la vie de Monsieur Hamon, faite par lui-meme sur le modèle des Confessions de S. Augustin* (no place or editor, 1734), p. 1.

[72] *Ibid.*, p. 3.

[73] *Ibid.*, p. 8.

être fidèle pour rendre honneur à la verité".[74] Similarly, Du Fossé (no doubt bearing in mind the problems which arose from his memoirs of Pontis) explains:

> Je puis protester que mon intention est très droite, que je n'ai dessein directement de choquer personne, et que si quelqu'un se trouve blessé contre mon intention, il ne doit l'imputer à d'autre qu'à lui, puisqu'un Historien n'est point responsable des fautes d'autrui, et qu'il ne peut être blâmé, lorsqu'il rapporte simplement les choses comme elles se sont passées, sans en alterer la verité.[75]

Whereas Lancelot is able to subsume his voice into that of his subject, Saint-Cyran, Du Fossé is aware of the possible accusation of self-aggrandisement in using the "je" so prominently. Yet, unlike his fellow memoir-writers, he does not attempt to diminish his role as author. In fact, the veracity of his observations is given further weight by the authority of his eye/I:

> je suplie ceux qui pourroient avoir de moi ces pensées de considerer que des Memoires n'ont de force qu'autant qu'ils sont appuyez par celuy qui les écrit; puisque celuy qui les écrit, et qui raporte ce qu'il a veû, n'a droit d'exiger la creance de ses lecteurs qu'autant qu'il se fait connoistre. [...] Desirant donc qu'on regarde ces memoires comme un temoignage que je rends à la verité et l'innocence, je me nomme exprès et je prétends y donner par là une autorité, sans laquelle on pourroit les rejeter.[76]

Significantly, the authority of his testimony is derived principally from his memory rather than that of others. He tells us that he first embarked on writing his memoirs because in a conversation with some friends, his sister-in-law had told "une histoire que je savois beaucoup mieux qu'elle, comme ayant été present à la chose",[77] which prompted him to write down the true story. It is clear that Du Fossé recognizes the value of a good memory. As

---

[74] C. Lancelot, *Memoires touchant la vie de Monsieur de S. Cyran pour servir d'éclaircissement à l'histoire de Port-Royal* (Cologne, 1738), 2 vols, vol. 1, p. 225.

[75] P. T. Du Fossé, *Memoires pour servir à l'histoire de Port-Royal* (Cologne, 1739), p. 6. I shall refer to both the eighteenth-century edition and Bouquet's nineteenth-century edition of Du Fossé's original manuscript.

[76] Du Fossé, *Memoires*, ed. F.Bouquet (Rouen: Ch.Métérie, 1876, Geneva: Slatkine Reprints, 1976), 4 volumes, IV, p. 268.

[77] Du Fossé, *Memoires* (1739), p. 4.

we shall see in the next chapter, his account of his experience as a pupil at the Port-Royal petites écoles gives precious indications of the way in which the children were taught. Whenever he admiringly remembers a teacher or old school friend, almost invariably he mentions the strength of their memory. M. de la Rivière, who retired to Port-Royal and who taught him Spanish, for example, "apprit par cœur tous les mots qui sont dans la Bible",[78] while M. de Villeneuve, the youngest son of Arnauld d'Andilly and his closest school friend, "avoit beaucoup de disposition pour les études, et sa memoire jointe à la penetration et à la vivacité naturelle de son esprit, le rendoit capable de soutenir avec éclat la gloire et la reputation de tous ceux de sa famille".[79] Now, in his old age, as with Fontaine, Du Fossé's memoirs form a substitute for the conversations which he had with his friends. Yet, for Du Fossé, this is literally the case, for at the time of writing, he has been beset by a paralysis of the tongue which has deprived him of the ability to speak. Instead, he tells us, God has given him "une faculté plus grande que jamais à écrire".[80]

By writing down his memories, Du Fossé hopes to bear witness to one of his teachers, Antoine Le Maître, who himself saw conversation on appropriate subjects as a way of remembering one's duty to God. As Du Fossé writes,

> Ç'a esté la dévotion particuliere d'un des plus grands hommes de ce siècle [Antoine Le Maître], avec lequel j'ay eu le bonheur de vivre longtems durant ma jeunesse, de se faire raconter par ceux qui venoient se retirer avec luy dans la solitude, la maniere dont Dieu les y avoit amenez. Et il sentoit un plaisir sans comparaison plus grand et plus solide, à entendre ces récits des avantures spirituelles qui regardoient la conversion des ames, que les gens du monde n'en goûtent dans la lecture sterile des plus beaux romans. Car il admiroit le doigt de Dieu dans ces ouvrages miraculeux de sa grace; et il se croyoit heureux de pouvoir se joindre à ses amis, pour luy offrir avec eux un sacrifice de reconnoissance, qui le faisoit souvenir luy même de plus en plus de ce qu'il devoit à Dieu pour le miracle de sa propre conversion.

---

[78] *Ibid.* (1876), I, p. 123.

[79] *Ibid.*, I, p. 250.

[80] *Ibid.*, IV, p. 349.

Il seroit utile que chacun instruisist les autres de ce qui le regarde en particulier, afin que l'histoire en fust d'autant plus fidelle qu'elle seroit originale.[81]

*

* *

With the example of Port-Royal, therefore, we find ourselves at the crossroads of Memoirs and History, private and public, past and future, survival and destruction, and perhaps above all memory and forgetfulness.

III. Memory Sources

It is therefore hardly surprising that memory as a concept should assume such an important position in both the theory and practice of Port-Royal. Having started this chapter in effect with the post-history of Port-Royal, I shall end it with an essential element of its pre-history: the ancient and more recent authorities on memory which would have been read by those attached to Port-Royal. This is intended neither as a comprehensive survey of all theorists of memory nor as a detailed analysis of the authors that those at Port-Royal read. Rather, in order to understand better the background to the prominence attached to memory and education at Port-Royal, a brief summary of those authors on memory most commonly studied at Port-Royal is necessary. Some authors mentioned only briefly in the next few pages, notably Aristotle, Cicero, Quintilian and Augustine, will be discussed in most chapters of this book. Other authors not mentioned here, such as Montaigne, will be considered within the context of individual authors.

It is inevitable that such a short summary will simplify some very complex concepts. In this section and throughout the book, I have relied upon a number of excellent critical studies which have been devoted to memory and which will provide the reader with a more sustained analysis. Of those books which will be referred to most frequently, there are some which merit particular mention here. Mary Carruthers's two works *The Book of Memory: a study of memory in medieval culture* (Cambridge: Cambridge University Press, 1992) and *The Craft of Thought: meditation, rhetoric, and the making of images, 400-1200* (Cambridge: Cambridge University Press, 1998) have provided a most stimulating starting point for

---

[81] *Ibid.*, I, pp. 2-3.

my analysis of memory within the context of education. Janet Coleman's *Ancient and medieval memories: studies in the reconstruction of the past* (Cambridge: Cambridge University Press, 1992) includes perhaps the most detailed synthesis of early writers on memory. More recently, Jean-Yves and Marc Tadié's briefer and wider ranging study, *Le sens de la mémoire* (Paris: Gallimard, 1999), makes interesting links between pre- and post-seventeenth-century texts. Paul Ricœur renews his interest in memory and time in *La Mémoire, l'histoire, l'oubli* (Paris: Seuil, 2000), a work which is always challenging and often illuminating. Frances Yates's seminal study, *The Art of Memory* (London: Pimlico, 1994, first published 1966), cannot escape mention. However, her analysis of the metaphysical mnemonics of the Renaissance, with the emphasis on mechanical memory systems, did not impinge either on Port-Royal educationalists or on writers associated with Port-Royal, and so will not feature prominently in this book. Angelica Goodden's *The Backward Look: memory and the writing self in France 1580-1920* (Oxford: Legenda, 2000) is a constantly engaging and valuable contribution to discussion of memory, but, despite its title, the overwhelming focus of attention is on the eighteenth century, especially within the context of selfhood in narrative, and is therefore of less immediate application to my subject-matter. I hope at least that my study will question her assertion that "the issue of memory engaged the seventeenth century less than it did the sixteenth or the eighteenth" (p. 163).

a) Plato

Although Plato was neither widely mentioned nor translated by writers at Port-Royal, his influence on many Christian writers (especially in the recollection of immaterial Forms), most notably Augustine, makes him an essential figure when considering memory. He was less interested in describing memory than analysing its role in the acquisition of knowledge. In *Meno* (81d-86b) and *Phedo* (75e-76b), for example, Plato (or, more strictly, Socrates) equates knowledge with recollection (*anamnesis*). Knowing is in effect remembering. In other words, all knowledge remains latent in the mind, and it is the process of recollection which extracts that knowledge from the mind, raising it to consciousness.[82] As Janet Coleman puts it, for Plato, "the truth that is to be recollected preexists and transcends

---

[82] See Coleman, pp. 11-12; Tadié, pp. 20-21.

language".[83] In the *Theetetus* (191d-194c), the memory is compared to a piece of wax, where remembering is dependent upon the effectiveness of the imprint made. Moreover, in the *Philebus* (38e-39e), the encounter between memory and sensations is related to the image of a writer and then a painter, where an inner discourse is viewed as being written onto the soul by memory, upon which images are imposed. The writer within us can write either true or false discourses, leading to true or false opinions.

b) Aristotle

Plato's pupil Aristotle, who will be considered specifically within the context of tragedy in chapter 4, is more interested in the workings of memory and in techniques of memorization. In the central text by Aristotle on memory, the section of *De anima*, entitled *De memoria et reminiscentia*, perhaps most importantly he distinguishes between *mnesis/memoria*, defined by Paul Ricœur as "le simple souvenir [qui] survient à la manière d'une affection",[84] and *anamnesis/reminiscentia*, defined variously as "recollection",[85] "rappel"[86] and "réminiscence".[87] Jean-Yves and Marc Tadié have summarized most succinctly these two kinds of memory,

> La première donne le souvenir entier, la seconde le reconstruit à partir de fragments. Elle suppose un effort de l'esprit. Le souvenir relève du sensible, est analogue à un tableau, à une image de l'objet absent, à l'empreinte d'un cachet sur la cire. La réminiscence, qui ne donne qu'une partie de l'objet, appelle un travail […].[88]

According to Aristotle (*De memoria et reminiscentia* 450a31-2, 451a4), memory and imagination belong to the lowest, perceptual part of the soul most dependent on sense images.[89] Aristotle was the first explicitly to associate memory with the lapse of time: "Memory is of the past", he tells

---

[83] Coleman, p. 35.

[84] Ricœur, p. 22.

[85] R. Sorabji, *Aristotle on Memory* (London: Duckworth, 1972).

[86] Ricœur, p. 22.

[87] Tadié, p. 27.

[88] *Ibid.*, p. 27.

[89] See Coleman, pp. 17-18.

us (*De Memoria et reminiscentia*, 449b15).[90] In his *Rhetoric*, Aristotle makes a similar distinction. In the 1654 translation by François Cassandre, a copy of which Sacy kept in his library,[91] he writes, "on sçait que la jouissance regarde toujours le Present, la Memoire toujours le Passé, et l'Esperance toujours l'Avenir".[92] Aristotle notes that pleasure, which he defines as a movement of the soul, consists in the sensation of an emotion.[93] As he writes in his *Rhetoric*, as translated by Cassandre,

> Il est donc constant que la Memoire ne represente jamais rien qu'elle n'apporte du plaisir: car non seulement elle donne du plaisir lors qu'elle vient à rappeller les images des choses qui estoient agreables dans le temps qu'on en avoit la joüissance; mais méme encore lors qu'elle en represente d'autres d'une nature toute contraire, et qui autrefois estoient tres-fâcheuses à supporter; principalement quand les personnes qui les ont souffertes ont changé d'estat, et qu'à leurs travaux passez, et à toutes leurs disgraces a succedé beaucoup de repos et beaucoup de gloire.[94]

Within the context of rhetoric, Aristotle states therefore that pleasure is attendant upon remembering. I shall consider some of these ideas in chapter 4, especially with reference to "le plaisir de la tragédie".

c) Cicero

It is clear that Cicero was both widely read and taught by those at Port-Royal, in the tradition of all colleges in France where rhetoric formed an important part of the syllabus. Sacy possessed two sets of Cicero's complete works,[95] and, as we shall see in chapter 4, Racine made notes on Cicero while at the petites écoles. Whereas Aristotle views rhetoric as secondary to logic or dialectic, Cicero (ever the public orator) places rhetoric at the highest pinnacle, considering it as the key to human virtue.[96] In *De Inventione*, memory forms one of the three parts of prudence

---

[90] See Ricœur, pp. 19ff.

[91] See O.Barenne, *Une grande bibliothèque de Port-Royal* (Paris, 1985), p. 128.

[92] *La Rhetorique d'Aristote en francais* (Paris, 1654), translated by F. Cassandre, p. 130.

[93] See Coleman, p. 33.

[94] *La Rhetorique, op. cit.*, pp. 130-1.

[95] See Barenne, p. 75.

[96] See Coleman, p. 46.

(memory, intelligence and foresight) and is the faculty which presents or re-presents experience, the foundation upon which moral judgements are made.[97] In *De Oratore*, where memory is described in a seventeenth-century translation as "la depositaire des thresors de l'esprit",[98] Cicero rehearses the technical art of memory, telling the story of Simonides. Although those at Port-Royal seemed less interested in the art of memory as such, Cicero's assertion that "la memoire des mots est la moins necessaire à l'Orateur, [...] c'est la memoire des choses dont l'Orateur a particulierement besoin"[99] was to strike a chord in the emphasis placed on memory in a pedagogical context. The orator, according to Cicero in *De Divinatione* (I. 50), is obliged to preserve collective memory by recalling the exemplary nature of the past. Moreover, as Janet Coleman puts it, he "prefers to see the memory as a divine power of the mind which is somehow distinct from the immortal soul".[100]

d) Quintilian

Quintilian's *Institutio Oratoria* remained a seminal text at the Port-Royal schools. The list of Sacy's library shows that he possessed two copies of the *Institutio*.[101] The text has particular relevance for the teaching of rhetoric, for its own impetus is primarily pedagogical, in that its aim is to educate the perfect orator. Memory is viewed by Quintilian as primarily responsible for the high status accorded to eloquence (XI,ii,7), and he devotes passages to ways of memorizing long speeches as well as to the operations of the memory. Much of the first part of chapter 4 will be devoted to Racine's copious notes on memory in the *Institutio* which he made while he was a pupil at Port-Royal.

e) St Augustine

Augustine's influence on those at Port-Royal cannot be over-empasized. Not only did they prefer to call themselves "disciples de saint

---

[97] See Carruthers, *The Book of Memory*, pp. 68-9.

[98] *La Rhetorique de Ciceron ou les trois livres du dialogue de l'Orateur*, translated by J. Cassagnes (Paris: Barbin, 1673), p. 10.

[99] *Ibid.*, p. 405.

[100] Coleman, p. 58.

[101] Barenne, p. 76.

Augustin" but also, as we have seen in this chapter, many Port-Royal writers modeled themselves on Augustine. A massive translation exercise was embarked upon, and Robert Arnauld d'Andilly's translation of the *Confessions* was a major event. Much of Book X of the *Confessions* is devoted to memory. Although the memoir writers and leading figures at Port-Royal mention the *Confessions* as an essential text, it is perhaps surprising that, especially in polemical texts, they tend more frequently to quote from other later works by Augustine. Philippe Sellier has offered a plausible explanation for this: "la violence et l'urgence des controverses sur la grâce divine a conduit ces penseurs à mettre au premier plan les dernières œuvres d'Augustin".[102] However, as far as memory is concerned, although Book X is directly quoted relatively rarely, the prominence which Augustine accords memory is one which was imitated in Port-Royal circles, as we shall see in the forthcoming chapters.

Memory makes an appearance in Augustine's early works. In *De Magistro*, for example, Augustine considers the operation of language as both commemorative and indicative; the commemorative function of speech becomes prominent for the Christian especially within prayer, for in this way his/her memory is stimulated.[103]

It is in chapter viii of Book X of the *Confessions* that Augustine's metaphor of a palace gives, in Ricœur's words, "à l'intériorité l'aspect d'une spatialité spécifique",[104] as communicated in Arnauld d'Andilly's translation:

> Je passerai donc au-delà de ces puissances naturelles qui sont en moi pour m'élever comme par degrés vers celui qui m'a créé, et je viendrai à ces larges campagnes, et à ces vastes palais de ma mémoire où sont renfermés les trésors de ce nombre infini d'images qui y sont entrées par les portes de mes sens. C'est là que nous conservons aussi toutes nos pensées en y ajoutant ou diminuant, ou changeant quelque chose de ce que nous avons connu par les sens, et généralement tout ce qui y a été mis comme en dépôt et en réserve, et que l'oubli n'a point encore effacé et enseveli. (X,viii,12)

---

[102] P. Sellier, 'Des *Confessions* aux *Pensées*: les seuils platoniciens', *Transversalités* 60 (octobre-décembre 1996), p. 22.

[103] See Coleman, p. 82.

[104] Ricœur, p. 118.

In contemplating memory and time, Augustine recognizes that knowledge of God stems from a particular time, since when it has been stored in the memory. Within the memory storehouse, everything is in disorder, and it is the mind which provides order, for, according to Augustine, the Latin word 'cogito' (I think) is related to 'cogo' (I put together): "le mot qui signifie penser ne veut dire autre chose dans son origine que rassembler" (X,xi,18). In remembering things, I am also remembering myself: "je me souviens donc de m'être souvenu, tout de même que si je me ressouviens dans quelque temps des choses dont j'ai pu maintenant me souvenir, ce sera par le moyen et par la puissance de ma mémoire que je m'en ressouviendrai" (X,xiii, 20). Indeed, at a later stage (X, xiv,21), he goes so far as to state that "il paraît que la mémoire est une même chose que l'esprit". As far as forgetfulness is concerned, Augustine recognizes a seeming paradox, for, in order to understand the meaning of forgetfulness, one has to have an image of forgetfulness in one's memory (X,xvi,24).

In chapters xx- xxiv, Augustine tries to give meaning to the love of God, and traces a trajectory, seeing this love as coming from a desire for happiness which itself is understood through our memory of what constitutes happiness. Spiritual happiness is born out of truth. He therefore is able to ascertain that God has been present in his memory ever since he discovered truth:

> Aussitôt que j'ai trouvé la vérité, j'a trouvé mon Dieu qui est la vérité même, laquelle je n'ai point oubliée depuis qu'une fois que je l'ai connue. Ainsi depuis ce moment que je vous ai connu, mon Dieu, vous êtes toujours demeuré dans ma mémoire, où je vous retrouve lorsque je me souviens de vous, et trouve en vous ma consolation et ma joie. (X,xxiv,35)

He then asks himself in which part of his memory he finds God, for he cannot be found either in "une image corporelle" or in "une passion de l'esprit" (X,xxv,36). He concludes that "il me suffit de savoir que vous y demeurez, puisque je me souviens de vous depuis le temps que j'ai commencé à vous connaître, et que c'est en elle [la mémoire] que je vous trouve toutes les fois que je m'en souviens" (X,xxv,36).[105]

---

[105] For a subtle analysis of memory in the *Confessions*, see T.Breyfogle, 'Memory and Imagination in Augustine's *Confessions*', in *Literary Imagination, ancient and modern*, ed. T.Breyfogle (Chicago: University of Chicago Press, 1999), pp. 139-154. See also A.Solignac, 'L'idée de la mémoire chez Augustin', in *Mémoire et Oubli au*

In *De Trinitate*, Augustine continues his discussion of memory, seeing the soul as an interrelated trinity which comprises memory, understanding and will. In XI,viii,13, as Janet Coleman explains, "although we preserve memories of corporeal forms according to the various capacities of our sense organs and the intensity of experiences, all these visions of representation have their origins in these realities present in the memory, which, thereafter, are multiplied and diversified by thought".[106] The soul's knowledge of itself is in effect a memory of itself . However, false representations are seen as being the fault of the will, which, while determining our response to personal experiences, is also responsible for turning the soul's gaze away from the memory (XI,viii,15). We shall see the influence of Augustine's theory of memory on Port-Royal writings on prayer in the following chapter.

f) St Bernard de Clairvaux

After Augustine, St Bernard can justifiably be regarded as one of the most important authorities for Port-Royal. In the epigraph to the *Constitutions du monastère de Port-Royal*, Mère Agnès Arnauld writes that the major impulse of Mère Angélique Arnauld had been to "faire revivre dans cette maison le premier esprit de saint Bernard".[107] Moreover, Bernard's rigorous ideas on monasticism had appealed to the Messieurs de Port-Royal. Sacy's library again acts as a useful barometer of Bernard's importance at Port-Royal, for he possessed a 1645 edition of Bernard's works in Latin, a 1649 translation by Gabriel de St Malachie, and Antoine Le Maistre's very influential *Vie de S. Bernard* (Paris: A. Vitré, 1648).[108] Le Maistre followed up this work with a translation in 1649 of various works by St Bernard.

---

temps de la Renaissance, ed. M. T. Jones-Davies (Paris: Honoré Champion, 2002), pp. 13-22.

[106] Coleman, p. 104.

[107] *Cf.* Racine, in his *Abrégé de l'histoire de Port-Royal*, ed. A.Couprie (Paris: La Table Ronde, 1994), who writes that when the Port-Royal house was instituted, they wished to "joindre en elles le nom glorieux des filles du Saint-Sacrement à celui de filles de saint Bernard", p. 55.

[108] Barenne, p. 38. See J.Lesaulnier, '*La Vie de saint Bernard, premier abbé de Clairvaux et père de l'Eglise, d'Antoine le Maistre*', in *Port-Royal et les Mémoires*, pp. 249-276.

De conversione is the most important work by Bernard to be concerned with memory. Janet Coleman effectively sums up Bernard's pessimism in this book with respect to memory:

> For Bernard, all past events are to be censured. The memory stores up in its secret recesses the remembrance of past evil deeds, either our own or those of others. For Bernard, man's memory is stained.[109]

In Le Maistre's translation, Bernard's words make grim reading:

> Cette puissance de l'ame est comme la sentine du vaisseau, toute l'abomination y entre, toute l'impureté s'y amasse. Ou plustost elle est ce grand livre où tout est escrit de la main et de la plume de la verité, qui est doux à la bouche, mais qui est amer à l'estomac. Le miserable pecheur se plaint de cette amertume: cet amas de corruption dont sa memoire est remplie le fait gemir et soupirer.[110]

Whereas Augustine blames the will for corrupting memory and the mind, Bernard condemns both the will and memory. Although the extremity of Bernard's pessimism is rarely taken up by Port-Royal commentators on memory, the latter group's wariness of the possible dangers of memory can certainly be ascribed to Bernard's influence. Of even greater significance for our purposes is Bernard's meditation on forgetfulness of self through prayer, for it resonates strongly in Pascal's writing. I shall discuss this at greater length in chapter 3.

g) Descartes

It is well known that Descartes had admirers at Port-Royal, most notably Antoine Arnauld, who corresponded with him and who published his response to Descartes's *Meditationes* in 1641.[111] However, Descartes's interest in memory was primarily anatomical, and, as we shall see, this aspect of memory did not form part of the more general musings on the functions of memory by Port-Royal educators, although we shall find that Nicole uses some of Descartes's terminology. In the second part of *Le*

---

[109] Coleman, p. 181.

[110] St Bernard, *Traduction de trois excellens ouvrages de S. Bernard: de la conversion des mœurs, de la vie solitaire, des commandemens, et des dispenses*, trans. A.Le Maistre (Paris, 1649), pp. 12-13.

[111] See H. Gouhier, *Cartésianisme et Augustinisme au XVIIe siècle* (Paris: J. Vrin, 1978), pp. 33-37.

Monde, entitled *Traité de l'homme*, for instance, Descartes considers a corpuscular and mechanistic description of human physiology, focusing in particular on the cognitive faculties, which include memory, imagination and the senses. His explanation for memory was based on a brain trace.[112] Descartes perceived faculties as powers of the soul, but, of the different faculties, he saw memory, along with sense perception and imagination, as dependent on mind-body interaction, whereas pure intellect can function without any corresponding change in bodily state. There are some similarities between Augustine and Descartes in that for both, as Jean-Yves and Marc Tadié put it, "la mémoire provient des vestiges que les impressions sensibles ou les modifications de la pensée laissent en nous".[113] But they differ most markedly in the way that Descartes distinguishes between material and intellectual memory, whereas Augustine does not. At several points, we find Descartes making this distinction. In a letter written on the 1st April 1640 to Mersenne, for example, he states, "Mais, outre cette memoire, qui dépend du cors, j'en reconnois encore une autre, du tout intellectuelle, qui ne dépend que de l'ame seule".[114] Descartes engaged in a lively correspondence on these matters with Arnauld. In a letter from 29 July 1648, for example, he makes the following points:

> l'exercice de la mémoire ne s'accommode pas de toutes les traces qui ont été laissées dans le cerveau par les pensées précédentes, mais de celles-là seulement qui sont telles que l'esprit reconnaisse qu'elles n'ont pas toujours été en nous, mais qu'elles sont un jour nouvellement survenues. Or, pour que l'esprit puisse reconnaître cela, j'estime qu'il a dû lors de la première impression se servir de l'intellection pure, pour remarquer que la chose qui s'offrait alors à notre esprit était nouvelle, c'est à dire qu'elle n'avait jamais été aperçue auparavant; car il ne peut y avoir aucune trace corporelle de cette nouveauté. C'est ainsi que si j'ai écrit quelque part que les pensées des enfants ne laissent aucunes traces dans leur cerveau, j'ai entendu parler de ces traces qui sont propres à l'exercice de la mémoire, c'est à dire de celles que lors de leur impression nous reconnaissons comme nouvelles par l'intellection pure. En même façon, nous disons qu'il n'y a point de traces d'homme sur le sable où

---

[112] See Descartes, *Œuvres complètes*, ed. Adam and Tannery (Paris: J. Vrin, 1996), vol. XI, pp. 177-9 (henceforth referred to as A-T).

[113] Tadié, p. 37.

[114] Descartes, *Œuvres complètes*, A-T, vol. III, p. 48. *Cf.* vol. III, pp. 84-5, 580.

nous ne voyons aucune empreinte d'un pied humain, encore qu'il
puisse s'y trouver bien des inégalités faites par des pieds humains, qui
par conséquent peuvent en un autre sens être appellées des traces
d'hommes.[115]

For Descartes, a self-evident proposition like 'cogito, ergo sum'
cannot be doubted, because by having such a proposition before the mind
means that we have understood what makes it certain, but other so-called
certain propositions can be doubted, because we may remember showing
them to be certain but are no longer attending to the reasons why they are
certain.[116] Indeed, in the *Discours de la méthode*, which commences with
Descartes claiming that he does not have "la memoire aussy ample, ou
aussy presente, que quelques autres",[117] memory and forgetfulness do play
a part, divided into two distinct stages, divided between what Harald
Weinrich calls "l'oubli méthodiquement induit", where readers are urged to
eliminate from their consciousness all false or misleading thoughts, and the
subsequent state of "la réminiscence méthodiquement contrôlée".[118]
Forgetfulness is of the utmost importance in this regard, for, as Ralph
Heyndels puts it, "c'est, en quelque sorte, par lui [l'oubli] qu'il faut
toujours commencer. Lui seul permet le renouvellement de la mémoire. Il
s'inscrit par là dans la déontologie d'avènement du *cogito*, à la fois comme
certitude et activité de la pensée".[119] In the *Méditations*, especially
Meditatio III, sceptical doubt does involve memory, but it would not seem
to be a doubt about the reliability of memory itself.[120] As Charles Larmore
has argued, "the doubt assumes that we correctly remember having shown
that a proposition is certain, but, as a doubt about whether what is certain is
indeed true, it can arise when we are no longer attending to what makes
that proposition certain, because we are thinking instead about what an

---

[115] Descartes, *Œuvres* (Paris: Pléiade, 1953), ed. A.Bridoux, pp. 1306-7. For the Latin
original, see A-T, vol. V, pp. 219-20.

[116] See the *Secundae Responsiones* to the Objections against the *Meditationes*, A-T, vol.
VII, pp. 145-6.

[117] Descartes, *Œuvres*, vol. VI, p. 2.

[118] H. Weinrich, *Léthé: art et critique de l'oubli* (Paris: Fayard, 1999), translated from the
German by D. Meur, p. 91. *Cf.* also pp. 87-9. See also A. Goodden, *The Backward
Look*, pp. 20-3, for a stimulating analysis of memory in the *Discours*.

[119] R. Heyndels, '*Camera obscura* de la mémoire: Descartes', in *Les lieux de mémoire et
la fabrique de l'œuvre*, ed. V. Kapp (Paris-Seattle-Tübingen, 1993), p. 260.

[120] A-T, vol. V, p. 148.

omnipotent God might do. It is this understanding of assent, of when it is compelled and when it can be withheld, that makes possible Descartes's supreme doubt".[121]

*
*　*

We shall see in the course of this book how a number of these authorities on memory are filtered into Port-Royal writings. Having considered some theories of memory, I shall turn in chapter 2 to the practice of memory in the Port-Royal schools.

---

[121] C. Larmore, 'Scepticism', in *The Cambridge History of Seventeenth-Century Philosophy* (Cambridge: Cambridge University Press, 1998), ed. D. Garber and M. Ayers, 2 volumes, vol. 2, pp. 1171-2.

CHAPTER 2

THE PETITES ECOLES

Although the petites écoles at Port-Royal were relatively short-lived, lasting in different guises from 1637 to 1660, and involving only between 120 and 150 pupils,[122] their importance cannot be over-emphasized. Many significant treatises on education (to be discussed in this chapter) emanated directly from Port-Royal, written by those involved in the teaching of pupils there. Among those who were engaged as teachers at Port-Royal, we find a number of prominent names (many of which we have met already), such as the founder of the schools, Saint-Cyran (1581-1643), Pierre Nicole (1625-95), Claude Lancelot (1615-95), Pierre Coustel (1621-1704), Antoine Singlin (1607-64) and Nicolas Fontaine (1625-1709). Other teachers at the schools whom we shall meet, François Dirois (1625-1690) and François Le Bon (dates unknown), played no important part in the published output of Port-Royal but were significant witnesses through their conversations, which were transcribed. Others attached to the various Port-Royal religious communities can justifiably be seen to have played a large role in its education policies. They include Blaise Pascal (1623-62), his sister Jacqueline (1625-61), Antoine Arnauld (1612-94), his brother Robert Arnauld d'Andilly (1588-1674), Antoine Le Maître (1608-58), Louis-Isaac Le Maître de Sacy (1613-84) and Alexandre Varet (1632-76). Of the pupils at Port-Royal, undoubtedly the most famous name is that of Jean Racine (1639-99). Another pupil, Pierre Thomas Du Fossé (1634-98), whom I discussed in the last chapter, left valuable information about the education policies of Port-Royal in his *Mémoires*. Other pupils, such as Sébastien Le Nain de Tillemont (1637-1698), will make an appearance in this chapter.

We saw in the first chapter the strands of memory theories which were passed from the ancients and early Church Fathers down to the seventeenth century. In the realm of education at Port-Royal, it is important not to forget the different ways in which these writings on memory might have filtered into the treatises on education. Moreover, as we saw in the last chapter, the contrasting views at Port-Royal on the function of memory and its usefulness can easily be seen in the influence of the varied accounts of

---

[122] See F. Delforge, *Les Petites Ecoles de Port-Royal 1637-1660* (Paris, 1985), pp. 213-4.

memory by writers as diverse as Quintilian, St Augustine, St Bernard of Clairvaux and Descartes.

I. Jesuit Education Policies

Bearing in mind the overwhelming Jesuit dominance of education in France[123] in the seventeenth century and the role of the Jesuits in the eventual destruction of the Port-Royal schools, it is inevitable that the educators at Port-Royal would shape themselves in opposition to the Jesuit Colleges. Indeed, in his *Abrégé de l'Histoire de Port-Royal*, Racine goes so far as to assert that "cette instruction de la jeunesse fut [...] une des principales raisons qui animèrent les jésuites à la destruction de Port-Royal".[124] Robert Arnauld d'Andilly makes similar and more detailed claims in his *Mémoires*:

> On élevoit à Port-Royal des Champs dans la piété et dans les sciences, avec un soin extraordinaire, un très-petit nombre de jeunes enfans; et une éducation si chrêtienne qui pouvoit leur faire faire également tant de progrès dans la vertu et dans les lettres, fut insupportable aux J.***. Ils résolurent d'employer tous leurs efforts pour détruire cette bonne œuvre, et ils en vinrent à bout. Car ils assûrérent si hardiment que le nombre de ces enfans étoit (138-9) fort grand, et que c'étoit un véritable Seminaire, où on leur enseignoit ce qu'ils nommoient les maximes du Jansenisme, sans pouvoir dire ce que c'est, non plus que ce prétendu Jansenisme, que les parens furent obligés de retirer leurs enfans avec la douleur de les voir privés d'une instruction que les seuls commencemens ont fait connoître être si bonne, que la plûpart ont parfaitement bien réussi.[125]

Certainly we find both implicit and explicit criticism of Jesuit teaching practices by figures connected with Port-Royal. In Lancelot's *Memoires touchant la vie de Monsieur de Saint-Cyran*, for example, Saint-Cyran's educational principles are discussed. His criticism of the state of education at the time must surely involve the implicit condemnation of the Jesuits:

---

[123] François de Dainville estimates that in 1627 there were 40 000 pupils taught in Jesuit institutions, *L'Education des Jésuites* (Paris, 1978), ed. Marie-Madeleine Compère, p. 122.

[124] J.Racine, *Abrégé de l'histoire de Port-Royal*, p. 90.

[125] R. Arnauld d'Andilly, *Memoires de Messire Robert Arnauld d'Andilly écrits par lui-même*, pp. 138-9.

> Car la grace de la bonne éducation est si grande en soi, et si rare au
> siecle où nous sommes, que le mauvais usage qu'en font ceux qui en
> sont gratifiés de Dieu, ne peut qu'il n'attire sur eux une suite
> effroyable de malédictions.[126]

Pierre Thomas Du Fossé's explanation in his *Mémoires* of his father's
reasons for sending him and his brothers to the Port-Royal schools seems to
indicate above all a desire to avoid the Jesuit Colleges: "la connoissance
qu'avoit mon pere de la corruption des colleges luy donna un fort grand
éloignement d'y envoyer ses enfans".[127] Godefroy Hermant, who studied at
the Jesuit Collège de Clermont but later attached himself to Port-Royal, is
more direct in his criticism of Jesuit teaching practices, which he associates
with "ces annotations inutiles, ces explications hors de saison, ces discours
à contre-temps, ces thèmes étudiés et ces recherches curieuses".[128]

Hermant's view, whether justified or not, that Jesuit education
consisted of the accumulation of seemingly useless facts can be linked to
the perception, held by others, that unthinking memorization of material
played too great a role in the Jesuit schools. The *Ratio Studiorum* (1599),
which consisted of a detailed plan of Jesuit education policies and which
was followed closely by teachers in Jesuit colleges, certainly is filled with
references to frequent memory exercises in the daily routine of pupils at
every level. The first hour of every morning was devoted to recitation by
memory, for example, and for studies in the humanities several hours a day
were spent reciting poets or the catechism or sentences set by the teacher.
Moreover, as is stated in the *Ratio*,

> Puisque l'exercice quotidien de la mémoire est nécessaire au
> rhétoricien, et que, dans cette classe, les prélections se prolongent
> souvent trop longuement pour pouvoir être retenues facilement de
> mémoire, le professeur fixera lui-même la nature et la longueur de la

---

[126] Lancelot, *Memoires touchant la vie de Monsieur de S. Cyran*, vol.2, pp. 333-4.
Despite the great originality of the Jesuit education policies in the sixteenth century,
by the seventeenth and eighteenth centuries there was a general perception that this
quality was waning. Adrien Demoustier writes, "Quoi qu'il en soit de la valeur
personnelle de chaque enseignement, l'institution pédagogique qui les animait et les
soutenait deviendra de moins en moins adaptée à la société qu'elle voulait servir",
Avant-Propos to *Ratio Studiorum*, presented by A. Demoustier and D. Julia, translated
by L. Albrieux and D. Pralon-Julia, annotations and commentary by M.-M. Compère
(Paris: Belin, 1997), p. 26.

[127] Du Fossé, *Mémoires* (1876), I, p. 18.

[128] Quoted by Dainville, *L'Education des Jésuites*, p. 192.

leçon à apprendre, et comment il faut la réciter, s'il veut le faire faire.
De plus, il serait utile de faire réciter ensuite par un élève, depuis
l'estrade, des textes appris chez les meilleurs auteurs, afin d'associer
l'action oratoire à l'exercice de la mémoire.[129]

As a result of this freedom, teachers were known to put even greater an
emphasis on memory exercises. Jonathan Spence, in *The Memory Palace of
Matteo Ricci*, for instance, writes of the founder of the Jesuits, Ignatius of
Loyola, and the way in which his advice was perhaps misinterpreted:
"Ignatius's terse instruction that the students 'should commit to memory
what their masters have assigned' was taken literally and was echoed by
other Jesuit directors of instruction".[130]

Another former pupil of the Jesuits, Claude Fleury, who succeeded
Lancelot as the teacher of the Prince de Conti's children and who distanced
himself from the *Ratio*, wrote a treatise on education, *Traité du choix et de
la méthode des études* (1686), in which he directly criticizes the over-
emphasis on memorization by the Jesuit teachers. As he mentions of the
pupils,

> Ils ont cultivé leur mémoire et leur imagination, sans exercer leur
> jugement: ils sçavent par cœur grand nombre de vers latins, la vie de
> Miltiade ou d'Epaminondas, quelques morceaux de l'histoire romaine,
> quelques curiosités des mœurs des anciens; quelques noms de leurs
> magistrats, quelques cérémonies de leur religion.[131]

Fleury then suggests that a child would benefit far more if one were to "luy
remplir la mémoire des connoissances qui sont d'usage dans la vie".[132] It is
important to bear in mind these perceptions of the Jesuits and their use of

---

[129] "Quoniam memoriae quotidiana exercitatio rhetori necessaria est, atque in hac classe
saepe longius praelectiones excurrunt, quam ut tradi commode memoriae possint,
praeceptor statuet ipse, quid quantumque ediscendum, et quomodo, si exigere velit,
recitandum. Immo ex usu esset, ut subinde, aliquis e suggestu recitaret, quae ex
optimis auctoribus didicisset, ad memoriae exercitationem simul cum actione
iungendam." *Ratio Studiorum, op. cit.*, paragraph 377, p. 167.

[130] J. Spence, *The Memory Palace of Matteo Ricci* (London/Boston, 1984), p. 135.

[131] Fleury, *Traité du choix et de la méthode des études*, quoted in Dainville, p. 48. Several
pages from Fleury are quoted by Dainville. See E. Bury, 'Fénélon pédagogue', *XVIIe
siècle* 206 (January-March 2000), pp. 47-57, in which he discusses Fleury.

[132] Fleury, in Dainville, p. 48. See Dainville, p. 175, for a more detailed account of the
role played by memorization in Jesuit classes.

memorization when considering the approach to memory in the Port-Royal schools.[133]

II. Conversation

Another major difference in the approach to education of the Port-Royal schools, which in some respects can be compared to their attitude towards memory, lies in their perception of the child and his/her abilities. As René Taveneaux writes,

> Les port-royalistes furent parmi les premiers à comprendre l'enfant, à le traiter non comme un adulte incomplètement formé, mais comme un être distinct, aux contours psychologiques propres, nettement différencié des autres humains. Leur conception marque, en ce domaine, une rupture avec l'universalisme classique.[134]

It is in this light that we can first consider the significant role played by conversation in the Port-Royal schools. The child was considered to be of sufficient importance to engage in discussions with the teacher and with other pupils. Indeed, the innocence and clarity of a child's words was held by some to be, to use Philippe-Joseph Salazar's words, "le souffle innocent de l'immatérielle voix divine".[135] Moreover, if we are to see the schools as being formed in contradistinction to previous styles of education, the popularity of conversation in the seventeenth century was, as Chrisoph Strosetzki has argued, in part inspired by an antipathy towards the pedantry of "l'éducation générale dispensée dans les écoles et les universités".[136] Port-Royal would have been especially keen to shape its education policies

---

[133] It must be stressed here that such criticisms of Jesuit education policies are inevitably partial. There were many prominent former pupils who professed themselves to be very satisfied with their education at Jesuit colleges. Even though Descartes, for example, starts his *Discours de la méthode* with the need to "sortir de la sujetion de mes Precepteurs" (*Œuvres complètes*, vol.vi, p. 9, se also p. 13), he nonetheless writes very approvingly elsewhere of his time at La Flèche, *Œuvres complètes* A-T, vol. I, pp. 383-4 and 377-8.

[134] R. Taveneaux, *La Vie quotidienne des Jansénistes* (Paris: Hachette, 1973), p. 65.

[135] P.-J.Salazar, *Le Culte de la Voix au XVIIᵉ siècle* (Paris: Honoré Champion, 1995), p. 268. One popular text, discussed by Salazar, is Philippe de Berlaymont's *Paradisus puerorum* (1618), in which the *vox puerilis* is deemed to surpass most gifts of eloquence. I shall return to this in chapter 4.

[136] C.Strosetzki, *Rhétorique de la Conversation* (Tübingen: Biblio 17, 1987), p. 190.

in opposition to the unconversational style of teaching in other establishments.

It might seem, and in many ways is, paradoxical that Port-Royal, so devoted to the solitary life and contemplation, should place (as we shall see in this and succeeding chapters) such emphasis on conversation, which is so greatly associated with worldly and *galant* circles in the seventeenth century.[137] It should not be forgotten, of course, that many of the Port-Royal *solitaires* left lives of success in salon society in order to embrace the spiritual retreat of Port-Royal des Champs. Although silence was highly prized, those who wrote memoirs, as we saw in chapter 1, all mention the valuable part played by conversation in their friendships. Indeed, salons such as those held by Mme de Sablé and collections like the *Recueil de choses diverses* (to be discussed in this chapter), exemplify certain links between these two very different worlds. As Antony McKenna mentions with reference to the mode for maxims in the seventeenth century, "le milieu social du salon de Mme de Sablé constitue un des liens importants entre la vie du couvent et des solitaires de Port-Royal d'une part, et d'autre part la vie mondaine des 'honnêtes gens'".[138]

None the less, many Port-Royal writers and thinkers remained aware of the possible dangers associated with conversation and worldly society, and we shall see this expressed at various points in this and the next chapter.

Of the theoretical writings on education which emanate from Port-Royal, two works in particular merit close attention: Pierre Coustel's *Les Regles de l'Education des Enfans* (1687), which will be discussed in Part III of this chapter, and Pierre Nicole's *Traité de l'Education d'un Prince* (1670), which will form the basis of Part V. Between analysis of these two primarily **theoretical** works, Part IV will be devoted to the collection of different pieces known as the *Recueil de choses diverses*, which, while not directly related to pedagogy, can to a large extent be viewed as the closest we as readers can get to the **practice** of the Port-Royal schools.

---

[137] Much has been written on the role of conversation in seventeenth-century society. See, for example, Strosetzki, *Rhétorique de la Conversation*; B.Bray and C.Strosetzki, eds, *Art de la lettre, art de la conversation* (Paris: Klincksieck, 1995); D.Denis, *La Muse galante* (Paris: Honoré Champion, 1997); M.Fumaroli, *La Diplomatie de l'esprit, de Montaigne à La Fontaine* (Paris: Hermann, 1998).

[138] A.McKenna, *De Pascal à Voltaire* (Oxford: Voltaire Foundation, 1990) vol.1, p. 101.

III. Coustel

It is generally acknowledged that Coustel was one of the most influential teachers at Port-Royal (Delforge, p. 179). Although his *Regles de l'Education des Enfans* appeared 27 years after the dispersal of the petites écoles, he stresses in the Preface the importance both of his early teaching experience and of the fact that he has read most books on education to assist him in his pedagogical theories. As he adds, "je mets, dis-je, ici sur le papier ces remarques et ces observations, qu'une assez longue experience m'a fait faire".[139]

From the very beginning, he names a number of authors who have provided him with most inspiration. Significantly, those authors which figure most prominently in his list are both influential at Port-Royal and important theorists of memory. Of sacred authorities, Coustel mentions St Augustine and St Bernard. Of ancient secular writers, Cicero and Quintilian are singled out. A direct link is made by Coustel between his quotation of these authors and memory, because he states that he has extracted "des maximes tres-salutaires" (Preface) from them, which will be useful to imprint on the pupils' memory. As he explains (following the advice of Quintilian), with regard to the teaching of children, "il faut tâcher de leur donner toûjours pour leurs exemples quelque sentence de l'Ecriture, ou quelque belle maxime de morale, dont ils puissent ressouvenir toute leur vie" (vol. 2, p. 24). Indeed, throughout the book, this emphasis on the importance of memorizing maxims is shown by the constant repetition of phrases such as "il faut se souvenir de cette belle parole de..." and "il faut bien imprimer ces maximes dans leur esprit...". I shall return to the connection between the maxim and memory in this chapter and later in the book.

It might be added here that the explicitly Christian basis of the children's education, although shared by all educational establishments in France, could well be accentuated by theorists like Coustel because of the perceived over-emphasis on non-Christian authorities in Jesuit schools. The albeit jocular comment by Fontenelle, who was educated at a Jesuit school in Rouen, that "notre éducation nous a tellement familiarisés avec les dieux

---

[139] Because of frequent references to the text, all page numbers will be included in the main text and will be taken from P.Coustel, *Les Regles de l'Education des enfans* (Paris: Etienne Michallet, 1687), 2 volumes.

d'Homère, de Virgile et d'Ovide, qu'à cet égard nous sommes nés presque
païens",[140] cannot be too far from the perception held by those at Port-
Royal of the Jesuit schools.

As one would expect with a writer attached to Port-Royal, the basis
of Coustel's teaching methods is explicitly Augustinian. Before quoting
Augustine to support his arguments, Coustel relates the value of good
education to the ability to become aware of one's natural sinfulness: "C'est
particulierement la bonne éducation qui dissipe peu à peu dans l'esprit des
enfans les *tenebres* de l'ignorance qu'ils apportent en venant au monde, et
qui sans cela leur seroient tout-à-fait pernicieuses" (vol. 1, pp. 21-2). In
other words, an appropriate education helps to minimize mankind's
inherent corruption (pp. 88-9).[141] Indeed, such a movement is transcribed
into the word itself, for etymologically "éducation" (coming from the Latin
"e-ducere") implies a transformation from one state to another. With one
major exception (Nicole's *Traité de la Priere*, to be considered at the end
of this chapter), Augustine's discussions on memory in the *Confessions* and
elsewhere have very little direct impact on Coustel and other Port-Royal
educators. We shall see a number of indirect reminiscences of Augustinian
memory, but far more explicit is the debt owed to secular writings on
memory, above all the commentary given by Quintilian on memory in his
Institutio Oratoria.

According to Coustel, memory is one of three "qualitez" which a
teacher should cultivate, the other two being "l'esprit" and "le jugement"
(vol. 1, p. 111). He follows Quintilian closely (*Inst. Or.* XI, 2), applying
these three aspects to the particular demands of his own teaching methods:

> Or l'on exerce la memoire des enfans, en leur faisant dire les leçons
> qu'on leur donne à apprendre par cœur. On cultive leurs esprits en leur
> faisant lire, et en corrigeant leurs themes, et en leur faisant traduire les
> Auteurs Latins ou Grecs qu'on leur met entre les mains. Enfin, l'on
> forme leur jugement en les interrogeant souvent, et en leur faisant
> rendre raison generalement de toutes choses: ce qu'on voit bien ne se

---

[140] Quoted in Dainville, p. 198.

[141] As Coustel mentions elsewhere in the *Regles*, "Il ne faut pas s'étonner de voir des
defauts dans les enfans; puisqu'estant hommes, il faut que la peine du peché originel
paroisse dans eux", vol.1, p. 175.

pouvoir faire, quand le nombre des écoliers est excessif. (vol. 1, p. 112)[142]

Three major facts about education at Port-Royal can be gleaned from this extract, all three of which will be discussed during the course of this chapter. First, as I have mentioned already, memory was perceived as a separate component from mind and judgement.[143] Second, at the petites écoles, small-group teaching was essential to their philosophy of effective education: each master took responsibility for only five or six pupils.[144] We shall see this also in relation to the oral nature of the classes. Third, translation formed an integral part of the learning process and was actively encouraged at Port-Royal, as shown particularly by the use of translation in learning languages (in Claude Lancelot's books) and the many translations of ancient writers by those associated with Port-Royal.

Of the three "qualitez" which the teacher should develop in a child, Coustel sees memory as the first to nurture, particularly for children under the age of seven: "les premiers commencemens des études n'ont particulierement besoin que de memoire, qui excelle d'ordinaire dans cet âge" (vol. 2, p. 17). It is only afterwards that the other two qualities can be developed: "A mesure que leur esprit se fortifie et que le jugement leur vient, on doit leur apprendre les principales maximes de la morale Chrestienne" (vol. 1, p. 211). In another passage, although Coustel does not mention the word "memoire", he uses the classical image of memory as wax to describe the souls/minds of children:

---

[142] *Cf.* Quintilian, in De Pure's 1663 translation of the *Institutio Oratoria*, XI,2, p. 310: "Il n'est rien qui profite tant des soins que la memoire; ny qui souffre tant de la negligence. C'est pourquoy il faut que les enfans apprennent comme j'ay dit beaucoup: et en quelque aage qui puisse luy permettre de cultiver sa memoire par quelque estude, qu'il devore dés le commencement ce petit chagrin de repasser souvent les mesmes choses, qu'il aura ou leuës ou escrittes, comme s'il remaschoit les mesmes morceaux."

[143] *Cf.* the comment by Saint-Cyran in his hugely influential *Theologie familiere* that "comme l'entendement, la volonté et la memoire sont trois facultez differentes, et neantmoins une méme ame: ainsi les trois Personnes Divines sont veritablement distinctes l'une de l'autre, et ne sont neantmoins qu'un méme Dieu" (Paris, 1639), pp. 14-15.

[144] This is in marked contrast to the very large classes in Jesuit schools. Dainville writes of there being as many as 200 students assigned to a single teacher in the seventeenth century, *L'Education des Jésuites*, p. 175.

L'on compare d'ordinaire l'ame des enfans à une table raze, sur laquelle on peut tracer toutes sortes de figures; ou bien à une cire molle, qui est susceptible de toutes les impressions qu'on luy veut donner. D'où il s'ensuit qu'il est important de remplir d'abord leur esprit des plus pures lumieres de la verité, et des plus solides maximes de la morale. (vol. 1, pp. 33-4)

In the major section devoted to memory in the *Regles* – Book 3, chapter 3 in the second volume – Coustel unequivocally cites ancient writers on rhetoric as his major influence and reiterates the importance of memory in the young child's learning process. It is worth quoting his comments at greater length.[145]

(i) C'est avec beaucoup de raison que les Anciens ont donné tant de louanges à la memoire, et qu'ils l'ont appellée, le precieux tresor de la nature, la mere des muses, et la depositaire de toutes les sciences.

(ii) Et en effet, il sert peu de se donner bien de la peine d'apprendre quoi que ce soit, si l'on ne s'en ressouvient, pour s'en pouvoir servir dans l'occasion.

(iii) Un des principaux soins d'un Maître doit donc estre de la bien exercer, tandis que les enfans sont encore jeunes; parce qu'elle se dilate, et se fortifie de plus en plus, quand on la cultive; et qu'au contraire elle diminuë et se perd quand on la neglige. *Cura augetur, negligentia intercidit*, dit Quintilien.[146]

(iv) C'est aussi la seule chose qui soit capable de donner de la consolation ou du soulagement à un Maître; tandis que les enfans ne peuvent encore rien produire d'eux-mesmes.

(v) La memoire regarde les choses passées, comme le sens est seulement des choses presentes, et que l'esperance et l'attente sont pour les choses futures.

(vi) Ses deux principales qualitez sont de recevoir aisément ce qu'on luy confie, ce qui marque l'étenduë de l'esprit; et le conserver fidelement, ce qui en marque la solidité.

---

[145] The paragraphs are numbered for ease of reference.

[146] This comes from Quintilian, *Institutio oratoria*, XI.ii.40, and was a passage copied down by Racine when he was a pupil at the petites écoles (see chapter 4): "Si quis tamen unam maximamque a me artem memoriae quaerat, exercitatio est et labor; multa ediscere, multa cogitare, et si fieri potest cotidie, potentissimum est. Nihil aeque vel augetur cura vel negligentia intercidit." (However, if anyone asks me what is the one supreme method of memory, I shall reply, practice and industry. The most important thing is to learn much by heart and to think much, and, if possible, to do this daily, since there is nothing that is more increased by practice or impaired by neglect than memory.)

(vii) Il faut donc faire apprendre aux enfans les plus excellentes choses qui sont dans les bons Auteurs, afin que le jugement s'en puisse avantageusement servir ensuite dans les occasions, comme il faut remplir ses coffres avant que d'avoir de quoy exercer ses liberalitez.

(viii) Trois choses peuvent encore contribuer beaucoup à la memoire, sçavoir 1. L'intelligence parfaite de ce qu'on desire apprendre par cœur. 2. L'ordre. 3. L'application.

(ix) Le silence exterieur sert aussi extremement: c'est à dire, de n'estre pas dans un lieu, où l'on fasse continuellement un bruit importun [...].

(x) Il est aussi bon d'écrire soy-mesme ce qu'on veut apprendre par cœur, et de le lire avant que de se mettre au lit. (pp. 54-6)

It has all too often been assumed that, within the context of the five traditional parts of rhetoric, memory was regarded as less important than the others, especially after the written word began to take precedence over oral communication. However, as Mary Carruthers has demonstrated,[147] in the Middle Ages access to printed books increased rather than decreased the interest in memory. Coustel's strong endorsement of the ancients' enthusiasm for memory (in paragraph i) only serves to accentuate the fact that memory remains significant in pedagogical literature of the seventeenth century.

Indeed, memory plays an essential role in Coustel's pedagogical concerns (ii, iii and iv), for he sees it as the teacher's *duty* to exercise the child's memory. Not only does this benefit the child before he (the pupils about whom Coustel writes were all boys) develops his other faculties but it can give satisfaction to the teacher (iv). As far as teaching young children is concerned, within a rhetorical scheme, *memoria* precedes *inventio*: "tandis que les enfans ne peuvent encore rien produire d'eux-mesmes" (iv). Creativity will only be attained at a later age. In addition to this, as he states in paragraph viii, *dispositio* ("l'ordre") is one of the three components which most assist memory. Without the ordering effect of thought, the memory can remain in a state of disorder. This is clearly the point of view of Augustine in Book X of his *Confessions*, which was well known to Coustel, when he talks of the learning process, as is shown in Arnauld d'Andilly's translation:

Ainsi, apprendre les sciences dont nous n'avons pas reçu les images par les sens, mais que nous considérons dans notre esprit sans aucunes images comme elles sont en elles-mêmes, n'est autre chose que

---

[147] *The Book of Memory.*

rassembler par notre pensée les choses qui étaient éparses deçà et delà sans aucun ordre dans notre mémoire […]. (X, xi)

The final paragraph of the extract from Coustel's discussion of memory (x) introduces another traditional part of rhetoric, *actio*, which itself helps memory. The writing down and reading of the piece to be learned is in essence a performance which aids the memory. As Coustel emphasizes in a later section devoted to *actio*, "elle [action] exerce l'esprit, elle fortifie la memoire, elle forme la voix, et enfin elle donne moyen de tirer du fruit de ses études, qui seroient souvent presques inutiles sans elle" (vol. 2, p. 205). The one remaining part of rhetoric, *elocutio*, is implied in both paragraphs vii and x: by learning good examples (vii) and writing them down (x), so can one's style improve.[148] I shall return to the relationship between *elocutio* and *memoria* in this chapter, but this subject will be explored most fully in the chapter on Pascal.

For Coustel, the most important educational application of memory is one which is shared by many educators and writers attached to Port-Royal, as we shall see: namely, the *correct* use of memory. One must not learn by heart any random maxim or thought; rather, it should be "les plus excellentes choses qui sont dans les bons Auteurs" (vii).[149] Moreover, the mindless absorption of facts has no inherent value. Instead, the child should try to understand, to have "l'intelligence parfaite" (viii) of what he is learning. Rather than being useful on it own terms, memory, therefore, should be the launch-pad for other faculties, such as "jugement".[150] The

---

[148] *Cf.* Albert de Paris in *La Veritable Maniere de prescher selon l'esprit de l'Evangile* (Paris, 1691): "il est certain que lors qu'on parle par memoire, le stile est bien plus exact et plus net", pp. 296-7.

[149] *Cf.* Du Fossé in his *Memoires*, who writes of his experience as a pupil at the petites écoles, where they read various authors, "tâchant de nous remplir la memoire de ce que nous trouvions de meilleur dans les Livres des Anciens", pp. 131-2. *Cf.* also Arnauld and Nicole in *La Logique* (Paris: J.Vrin, 1981):"comme on doit avoir pour but de rendre tout ce qu'on écrit aussi utile qu'il le peut être, il faut tâcher de choisir des exemples de fautes qu'il soit bon de ne pas ignorer, car ce seroit fort inutilement qu'on se chargeroit la memoire de toutes les réveries de Flud, de Vanhelmont et de Paracelse. Il est donc meilleur de chercher de ces exemples dans des Auteurs si celebres, qu'on soit même en quelque sorte obligé d'en connoître jusques aux defauts." (II, p. 32). Arnauld and Nicole speak also of the need not to overburden the memory in I, pp. 17-18 and 23.

[150] *Cf.* elsewhere in the *Regles*, where the need for "jugement" is stressed: "l'on se contente d'ordinaire de bien exercer l'esprit et la memoire des enfans; et l'on est

teacher himself is not exempt from this necessity. As Coustel reiterates elsewhere, "ce n'est pas mesme assez qu'un Maître ait la memoire remplie d'une infinité de belles choses; mais il faut outre cela souhaiter qu'il ait beaucoup de justesse d'esprit" (vol. 1, p. 133).[151]

    Closely related to this concept of "justesse d'esprit" and memory is that of prudence. *Memoria* formed an essential part of the virtue of prudence, that which enables one to make moral judgements.[152] Cicero, whose writings were well known to Coustel (as Coustel had edited and written a preface for a work entitled *Les Paradoxes de Ciceron*, published in Paris in 1666), lists the three parts of prudence (*memoria*, *intellegentia* and *providentia*; memory, intelligence and foresight) in his *De Inventione*.[153] Just as Coustel refers to the past ("memoire"), present ("sens") and future ("esperance" and "attente") in paragraph iv, so too can the three parts of prudence be applied to the three time zones: *memoria* – past, *intellegentia* – present, *providentia* – future.[154] Moreover, Coustel makes a direct connection between prudence and moral judgement. The teacher, in his words, must have "prudence, pour pouvoir regler les mœurs" (vol. 1, p. 134). Not unlike the care which one should take in memorizing the correct authors, this prudence is extended by Coustel to one's choice of

---

entierement satisfait [...]. Mais il n'en faut demeurer là. Comme le jugement est la principale faculté de l'homme..." (vol.2, p. 70).

[151] *Cf.* Bernard Lamy, who himself was greatly influenced by Port-Royal thought and who writes in his *La Rhétorique ou l'art de parler* (1675): "On s'imagine devenir éloquent pourvu qu'on charge sa mémoire de phrases ramassées dans les livres de ceux dont l'éloquence est estimée. On se trompe fort, et ceux qui suivent cette méthode ne parlent jamais juste. Car ils accommodent les choses qu'ils traitent à ces phrases sans se souvenir du lieu où les auteurs de qui ils les ont prises les avaient placées", Book I, ch. 18, ed. B.Timmermans (Paris: PUF, 1998), p. 139.

[152] See M. Carruthers, *The Book of Memory*, p. 9.

[153] See J. Coleman, *Ancient and Medieval Memories*, p. 42 for a discussion of this.

[154] *Cf.* Aristotle in his *Rhetoric*. In François Cassandre's 1654 translation, well known to Port-Royal (for example, we know that Sacy possessed a copy; see O. Barenne, *Une grande bibliothèque de Port-Royal*, p. 128), the words "memoire", "sens" and "esperance" are used: "Qu'il y aura du plaisir à se souvenir parfaitement d'une chose, et à estre dans une tres-grande esperance de l'avoir, puis que, selon ce que nous venons de dire, ce sera en joüir alors en quelque sorte, et l'avoir present a nos sens, et qu'en effet nous en joüirons; ou quand il nous souviendra qu'autrefois nous en avons joüi; ou enfin lors que nous aurons esperance d'en joüir quelque jour: Car on sçait que la jouissance regarde toujours le Present, la Memoire toujours le Passé, et l'Esperance toujours l'Avenir" (I, xi, p. 130).

conversation partners: "un des principaux effets de la prudence consiste dans le choix de ceux avec qui l'on doit converser" (vol. 2, p. 351).

This idea of conversation is central to the philosophy of education at Port-Royal; and once again memory plays an important part. The emphasis at the petites écoles on the memorization of extracts from approved authors derives not only from a belief in the educational value of exercising the memory but also from mistrust of the possible corrosive effect of the written word. As we shall discover in the course of this book, the Port-Royal authorities continually stressed the need not only to choose one's books carefully but also to pick out the best passages. But above all, it was felt that the small-group system of teaching would encourage active discussion of important issues, which could never be achieved if one were left alone to read the work of dead authors. As Coustel states,

> il faut toûjours, autant qu'on peut, joindre la conference des hommes sçavans avec la lecture des bons Auteurs; puis qu'on apprend avec bien moins de peine, et plus agreablement, ce qu'on ne sçait pas, en conferant avec les vivans, qu'en s'entretenant dans son cabinet avec les morts. (vol. 2, pp. 213-4)

The oral nature of learning at Port-Royal is confirmed by Fontaine's record of a letter written by Claude Lancelot to Sacy on the subject of the education of the princes de Conti. Having spoken of how the princes learnt various Latin phrases by heart, repeating them each night before going to bed, Lancelot adds:

> Mais tout cela se fait presque en se divertissant, parce qu'ils ne travaillent jamais seuls, et qu'ils ne cherchent jamais rien dans les livres. On est leur dictionnaire vivant, leur règles, leur commentaire; tout se fait par la parole.[155]

---

[155] N. Fontaine, *Memoires ou histoire des Solitaires de Port-Royal*, ed. P. Thouvenin, p. 916. *Cf.* Nicole's methods of teaching his pupil Le Nain de Tillemont (who himself is praised for his "grande memoire" in the *Recueil de choses diverses*, p. 479). As C-P. Goujet in his *Vie de M. Nicole* describes it, "Il ne lui dictait aucun cahier, mais lui parlait très sensément, et pour rendre plus claires les choses qu'il lui disait, il les appuyait d'exemples sensibles et de comparaisons justes; il laissait à son disciple la liberté de faire ses objections, il y répondait simplement et avec netteté, et jamais il ne sortait des entretiens qu'il avec lui qu'il ne vît clairement qu'il avait entièrement compris ce qu'il lui avait dit", in Nicole, *Essais de Morale* (Luxembourg, 1732), vol.14, p. 32. Antoine Arnauld, in his *Mémoire sur le règlement des études dans les lettres humaines* (c.1662), similarly criticizes thoughtless memorization by pupils, and

Although in the above examples the pupils learn Latin phrases, one of the major innovations of Port-Royal was the insistence on learning to read first in French rather than Latin. Moreover, much attention was paid to the sound of words rather than to the names assigned to specific letters of the alphabet, thereby confirming the priority accorded to orality in their teaching methods. Thomas Guyot, one of the teachers at the petites écoles, stresses how this way of teaching pupils to read is most effective:

> Le seul effort serieux consisteroit à retenir les figures des lettres et leurs combinaisons ou assemblages; les choses estant connues et les mots souvent entendus, il n'y auroit guere de difficulté à memoriser et donc à apprendre à lire rapidement.[156]

Blaise Pascal is generally credited with devising a reading system based on learning letters from their sound rather than their name. Although no document survives of Pascal's own ideas on this system, not only does Antoine Arnauld write to his niece Angélique about a young boy learning to read through "la methode de M. Pascal"[157] but also a letter from Jacqueline Pascal to her brother exists in which she asks him questions about "toutes les circonstances de votre méthode pour apprendre à lire par *be, ce, de*, etc. où il ne faut point que les enfants sachent le nom des lettres".[158] The fullest exploration of the method can be found in Arnauld and Nicole's *Grammaire de Port-Royal* (1660) in a chapter entitled 'D'une nouvelle manière pour apprendre à lire facilement en toutes sortes de langues', where "quelques gens d'esprit" are credited with having been instrumental in devising such a method.[159]

Such an oral way of learning to read forms an essential part of the idea of conversation as a pedagogical technique which we have seen reiterated in Coustel's writing. Indeed, the interactive nature of conversation is even perceived by Coustel as God-given. In the following

---

instead suggests that "on doit leur enseigner de vive voix et par pratique tout ce qu'on appelle règles et les engager seulement à les rapporter comme une petite histoire dans les petites classes", in I. Carré, *Les Pédagogues de Port-Royal* (Paris, 1887), p. 212.

[156] T. Guyot, *Billets que Ciceron a ecrits tant à ses amis communs qu'à Attique* (Paris, 1666), preface.

[157] See Delforge, p. 291.

[158] See Pascal, *Œuvres complètes*, ed. Mesnard, vol.3, p. 439.

[159] Part I, chapter 6, quoted by Mesnard in his edition of Pascal's *Œuvres complètes*, vol.3, pp. 442-3. See also F.Delforge's article, 'Le Ministère pédagogique de Jacqueline', in *Chroniques de Port-Royal* 31 (1982), pp. 107-119.

passage, although he does not use the term "memoire", it is strongly implied in his use of two other terms which (as we saw earlier) encapsulate the "qualitez" that a teacher must cultivate in his pupils – "esprit" and "jugement":

> Ce n'est pas par la bizarrerie et par la mauvaise humeur de certains melancoliques, qu'il faut juger de la conversation: mais par le sentiment general que l'Auteur de la Nature a imprimé dans l'esprit de tous les hommes. Dieu ne leur a pas donné l'usage de la parole, pour leur faire passer toute la vie dans les deserts; mais ç'a esté pour converser les uns avec les autres; afin qu'ils pussent apprendre ce qu'ils ne sçavoient pas, et qu'ils se perfectionnassent dans l'intelligence de ce qu'ils sçavoient déja. Comme donc la conversation aiguise l'esprit, forme le jugement, fait qu'on se connoist soy-mesme. (vol. 2, pp. 347-8)

The way in which self-knowledge is cited as the direct result of conversation will find its most striking counterpart in the self-exploration which lies at the heart of Pascal's *Pensées*, as we shall see in the following chapter.

IV. *Le Recueil de choses diverses*

Although Coustel is not mentioned by name in the *Recueil de choses diverses*, *Les Paradoxes de Ciceron* – the work which he edited and for which he wrote the preface – is referred to within the text.[160]

Jean Lesaulnier's comment that "le *Recueil de choses diverses* nous offre un témoignage de première importance sur Port-Royal, sur la vie intellectuelle et religieuse de son temps, comme sur la littérature française du XVIIe siècle"[161] might be dismissed as the hyperbolic praise of an over-enthusiastic editor but in fact reflects accurately the significance of this volume. Made up of over 1460 passages of unequal length, all accompanied by brief titles and names of those reporting or speaking, the manuscript is composed of conversations held mostly between 1670 and 1671 at the Hôtel de Liancourt between various supporters of Port-Royal. Lesaulnier has managed to establish the identity of the compiler of the fragments as almost certainly Jean Deslyons (1615-1700), who frequently

---

[160] *Recueil de choses diverses*, f300. All references to the *Recueil* will be to the original pagination (f=folio; v=verso) which is marked in Jean Lesaulnier's edition.

[161] J.Lesaulnier, Introduction, p. 167.

resided at the hôtel de Liancourt at that time.[162] For our purposes, perhaps the most significant aspect is that over half the text involves discussions between or on former teachers and pupils at the Port-Royal petites écoles.[163] In other words, we find, only a few years after the dissolution of the schools, many of the major participants engaged in what we have already seen to be one of the most important pedagogical features at Port-Royal, conversation. Moreover, although there are many passages which are distinctly gossipy in character, the majority of the conversations remain resolutely high-minded, with discussions on the Bible, the saints, recent Port-Royal translations and various religious controversies of the day, and so therefore would not have been far removed from the conversations held in small-group teaching. Yet, whereas the various Port-Royal memoirs and histories would be expected to be largely hagiographical, in these passages we find both praise and criticism of leading Port-Royal figures. One past pupil, Pierre Lombert (1636-1710), for example, spends much of his time in the text criticizing his former teachers and fellow pupils. Sacy is lambasted both for sounding provincial in his writing (f31) and for not being "simple" or "naturel" (ff400v-401) enough, Nicole "n'a gueres profitté des avis de son maistre feu M. Paschal" (f401v), and his fellow pupils Racine (f402) and Tillemont (f331v) do not escape censure. Lombert's father even joins in by criticizing the way in which Antoine Le Maistre taught his pupils Tillemont and Du Fossé, claiming that they were "elevés par Monsieur le Maistre dans un stile enflé" (f326).

François Dirois (or Diroys), who, along with his two brothers Pierre and Etienne, taught at the petites écoles between 1656 and 1659, is the leading participant in the conversations recorded in the *Recueil*, appearing in over a third of the documents. His comments often veer between criticism and praise of people at Port-Royal, reflecting to a certain extent the fluctuations of his relationship with the community.[164] After his time as

---

[162] *Ibid.*, pp. 135-164.

[163] I shall consider some of these names in this section, but for a full list of those who appear in the *Recueil*, we find the following:

Teachers or those who played some kind of supervisory role at the schools: Sacy, A.Arnauld, P.Nicole, C.Lancelot, F.Le Bon, J-G.de Flécelles, F.Dirois, J.Bourgeois, J.Burlugai, P. Floriot, L.Fournier, G.Guillaume, Collé.

Pupils: P. Thomas Du Fossé, S.Le Nain de Tillemont, J.Arnauld de Villeneuve, P. Lombert, P. Berrand, C. de Laval marquis de Boisdauphin, S.Roynette.

[164] *Cf.* Richard Simon's assessment of Dirois in a letter dated 25 August 1670: "M. Diroys, qui est lié d'amitié avec M. Arnauld, me vient voir quelquefois. Comme il a

a teacher, he distanced himself from Port-Royal and even signed the *formulaire*, declaring that Jansenius was heretical, which led to a furious polemical exchange with Arnauld and Nicole. However, by the time of the conversations recorded in the *Recueil*, he had resumed links with Port-Royal. He is described in the *Recueil* by a speaker called Le Vasseur (who appears elsewhere in the volume) as having "beaucoup d'imagination, beaucoup de veue; parce qu'il medite trop, il n'a pas de stile. Il peut donner de bons memoires" (f399v). He certainly shows himself to be both erudite and in touch with publications and manuscripts emanating from Port-Royal. St Bernard, who after St Augustine is possibly the saint most often quoted by Port-Royal writers, is acclaimed by Dirois as "un homme né eloquent, quoyqu'il ne soit pas pas poli; esprit penetrant, subtil, beau, fecond" (f324), which is backed up by his praise elsewhere in the volume of Le Maistre's *La Vie de saint Bernard* as "belle" (f33). He also still seems attuned to pedagogical matters, stating, for example, that a supporter of Port-Royal, Jacques de Sainte-Beuve (1613-1677), "est né pour enseigner" (f356).

Education plays a significant role in the conversations of the *Recueil de choses diverses*, appearing in different guises. References are made to Nicole's *Education du Prince* (f262v), which I will be considering shortly, also to a work by Philippe Goibaut du Bois on *L'Education de M. le Dauphin*, which was first published in 1670 with Nicole's piece (f68B), and to a projected work by the chevalier de Méré on the education of a prince (f255v). Additionally, the teaching of the Dauphin, who "ne scauroit rien apprendre" (f352v), is discussed. The petites écoles are mentioned explicitly only once, in a passage reported by a former teacher at Les Granges, Jean Bourgeois (1604-1687), whose pupils included Du Fossé, Villeneuve and Tillemont:

CONDUITTE DES ENFANS

M. Nicole leur faisoit lire trois volumes tous les ans.
A Port Royal les ecoliers n'alloient pas tous les jours a la messe affin qu'ils y allassent avec plus de devotion.
Quand on ne prioit point par routine, mais quand on en avoit l'esprit, de peur qu'on ne priast que des levres et non du cœur.
Bourgeois.
(f97)

---

de l'érudition et du bon sens, il ne s'est pas laissé prévenir entièrement des opinions de Messieurs de Port-Royal. Il loue en eux ce qu'il croit louable, sans approuver pour cela toutes leurs actions", quoted by Lesaulnier, Introduction, p. 83.

We shall discover in part VI of this chapter the importance of prayer at Port-Royal, especially in Nicole's treatise on prayer. The careful selection of books for children to read conforms also with Coustel's advice to choose appropriate passages.

Indeed, the choice of which writers, both ancient and modern, should be studied at Port-Royal is a question which is reiterated in the *Recueil*, and many of the authors who have written on memory and whom we have met already are mentioned at various points. In one passage, for example, it is stated that "Saint Augustin est plus propre pour enseigner que saint Ambroise" (f173v). In another extract, entitled "Jugement des auteurs", we find the following analysis:

> Messieurs de Port Royal estiment Terence et Virgile pour ses differents caracteres et son jugement, Ciceron pour sa philosophie et ses lettres, Quintilien pour sa morale, Montagne qui ne doit pas estre mis entre les mains de tout le monde, peu Scarron.
> Seneque est plein de faux raisonnemens; c'est un autheur celebre. Ils estiment peu Lucain.
> M. Lancelot a le recueil de tous les bons auteurs.
> (ff96v-97)

The wariness with regard to Montaigne is one which we will see reflected in Pascal's *Entretien avec M. de Sacy*, to be considered in the next chapter. The reference to Lancelot's "recueil de tous les bons auteurs" again shows the concern of Port-Royal to pick out those writers who are deemed to be useful. Of the authors above, two who are mentioned by Coustel, Cicero and Quintilian, are singled out in another passage from the *Recueil*. Additionally, Quintilian, although estimated by Sacy ultimately to be of less worth than Cicero, is nonetheless considered appropriate for memorization:

CICERON. QUINTILIEN

> M. de Sacy compare Ciceron a une statue d'or et Quintilien a une statue de bois. Il dit que ces deux statues sont parfattement achevées, en sorte que lorsqu'elles viennent a se rompre, les morceaux de celle d'or sont encore bons, mais les morceaux de l'autre ne vallent plus rien; car les mots de Ciceron, quelques (sic) derangés qu'ils soient, sont tousjours très propres.
> Il y a des auteurs dont il faut tout retenir, comme les petites declamations de Quintilien.
> (f112v)

Memory plays a very important part throughout the *Recueil de choses diverses*. At several points, leading figures of the day are assessed for the effectiveness of their memory. It is enlightening to find that, very much in keeping with Port-Royal's attitude to Jesuit education, where, as we saw earlier, quantity rather than quality of memory appeared to be emphasized, often when a Jesuit is praised for his good memory, he is simultaneously criticized for his lack of judgement. The historian Denis Petau (1583-1652), for example, who had been a teacher at the Jesuit Collège de Clermont, receives precisely such treatment:

PERE PETAU

> Il avoit beaucoup de memoire et de lecture. Il scavoit les langues; il escrivoit bien. Il raisonne mieux ou aussi bien que les scolastiques qui le blasment. Il n'avoit pas assés d'elevation d'esprit ny de penetration ny de discernement pour se determiner…
> (f5v)

Similarly, another Jesuit historian who taught at various Collèges, Philippe Labbe (1607-1667), is described in one passage as having had "une prodigieuse memoire", but "il n'avoit pas l'esprit si elevé" (f130), and in another as someone who "se fioit a sa memoire" but who "n'est qu'un almanach" (f176v). Yet another Jesuit author, Théophile Raynaud, who had died in 1663, is praised on the one hand for "une memoire prodigieuse" but is implicitly criticized on the other hand for his works which "peuvent passer pour un bon dictionnaire a cause des choses qu'il a ramassées" (f130v). An Augustinian theologian, Amable de Bourzeis (1606-1672), who had signed the *formulaire*, thereby cutting his ties with Port-Royal, but who, unlike Dirois, had not renewed his links, is tarred with the same brush, for he is seen as having "grande memoire, grande facilité, pas tant de jugement" (f89v).[165] Interestingly, the great founder of the Oratory, Pierre de Bérulle (1575-1629), is referred to as having made a distinction between memory and judgement with reference to preaching:

> M. de Berulle disoit qu'il estoit difficile qu'un grand predicateur fust homme de grand jugement. Il faut de la memoire pour un predicateur et le jugement ne se rencontre pas tousjours avec la memoire. (f45)

---

[165] *Cf.* f404v, where Bourzeis is described as having "de l'esprit, de la memoire, de la facilité et mediocrement du jugement". Similarly, a doctor from the Sorbonne, Antoine Faure, is credited with "beaucoup de memoire" but "mediocrement du genie" (f62).

Although it is reported that a friend of Port-Royal like Hermant "retient les bagatelles" (f52v) (a hang-over perhaps from his studies at a Jesuit college?),[166] almost overwhelmingly those close to Port-Royal are praised for their excellent memories but are not criticized for a lack of judgement. Pierre Berrand, a former pupil at the schools and a friend of Dirois, reports, for example, that a supporter of Port-Royal, Barbereau, has a "grande presence d'esprit et de memoire et grande facilité a s'exprimer" (f145v). This view is backed up by a (not completely uncritical) comment made by Bourgeois about Barbereau's favourite authors, all of whom found favour at Port-Royal: "M. Barbereau ne cite presque que saint Augustin, saint Gregoire, saint Bernard" (f153v). Barbereau himself reports in another section that Louis Touret, a hardline supporter of Port-Royal, "scavoit par cœur Jansenius" (f400v). François Le Bon, whose discussions are widely noted down in the *Recueil*, spent some time talking to Matthieu de Morgues, abbé de Saint-Germain (c. 1585-1670), shortly before the latter's death (in other words, just at the time when the conversations were being transcribed). It is again interesting to note how Le Bon, another former Port-Royal teacher, seems fascinated by de Morgues' excellent memory. At one stage, Le Bon asserts that "il a grande memoire; il apprend tous les jours quelque chose par cœur" (f81) and at another point, we are informed that "c'estoit un homme de feu et de memoire et ne pouvoit souffrir qu'on l'interrompit dans un discours" (f346v). Perhaps most tellingly, given the carefulness with which the Port-Royal educators treated memory, the report that Antoine Arnauld "ne se fie en rien sur sa memoire, qu'il a grande" (f86v) shows us both how memory was prized and how it was to be used sparingly.[167]

The *Recueil de choses diverses* can therefore be seen as living proof both of the importance of conversation within Port-Royal circles and of the role which memory and education played in those conversations.

V. Nicole

We have already seen the way in which Nicole was integral to the conversations recorded in the *Recueil*. Indeed, Dirois reports that "M. Nicole a escrit, dit-on, quelques faits des plus memorables de son temps"

---

[166] It should be noted that elsewhere in the *Recueil*, Hermant is praised for his "memoire prodigieuse" (f367Av).

[167] For other references to memory in the *Recueil de choses diverses*, see ff 85v, 141v, 157, 162v, 203, 245v, 260v, 353, 379, 389.

(f85v), and another comment that "Monsieur Nicole scavoit les humanités, les belles lettres" (f86) is supported by Ruffin's statement that Nicole "savait parfaitement les belles-lettres. Peu de temps avant sa mort, il récitait encore imperturbablement plusieurs vers de l'*Enéide* et les plus beaux endroits. Il m'avait dit ceux qu'il fallait apprendre par mémoire".[168]

Before concentrating on Nicole's *Traité de l'éducation d'un prince* (1670), it is worth mentioning briefly two works which have been associated with the text. Two short works appeared in the first edition with Nicole's text, Pascal's *Discours sur la condition des grands*, which I will consider in chapter 3, and Du Bois's *Education de M. le Dauphin*, which was mentioned in the discussion of the *Recueil*. Du Bois's text is of less interest to us, because it concerns almost exclusively education within the context of worldly *honnêteté*. He refers to the fact that children's memories are filled in a useless way and that their bodies are formed through physical exercise but that they are given no training in how to be *honnêtes*.[169]

In the Preface to the *Traité de l'éducation d'un prince* (1670), Nicole points out "l'utilité particuliere" that his book has for those of noble birth, but also stresses "l'utilité generale que tout le monde en peut tirer". Indeed, only the first part is specifically directed at those "de grande condition". Parts 2 and 3 are concerned with Christian education as a whole. Nicole's theories, as we shall see, coincide strongly with both the teachings of other Port-Royal educators and the accounts by pupils of teaching methods at the petites écoles. Part 3 eventually appeared separately as *De la maniere d'etudier chretiennement*, immediately preceding the first two parts of the *Traité de l'éducation d'un prince* in the 1733 edition of Nicole's *Essais de morale*.[170]

---

[168] *Entretiens avec P. Nicole*, quoted by Lesaulnier, *Recueil de choses diverses*, n.3, p. 302.

[169] See J.Mesnard, *Pascal et les Roannez*, pp. 738-9, for a discussion of the Du Bois text.

[170] All references will be to P. Nicole, *De l'Education d'un prince* (Paris: veuve Charles Savreux, 1670), because in this first edition all three parts appeared together as a single work. A recent edition reproduces the later version, where part 3 appears as a separate piece. See P.Nicole, *Essais de morale*, choix d'essais introduits et annotés par L.Thirouin (Paris: P.U.F., 1999), pp. 245-307.

Like Coustel, Nicole specifies the usefulness of writers like Cicero and Quintilian, but he adds some interesting provisos.[171] Whereas Coustel does not mention Aristotle, Nicole goes so far as to say, "il faut étudier la Rhetorique dans Aristote et dans Quintilien" (p. 60). Yet he adds: "mais on peut faire de grands retranchemens dans ces Autheurs" (p. 61). This idea of extracting appropriate sections can of course be linked to the importance at Port-Royal of using easily memorable and carefully chosen maxims and short extracts. As Nicole elaborates,

> il ne faut jamais rien faire apprendre par cœur aux enfans, qui ne soit excellent. Et c'est pourquoy c'est une fort mauvaise methode que de leur faire apprendre des livres entiers, parce que tout n'est pas également bon dans les livres. (p. 57)

Countering what, as we have seen, they perceived to be the Jesuit schools' preference for unthinking memorization, those at Port-Royal reiterate the need to learn in an intelligent way. In Part 3, we learn further why it is important to fill the memory with useful things. Nicole's categorization of memory and intelligence as parts of the actions of the soul can be seen in Descartes also, as discussed at the end of chapter 1:

> Ce que nous lisons entre dans notre mémoire, et y est reçu comme un aliment qui nous nourrit, et comme une semence qui produit dans les occasions des pensées et des desirs, et qui ne se reçoit jamais même sans penser: car nous pensons toujours aux choses que nous apprenons, puisque la mémoire et l'intelligence sont des actions de notre ame. (p. 406)

Moreover, as we saw with Coustel, for Nicole in *De l'education d'un prince*, memory (*memoria*) assists style (*elocutio*):[172]

> Cet avis est de plus grande importance qu'on ne pense, et n'a pas seulement pour but de soulager la memoire des enfans, mais aussi de leur former l'esprit, et le stile: car les choses qu'on apprend par cœur,

---

[171] *Cf.* C-P. Goujet's comment in his *Vie de M. Nicole* on what Nicole taught his pupil Tillemont: "M. Nicole [..] fit lire particulièrement à M. de Tillemont, Quintilien, le livre de Cicéron *De Oratore*, et l'*Art poétique* d'Horace", in Nicole, *Essais de Morale* (Luxembourg, 1732), vol. 14, p. 32. This choice of reading is backed up by Jean-Marie Tronchay in *La Vie et l'Esprit de Monsieur le Nain de Tillemont* (Cologne, 1713), p. 2. Tronchay makes the additional point that in suggesting such reading "ses Maîtres ne suivoient pas la méthode des Colleges"(p. 2).

[172] To a large extent, this follows Quintilian's treatment of *memoria* as a subdivision of *elocutio* (Preface, Book I, *Institutio Oratoria*).

> s'impriment davantage dans la memoire, et sont comme des moules et des formes que les pensées prennent lors qu'ils les veulent exprimer. (p. 58)

However, related to the concept of learning in a more efficient and intelligent way, Nicole makes a further distinction: that between reading and memorizing. Using the example of Cicero, whom he praises not for his quotability but for the high quality of sustained passages of his writing, he asserts the need in certain cases to read with understanding:

> Il y a des livres à lire, et d'autres à apprendre par memoire. On choisit d'ordinaire Ciceron dans les colleges pour le faire apprendre par cœur aux enfans, et on le lit peu, cependant il semble que l'on devroit faire tout le contraire. Car il n'y a pas tant de choses vives et éclatantes dans cet Auteur qui meritent d'estre retenues en particulier; et il y a au contraire une infinité de choses étenduës et fort bien écrites qui meritent d'estre leuës. (pp. 59-60)

One author whose whole work was memorized by the most talented students at the petites écoles is Virgil. Pierre Thomas Du Fossé's report in his *Mémoires* of the memory games which he and his fellow pupils played underlines the high regard in which they held both memory itself and those who had the most retentive memories:

> Comme notre classe estoit composée de ceux qui étoient les plus avancez dans les études, nous faisions des défis d'émulation les uns contre les autres, à qui reciteroit un plus grand nombre de vers de Virgile, sans faire de fautes. Et il est vray que la memoire du sieur de Villeneuve l'emportoit sur nous. Car je me souviens de luy avoir entendu réciter des livres entiers de Virgile, sans presque faire de faute. Pour moy, j'étois fort content, quand je pouvois en reciter un, en faisant dix ou douze fautes.[173]

If Ruffin's comment (quoted earlier) about Nicole learning much of the *Aeneid* by heart is true, no doubt Nicole himself joined in the game. However, even if such a game were criticized by Nicole in his role as pedagogue for the lack of true interpretation of the verses learnt by heart, its performative dimension (as seen in the repetition of the verb "réciter") reveals that even amongst the students memorization played an important role in the interactive nature of their education.

---

[173] Pierre Thomas Du Fossé, *Mémoires pour servir à l'histoire de Port-Royal* (Rouen, 1876-9, Slatkine reprint, Geneva, 1976), 2 volumes, vol.1, p. 170.

Earlier we saw Coustel's differentiation between "mémoire", "esprit" and "jugement" in the learning process. Nicole makes slightly different distinctions, mentioning, in addition to "mémoire" and "jugement", "imagination" and "intelligence", which seems again to evoke distinctions made by Descartes. Significantly, memory plays a central role in his evaluation of the way one teaches. For Nicole, memory reinforces judgement and is itself aided by imagination and judgement. However, it should be added that, following the convention set by so many writers, notably Cicero and Quintilian,[174] he states also that memory cannot be created; it can only be fortified. In other words, to a large extent it is a natural gift:

> L'Instruction [...] ne donne ny la memoire ny l'imagination, ny l'intelligence; mais elle cultive toutes ces parties en les fortifiant l'une par l'autre. On aide le jugement par la memoire, et l'on soulage la memoire par l'imagination et le jugement. (pp. 34-5)

Nicole appears to use imagination exclusively in a positive sense here, quite unlike the negative associations which Pascal applies to the term (*Pensées*, L44/S78). Indeed, he sees imagination as vital to the practicality of teaching children. One needs to appeal to the pupils' senses of hearing and sight in order to enable them to remember what they have learnt. This formed an essential part of the pedagogical methods at Port-Royal:

> On peut dire neantmoins generalement, que les lumieres des enfans estant toûjours tres-dependantes des sens, il faut, autant qu'il est possible, attacher aux sens les instructions qu'on leur donne, et les faire entrer, non seulement par l'ouye, mais aussi par la veuë, n'y ayant point de sens qui fasse une plus vive impression sur l'esprit, et qui forme des idées plus nettes et plus distinctes. (p. 37)

This emphasis on the constructive use of memory is not simply an abstract concept for the Port-Royal educators: rather, it forms the very basis of their teaching, as can be observed in discussions by masters and pupils at the petites écoles of the teaching of Geography, History and Languages.

---

[174] See, for example, Cicero's *De Oratore*, in Cassagne's translation: "J'avoüe que la Memoire est un don naturel ainsi que l'esprit", p. 402; and Quintilian in *Institutio Oratoria*, in De Pure's translation: "Quelques-uns ont crû que la memoire estoit un pur avantage de la nature; et sans doute elle y a la meilleure part; toutefois, le soin et la culture peuvent l'augmenter", (XI.2, p. 302).

In the field of Geography, Nicole suggests a method which will be both "utile" and "agreable" (p. 38). The sight of pictures of towns will be of greater value than simply the names of towns and provinces. Additionally, "on leur peut conter quelque histoire remarquable sur les principales Villes, qui y attache la memoire" (p. 38). Nicole likens this combination of diverting the child with an interesting story and locating the place to artificial memory. As he states,

> Il faut joindre à cette estude de la Geographie que l'on fait exprés, un petit exercice qui n'est qu'un divertissement, et qui ne laisse pas de contribuer beaucoup à la leur imprimer dans l'esprit. C'est que si l'on parle devant eux de quelque histoire, il ne faut jamais manquer de leur en marquer le lieu dans la carte. Si on lit, par exemple, la Gazette, il faut leur faire voir toutes les Villes dont il est parlé. Enfin il faut tâcher qu'ils placent tout ce qu'ils entendront dire dans leurs cartes, et qu'elles leur servent ainsi de memoire artificielle pour retenir les histoires; comme les histoires leur en doivent servir pour se souvenir des lieux, où elles se sont passées. (p. 39)

These methods can be applied equally successfully to the study of History, which, as we saw in the last chapter, was so central in the reconstruction of the memory of Port-Royal both before and after its destruction. Yet Nicole and other Port-Royal teachers did not restrict themselves to the History of their own institution. Nicole advocates the use of pictures of Kings of France, Roman emperors and other illustrious historical figures, in order to "arrester les idées dans la memoire" (p. 42). Although he admits that such a visual method "ne consiste que dans la memoire", he adds nonetheless that "elle sert beaucoup à former le jugement" (p. 43). Yet again, thoughtless memory is deemed to be useless, and, as before, the correspondence between memory and judgement is stressed. He is careful to meet the criticism that the children might be indulging in potentially pernicious curiosity by playing such games: "cette curiosité n'est pas un vice à leur âge, puisqu'elle sert à leur ouvrir l'esprit et qu'elle peut les détourner de plusieurs déreglemens" (p. 42). As we are told also in Part 3, "les études que l'on fait avec plaisir entrent bien plus avant dans la mémoire, que celles que l'on fait avec dégoût et avec chagrin" (p. 416). The use of cards to learn history is reiterated and developed in a document which details the lives and practices of those at Port-Royal, the *Supplément au Necrologe de l'Abbaie de Notre-Dame de Port-Royal des Champs* (1735), where a description of the daily routine of pupils at the Le Chesnay school (one of the petites écoles) is given:

> Ces *Cartes* étoient un certain jeu, où l'on avoit renfermé tout ce qui
> regarde l'histoire des six premiers siecles: c'est-à-dire, le lieu et le
> tems auquel se sont tenus les principaux Conciles; auquel ont vêcu les
> Papes, les Empereurs, les grands Saints, les Auteurs prophanes, et
> auquel enfin se sont passées les choses les plus memorables du
> monde. A force de joüer à ce petit jeu, la plûpart s'étoient tellement
> imprimé dans l'esprit toutes ces choses. Et les circonstances des divers
> tems et lieux où avoient vêcu tous les grands hommes, qu'il n'y avoit
> pas de Docteur qui en pût parler plus pertinemment. [...] Comme les
> enfans ont de la memoire, ils remarquoient les moindres circonstances
> de l'Histoire. (p. 56)[175]

Moreover, Nicole insists that the pupils can most usefully remember scenes
from History by having them told as stories: "il faut leur apprendre à
joindre ensemble dans leur memoire les histoires semblables, afin que l'une
serve à retenir l'autre" (p. 45).

In the pedagogical field, Port-Royal is perhaps best known for its
theories on language, as exemplified by Lancelot's various *Méthodes* for
learning languages and his *Grammaire générale et raisonnée* (1660),
written with Antoine Arnauld. In the preface to the fourth edition of his
*Nouvelle méthode pour apprendre facilement et en peu de temps la langue
latine* (Paris, 1655, first edition 1644), which was composed while the
petites écoles were still in existence and which clearly emanates from the
teaching methods employed at Port-Royal, Lancelot mentions the technique
(popular at the time) of learning Latin by tables. However, he is adamant in
rejecting this method for the teaching of children:

> Mais quand bien les Tables pourroient servir à des hommes avancez
> en âge pour commencer d'apprendre la langue Latine, il est difficile
> qu'elles puissent servir generalement à des Enfans. Car il faut bander
> l'imagination pour se les imprimer dans l'esprit, ce que les Enfans
> sont peu capables de faire, ne pouvant s'appliquer de la sorte fixement
> à une chose qui leur est de soy extrémement penible, et ayant
> d'ordinaire l'imagination aussi foible que l'esprit. Il n'y a que la
> memoire qui soit forte et agissante dans eux; c'est pourquoy il faut
> establir sur elle le principal fondement de tout ce qu'on leur veut
> apprendre. (p. 25)

---

[175] A description of these card games can also be found in *Mémoires sur la vie de M.
Charles Wallon, sieur de Beaupuis*, in *Vie des amis de Port-Royal* (Utrecht, 1756),
vol. 7, pp. 1-362. See B. Neveu, *Un Historien à l'Ecole de Port-Royal: Sébastien le
Nain de Tillemont 1637-1698* (The Hague, 1966), pp. 40-42.

Instead, Lancelot (and Nicole after him) recommends that the rules of learning Latin should be put into verse, so that the rules can be made "plus aisez et plus agreables" (p. 26) while at the same time making them "claires" and "intelligibles" (p. 25). Interestingly, both Lancelot and Nicole argue that this method will help to "arrester" the children's memory (Lancelot, p. 25; Nicole, p. 53). Learning by memory is perceived as only the first step towards the full understanding of a language. As Nicole reiterates, "c'est un avis general et qui est d'une tres-grande importance pour les Maistres, d'avoir extrêmement present tout ce qu'ils doivent monstrer aux enfans, et de ne se contenter pas de les trouver simplement dans leur memoire lors qu'on les en fait souvenir" (p. 55). Nicole elaborates upon this point, showing again the way in which the memory should help to strengthen mind and judgement. Even a moral dimension is introduced within this context, recalling the role which memory plays as a part of prudence:

> il est neantmoins fascheux de charger la memoire des enfans d'un livre où il n'y a que des mots à apprendre, puis qu'une des plus utiles regles qu'on puisse suivre dans leur instruction, est de joindre toûjours ensemble diverses utilitez, et de faire en sorte que les livres qu'on leur fait lire pour apprendre les langues, servent aussi a leur former l'esprit, le jugement et les mœurs. (p. 54)

It is in the moral and religious realm that memory plays its most significant part, both in instilling a sense of morality within children but also in preventing impiety from being implanted in its place. We have seen already Coustel's insistence on imprinting Christian maxims in children's minds. Nicole warns of the possible harm of the opposite (impious maxims) on their minds while accentuating the role which faith should play in their lives:

> Tout doit tendre à former le jugement des enfans, comme j'ay déja dit, et à leur imprimer dans l'esprit et dans le cœur les regles de la veritable morale. Il faut prendre occasion de toutes choses de les en instruire; mais on peut pratiquer neantmoins certains exercices qui y tendent plus directement. Et premierement il faut tâcher de les affermir dans la foy, et de les fortifier contre les maximes de libertinage et d'impieté qui ne se répandent que trop dans la Cour. (p. 66)

Religion, then, should be essential in their instruction: "toutes ces choses estant imprimées de bonne heure dans l'esprit des enfans, les rendent incapables d'être touchés des discours des libertins" (p. 70).

The above reference to the *libertins'* "discours" introduces another side to the value of conversation, for, unlike with Coustel, who sees discussion as the cornerstone of good education, here conversation is seen as potentially dangerous. Silence, held so dear by the *solitaires* at Port-Royal, remains one effective way to erase bad memories and thoughts, as Nicole points out: "C'est ce qui rend le silence si utile, et qui l'a fait tant recommander par les Saints, parce qu'empeschant que ces fausses idées qui ont esté imprimées dans nos esprits par les discours des hommes, ne soient renouvellées par ces mesmes discours, il les rend moins vives et plus faciles à effacer" (pp. 343-4).

There remain, however, other ways in which to purify the memory from the corruption of the outside world. In addition to Coustel's exhortation to instil saintly maxims in the pupils' memories, Nicole counsels specifically the memorization of psalms (themselves filled with references to remembering) and maxims ("sentences") taken from the Bible, "dans le dessein de sanctifier la memoire par ces divines paroles" (p. 424). This is very much in keeping with the practice observed by the nuns at Port-Royal. Indeed, in their very Constitutions, the learning by heart of psalms is advised, so that they might be able to "remplir le tresor de leur memoire de la parole de Dieu".[176]

Nicole concludes *De l'Education d'un Prince* with yet another reference to memory, here alluding to the truths of religion and the importance of using memory in the correct way:

> il ne suffit pas de sçavoir ces veritez d'une maniere speculative, ny qu'elles soient cachées dans quelques recoins de nostre memoire: Il faut qu'elles soient vives et presentes à nostre esprit, et qu'elles se presentent lors qu'il est question de les mettre en pratique: ce qui ne se peut faire si nous n'avons soin de les renouveller sans cesse, et si nous ne tâchons de les imprimer, non seulement dans nostre memoire, mais dans nostre cœur. (p. 426)

Memory is once more judged to be useless when passive (in this case, when truths are simply hidden away and not put to good use), and valuable when used actively ("il est question de les mettre en pratique") and in conjunction with other faculties (here "nostre cœur").

---

[176] *Les Constitutions du Monastere de Port-Royal du S. Sacrement* (Mons, 1665), p. 46.

The Christian foundation of the children's daily lives underpins all Port-Royal discourses on education. As we have seen, memory plays an integral part of that education. Jacqueline Pascal's *Reglement pour les enfans*, found at the back of the *Constitutions* of the Port-Royal convent (Mons, 1665), charts the progress of the convent pupils' immersion in a Christian way of life, including confession, communion, confirmation and prayer. Writing of various seminal texts, including Saint-Cyran's *Théologie familière*, Jacqueline Pascal tells us, for example, that "chaque dimanche on consacre trois quarts d'heure à la memorisation et à la recitation de ces textes (p. 475). Although she follows her Port-Royal counterparts in stressing that "il faut beaucoup exercer la memoire des enfans; cela leur ouvre l'esprit, les occupe et les empesche de penser à mal" (p. 453), her attitude towards memory tends to be rigorous, more in the line of St Bernard than that of St Augustine or the Latin writers on rhetoric. While speaking of confirmation, for example, she states that "nous nous arrétons peu à ce qu'elles en sçavent de memoire, et nous considerons bien davantage si elles en ont les sentimens dans le cœur" (p. 516). Yet remembering still plays a crucial role, almost always in connection with the need to recall their fallen state. When speaking of confession, for example, she asserts the nuns' duty to make the children "ressouvenir de toutes les principales fautes dont elles ne se souviendront pas" (p. 507). If the children have been deprived of communion as a punishment, "il leur faut faire ressouvenir de la perte qu'elles ont faite, et leur montrer qu'elles doivent estre dans un continuël gemissement pour obtenir de Dieu la grace de recouvrer ce qu'elles ont perdu" (p. 514). When they do take communion, "il les faut exhorter de ne pas oublier Dieu qui s'est donné à elles, mais de s'occuper à luy rendre graces, l'adorer et le prier souvent" (pp. 514-5).[177]

VI. Memory and Prayer

This emphasis on regular prayer is central to the children's education both at the Port-Royal convent and at the petites écoles. Lancelot reports in his *Memoires touchant la vie de Monsieur de Saint-Cyran* that Saint-Cyran's hopes for the pupils were founded upon prayer.[178] Indeed, Lancelot goes on to use a phrase which would seem to imitate Saint-

---

[177] See also F.Delforge, 'Le Ministère pédagogique de Jacqueline', who states that "les éducatrices de Port-Royal accordent une importance particulière à la mémorisation", p. 113.

[178] Lancelot, vol.2, p. 334. See Delforge, pp. 274-6.

Cyran's own words and which evokes just the kind of rhyming device (beloved of Lancelot himself in his language manuals) which would act as a mnemonic aid to teacher and pupils alike, aimed specifically at not overloading the children's memories with too many pieces of information. As Lancelot writes of Saint-Cyran,

> Il avoit soin d'avertir que pour bien conduire les enfants il falloit plus prier que crier, et plus parler d'eux à Dieu que leur parler de Dieu; car il n'aimoit pas qu'on leur tînt de grands discours de piété ni qu'on les lassât d'instructions.[179]

Prayer formed a central and regular activity at the schools. At Le Chesnay, for instance, the children's day was punctuated by prayer, starting as soon as the children woke (at 5 a.m.), followed by communal prayers at 6 a.m., again at lunch-time (11 a.m.), with further communal prayers before bed-time (8.30 p.m.).[180] Part of that routine consisted also of learning by heart sections from Saint-Cyran's *Theologie familiere*, 'Leçon XIII' of which is entitled 'De la prière'. As we are informed in the *Supplement au Necrologe* (1735), before they went to bed,

> on leur faisoit toûjours aprendre par cœur, deux ou trois articles du catechisme de Mr. De St. Cyran, qui est estimé un des meilleurs qui aïent été faits.
> L'on commencoit toûjours par faire repeter aux petits ce qui avoit été dit la derniere fois, afin de le bien imprimer dans leur memoire. (p. 58)

The most striking link between memory and prayer is to be found in another text by Nicole: his *Traité de la Priere*. The *Traité* itself had had a fraught history which needs some elucidation, as it involved a fierce debate concerning the role of memory in prayer.[181]

In the 1660s, immediately after the closure of the schools, a number of texts relating to prayer began to emanate from Port-Royal. In 1663, for example, Fontaine (using the pseudonym Sieur de Saligny) published a translation of the 4th/5th-century mystic John Cassian's *Conferences*, which

---

[179] Lancelot, vol.2, p. 336.

[180] These times are recorded in the *Supplément au Necrologe de Port-Royal*, pp. 59-60.

[181] For an exhaustive bibliography on this subject and lengthy extracts from both Agnès Arnauld and Martin de Barcos, see Denis Donetzkoff, 'Les Sentiments et les Remarques de Martin de Barcos sur l'Oraison Mentale', in *Port-Royal et l'Histoire*, *Chroniques de Port-Royal* 46 (1997), pp. 257-351. My quotations from both Agnès Arnauld and Barcos will be taken from these extracts.

deals with inward meditation ('oraison mentale') as opposed to articulated prayer ('oraison vocale').[182] As the title, *Conférences*, implies, the Cassian text consists of conversations, held with various leaders in the Egyptian desert. Cassian rehearses various problems which are germane to those questions considered by the Port-Royal pedagogues: he uses what Mary Carruthers calls "the language of elementary schooling"[183] and stresses the need to replace those worthless things learned by rote in one's childhood with sustained meditation on spiritual writings (XIV.13). Above all for Cassian, to quote Carruthers again, "the art of meditation is fundamentally an art of thinking with a well-furnished memory".[184]

In 1665, *L'Image d'une religieuse parfaite et d'une imparfaite, avec les occupations intérieures pour toute la journée* by Mère Agnès Arnauld (sometimes wrongly attributed to Mère Angélique de Saint-Jean Arnauld[185]) was published. Saint-Cyran's nephew and successor, Martin de Barcos, then wrote a work, which was eventually published in 1696 as *Les Sentiments de l'Abbé Philérème sur l'Oraison Mentale* but which was circulated in manuscript form at the time, in which he refuted some of Agnès Arnauld's ideas on prayer. Nicole in turn wrote a tract in which he opposed Barcos's point of view. This was published in 1679, the year after Barcos's death, as *Traité de l'Oraison*. Nicole subsequently reordered this work and published it in 1695 as *Traité de la Priere*. Amongst Mère Agnès's assertions, she writes that

> c'est l'esprit qui parle à Dieu dans la méditation; et c'est aussi la mémoire qui lui fournit ce qu'il doit dire, ou plutôt ce qu'il doit penser. Mais quand ces deux puissances ne font point leur fonction, il n'y a que la volonté, qui est le cœur de l'âme, qui puisse s'entretenir avec Dieu.[186]

---

[182] *Les Conférences de Cassien* (Paris: C.Savreux, 1663). See P.-J.Salazar, *Le Culte de la voix au XVIIe siècle* (Paris: Honoré Champion, 1995), pp. 251-3. Cassian is mentioned at three stages of the *Recueil de choses diverses* (135v, 136r, 184v), and clearly Fontaine's translation of the *Conferences* is being evoked (see Lesaulnier's footnote on p. 415 of *Port-Royal insolite*). We know also that Sacy possessed a copy of Fontaine's translation.

[183] M.Carruthers, *The Craft of Thought*, p. 75.

[184] *Ibid.*, p. 115. See *The Craft of Thought* for a fuller analysis of Cassian and memory/meditation, pp. 60-115.

[185] See Donetzkoff, n.12, p. 316.

[186] Donetzkoff, p. 259.

Barcos reacted strongly to these thoughts, because he believed that human agency was being attributed far too strongly to such an activity, so much so that it would not constitute prayer at all:

> Si c'est notre esprit qui parle à Dieu dans la méditation, et si c'est la mémoire qui lui fournit ce qu'il doit dire, il s'ensuit que nous ne prions point dans cette méditation, puisque nous prenons de nous-mêmes ce que nous disons, et non de l'Esprit de Dieu, qui est néanmoins celui qui prie proprement, et duquel seul nous pouvons tirer la vraie prière.[187]

Nicole was inclined to agree with Agnès Arnauld by accentuating the role of human memory within prayer. Because of Nicole's closer association with the petites écoles and because of the greater time in which he had to assess the different sides of the debate before publishing his *Traité de la Priere*, I shall concentrate on this treatise.

Some of the themes that we have met already recur in the *Traité*, such as the dangers posed by the use of memory alone and the usefulness of its conjunction with the heart.[188] But, no other Port-Royal text contains such a developed analysis of ancient sources on memory, combined with the positive use of memory in religious contemplation.

One of Nicole's sources is St Basil, whose writings on solitary life appealed particularly to the *Solitaires* at Port-Royal.[189] For St Basil, the memorization of the psalms in particular or of other Biblical extracts is integral to meditation upon God and all holy things. In this way, not only would one perform one's external duties but also one's internal life would

---

[187] Donetzkoff, p. 279.

[188] E.g. Book II, chapter 6: "Jesus-Christ nous ayant appris que l'homme se nourrit de la parole de Dieu, nous a donné lieu de le considerer comme l'aliment de notre ame: de reconnoistre en la méditant le besoin que nous en avons, et la défaillance où nous tombons si elle ne nous soutient et ne nous fortifie. Et c'est ce qui nous oblige de nous en approcher comme du pain de notre ame, et de prier Dieu qu'il l'imprime tellement non seulement dans notre memoire, mais aussi dans notre cœur, qu'elle se repande de là dans tous nos mouvemens interieurs et dans toutes nos actions", p. 151. *Cf.* IV,6, pp. 267-72.

[189] It might be noted here that, when in 1661 Jacqueline Pascal was Mistress of the Novices at Port-Royal des Champs and was questioned during the affair of the *formulaire* about what she was currently reading, she replied, "presentement c'est les moralles de St Basile", *Le Journal de l'Abbaye de Port-Royal*, 1661, manuscript P. R. 37 at the Bibliothèque de Port-Royal, pp. 369-70.

be enriched (as Nicole adds in Book IV, chapter 4, p. 254). Nicole quotes
Basil's remark "que le bien d'un Solitaire est de se souvenir
continuellement de Dieu, que le moyen d'y parvenir est de s'accoûtumer à
mediter en soi-même" (p. 254). However, he adds the rejoinder, again
paraphrasing Basil, that the memory can become distracted ("emportée par
un autre passage qui se presente") and, paradoxically, can lead to
forgetfulness – "qui nous fait perdre la meditation de celui qui le precedoit"
(p. 255).

Most significantly, Nicole adopts Augustine as his principal source
in his analysis of memory and prayer. Augustine explicitly discusses
memory in conjunction with prayer, particularly in *De Trinitate* and the
Confessions.[190] Gérald Antoni, in his excellent study, *La Prière chez Saint
Augustin* (Paris: J. Vrin, 1998), locates many different areas where the two
appear together in Augustine's writings, most prominently with respect to
prayer and self-reflexivity, prayer as praise of God, and prayer as *cogitatio
dei*. Significantly, for Augustine the value of prayer teaches us as much
about ourselves as about God. As Antoni explains, "prier est
paradoxalement, dans cette dimension immanente de la mémoire, un acte
ordonné à soi-même avant d'être ordonné à Dieu".[191] This element of self-
instruction, as we have seen in this chapter and as we shall find in the
chapters on Pascal and Racine, is an essential component of the theory and
practice of memory at Port-Royal.

One of Augustine's most vivid metaphors in explaining the way in
which the memory functions is that of the digestion of food. Often he uses
this image to compare it with the mind. In Book X of the *Confessions*, for
example, he explains (in Arnauld d'Andilly's translation):

> Il faut donc dire que la mémoire est comme l'estomac de l'esprit, et que la
> joie et la tristesse ressemblent à des viandes douces ou amères, qui
> lorsqu'elles passent dans la mémoire y sont comme les viandes dans
> l'estomac, où elles peuvent bien demeurer, mais sans avoir aucune saveur."
> (X,xiv)

---

[190] See, for example, *De Trinitate* XI.3,6; XIV.11,14; XV.7,12; XV.28,51; *Confessions*
II.7; X.8; X.11; XI.28. Augustine also covers some of these ideas in *De Magistro*,
where language is treated as both commemorative and indicative. As Janet Coleman
puts it, "it is clearly the commemorative function of speech that is most important for
the Christian, for through prayer and the reading of Scripture, man's memory is
stimulated", *Ancient and medieval memories*, p. 82.

[191] G.Antoni, p. 122.

Where prayer is concerned, Nicole was clearly impressed by this image. In the chapter entitled "Utilité des bonnes pensées pour la priere prouvée par ce que les Peres enseignent du soin que nous devons avoir de repasser dans notre esprit les veritez qui sont dans notre memoire" (Book IV, chapter 6), he quotes Augustine at length, from works like the Commentaries on the Psalms, Contra Faustum manichaeum and Tractatus in Johannis Evangelium, usually following the Port-Royal custom of quoting in French translation. For Nicole, Augustine's image of ruminating serves perfectly to describe the function of prayer: "C'est ce que ce Saint appelle ruminer, c'est-à-dire, repasser dans son esprit les veritez que nous avons apprises ou par la lecture, ou de la bouche des Prédicateurs" (IV,6,p. 267). This image is explicitly linked by Augustine to memory in his Commentary on Psalm 141, as quoted in the *Traité de la Priere*, where swallowing without chewing is equated to forgetfulness and rumination is likened to remembering: "C'est en ce sens que Salomon dit que le Sage tient long-tems dans sa bouche un tresor desirable, et que le fou l'avale aussi-tôt. C'est-à-dire, en un mot que le sage le rumine, et que le fou l'oublie" (IV,6,p. 268).

Nicole then develops the importance of repeated rumination through prayer. As he explains,

> C'est donc un exercice utile et necessaire selon saint Augustin, que de repasser dans son esprit les veritez qu'on a entenduës, ou qu'on a luës; de s'en entretenir, de s'en occuper, d'y faire reflexion; et comme il conseille generalement cette pratique, et qu'il en condamne l'omission en des termes tres-forts, il auroit sans doute approuvé que pour empêcher que les affaires et les soins du monde ne vous la fissent oublier, et n'effaçassent ainsi ces veritez de notre esprit, on destinât chaque jour un certain temps à cet exercice, et que l'on s'en fit une regle, comme il approuve qu'on regle ses prieres et l'on y destine certaines heures. (p. 269)

As we have seen with the positive use of memory in teaching methods, here Nicole is not concerned with "une simple repetition et un simple ressouvenir" (p. 269). Rather, he stresses that the purpose of memorization in prayer is to provoke "des reflexions vives, animées et efficaces" (p. 271). Memory in this instance can again be equated to prudence in the way that it helps "pour regler ses mœurs" (p. 272). Nicole makes a comparison between prayer and "oraison mentale", showing how Christians have always practised a form of "oraison mentale" without necessarily applying a method to it in the way that students of Rhetoric might have done.

Ultimately, Nicole in the *Traité de la Priere* associates memory with the perfection which existed in our prelapsarian state. Although all humans are at present corrupt, it is within the memory that we have a sense of divine truths. Augustine in Book X of the *Confessions* emphasizes this point: "depuis ce moment que je vous ai connu, mon Dieu, vous êtes demeuré dans ma mémoire, où je vous retrouve lorsque je me souviens de vous" (X,xxiv). For Nicole, the Augustinian inheritance is vital to a full understanding of the value of prayer:

> on conclut clairement de ces passages de saint Augustin, qu'il est utile de s'entretenir l'esprit de bonnes pensées, et de saintes reflexions sur les veritez divines que l'on trouve dans sa memoire; à quoi personne ne peut nier qu'il ne soit bon aussi d'ajoûter le desir que Dieu fasse passer ces veritez de notre memoire dans notre cœur, ce qui formera une priere appuyée sur des pensées interieures; et c'est ce qu'on appelle Oraison Mentale. (pp. 271-2).

VII. Conclusion

For those attached to Port-Royal, memory played an essential role in both the practicalities of teaching and in the Christian basis of their daily lives, covering such diverse areas of the spiritual learning process as reading, conversation and inner meditation and prayer.

In the following chapter, we shall find how both the theory and practice of Port-Royal memory were assimilated and transformed by the greatest thinker associated with Port-Royal, Blaise Pascal.

CHAPTER 3

PASCAL AND MEMORY

Both Blaise and Jacqueline Pascal, as I mentioned in the previous chapter, can be linked to various teaching methods employed at Port-Royal, Jacqueline through her *Reglement pour les enfans*, and Blaise through his reading method.[192] Although this reading system was designed as a practical aid to those learning to read, we shall see in the course of this chapter how the more abstract figure of reading informs Pascal's use of memory and forgetfulness in the *Pensées*. Neither Blaise nor Jacqueline was educated at the Port-Royal schools, but their very individual education under the tuition of their father is in some respects comparable to the petites écoles, for Etienne Pascal assumed his pedagogical role partly in reaction to the failings of other educational establishments. Pascal's elder sister Gilberte Périer's *Vie de Monsieur Pascal* needs to be read with caution, given its primarily hagiographical purpose, but her comment that "mon père [...] ne put se résoudre de commettre son éducation à un autre, et se résolut dès lors de l'instruire lui-même, comme il a fait, mon frère n'ayant [*sic*] jamais entré en pas un collège et n'ayant jamais eu d'autre maître que mon père"[193] can clearly be accepted at face value. Moreover, the emphasis on conversation in the Port-Royal classes seems to be replicated in Etienne Pascal's lessons, where, according to Gilberte, "il l'entretenait de toutes les choses dont il le voyait capable" and "mon frère prenait grand plaisir à ces entretiens".[194] There is evidence also of other ways in which the Pascal siblings were involved in educational matters. While at Port-Royal, Jacqueline was the mistress of the novice nuns and was particularly concerned with the education of the girls at the convent, as

---

[192] Jean Mesnard writes that "c'est dans les œuvres pédagogiques issues de Port-Royal que se révèle surtout l'utilisation d'écrits, ou au moins d'idées de Pascal", in Pascal, *Œuvres complètes*, vol. 1, p. 229. Pascal's *Eléments de géométrie* in particular are believed to have been used for the pupils' education. *Cf.* Delforge, p. 316. See Pascal, *Œuvres complètes*, vol. 3, pp. 439-40, for Jacqueline Pascal's response to her brother's reading method.

[193] G.Périer, *La Vie de Monsieur Pascal*, in Pascal, *Œuvres complètes*, ed. Mesnard, vol. 1, p. 571.

[194] *Ibid.*, p. 572.

shown in the *Reglement pour les enfans*. Meanwhile, not only are some of Blaise Pascal's writings, such as his *Discours sur la condition des grands* and *Réflexions sur la Géométrie en général*, clearly pedagogical in origin, but also it seems that he played a role in the education of two of his nephews. Etienne Périer, his eldest nephew, who had previously been taught by his grandfather in Rouen,[195] had been sent to the petite école at Chesnay, but after its enforced closure, as the *Recueil d'Utrecht* informs us, "ayant été obligé de sortir du Chênai, l'une des Ecoles de Port-Royal, où il avoit fait ses Humanités, étoit venu demeurer chez son oncle, qui lui avoit fait faire sa Philosophie au College d'Harcourt, dont M. Fortin son ami étoit Principal".[196] The following year at the Collège d'Harcourt, Etienne Périer would have had Jean Racine as a fellow pupil.[197] Pascal's second nephew, Louis Périer, was also sent to his uncle, and, as the *Recueil d'Utrecht* informs us, Pascal's pedagogical methods were particularly successful:

> il [Louis Périer] avoit, étant enfant, un esprit enjoué et boufon, qui lui faisoit tourner en plaisanterie tout ce qu'on vouloit lui apprendre; en sorte qu'à l'âge de sept ans il sçavoit à peine son *Pater*. Mme Perier le mena en 1658 à Paris et dit à M. Paschal, qu'on ne pouvoit rien apprendre à cet enfant. Cet oncle habile se chargea de son éducation et en peu de tems, le jeune Perier devint fort serieux.[198]

Jean Mesnard makes the plausible supposition that education was a popular topic of conversation with Pascal and his friend the duc de Roannez, a subject which was discussed all the more intently within his circle of friends after the birth of Louis XIV's eldest son on November 1st 1661, which "commença à éveiller les ambitions de gouverneurs et de précepteurs éventuels".[199]

It is worth considering briefly the one text by Pascal which is explicit in its pedagogical purpose, the *Discours sur la condition des grands*, noted down by Nicole from a lecture which Pascal gave to a young nobleman,

---

[195] "M. Paschal [Etienne] qui y [=Rouen] étoit Intendant, avoit voulu qu'il [Etienne Périer] restât auprès de lui, et il s'étoit appliqué singulierement à son éducation, mais à sa maniere", *Recueil d'Utrecht* (1740), XI. Pièce, p. 282.

[196] *Recueil d'Utrecht*, XI. Pièce, p. 340.

[197] See A.McKenna, 'Les petites écoles de Port-Royal', p. 23.

[198] *Recueil d'Utrecht*, XI. Pièce, pp. 401-2.

[199] J.Mesnard, *Pascal et les Roannez* (Paris: Desclée de Brouwer, 1965), p. 740.

almost certainly the duc de Chevreuse, the son of the duc de Luynes.[200] It was first published in 1670 together with Nicole's *Traité de l'éducation d'un prince*, which I discussed in the previous chapter. Nicole's prefatory note demonstrates the interest which Pascal purportedly had in the education of a nobleman:

> Une des choses sur laquelle feu M. Pascal avait plus de vues était l'instruction d'un Prince que l'on tâcherait d'élever de la manière la plus proportionnée à l'état où Dieu l'appelle, et la plus propre pour le rendre capable d'en remplir tous les devoirs et d'en éviter tous les dangers. On lui a souvent ouï dire qu'il n'y avait rien à quoi il désirât plus de contribuer s'il y était engagé, et qu'il sacrifierait volontiers sa vie pour une chose si importante.[201]

The three short *discours* are remarkable in the way that they relate to sections of the *Pensées*, especially in Pascal's exposition of the need to have "une double pensée",[202] calling to mind the fragments devoted to *raison des effets*. Memory plays a part in the text also, where the nobleman is called upon never to forget the fact that his noble condition is more a matter of chance than natural greatness. In the first discourse, he accentuates the stupidity of those noblemen "qui vivent dans un si étrange oubli de leur état naturel".[203] Yet, as he then goes on to state, a certain forgetfulness of one's natural state is sometimes necessary in order to maintain an illusion of superiority over the common people: "il faut s'oublier soi-même pour cela".[204] Towards the end of this chapter, I will consider other ways in which Pascal makes use of the idea of forgetfulness.

In the previous chapter, the pedagogical and spiritual value of memory was shown to be crucial to the daily life and educational theories of the Port-Royal schools. In this chapter, we shall find how such theories and practices of memory can throw new light on Pascal's own writings on the subject. Pascal himself, it might seem superfluous to add, was known for his excellent memory. We shall see in the course of this chapter how his contemporaries praised his memory. Nicole, for example, in the *éloge* which he wrote after Pascal's death, stresses, after the manner of the

---

[200] See Mesnard in Pascal, *Œuvres complètes*, vol. 4, pp. 1014-7.

[201] *Ibid.*, p. 1028.

[202] *Ibid.*, p. 1031.

[203] *Ibid.*, p. 1031.

[204] *Ibid.*, p. 1031.

positive use of memory at the Port-Royal schools, Pascal's constructive use
of his memory:

> Il avoit une memoire prodigieuse, mais elle consistoit à retenir les
> choses plutôt que les paroles, en sorte qu'il disoit, sans s'en élever
> davantage, qu'il n'avoit jamais rien oublié de ce qu'il avoit une fois
> bien compris.[205]

In a joint letter written to their sister Gilberte on 1st April 1648,
Blaise and Jacqueline perceive memory to have a two-fold function similar
to the way memory is perceived in the pedagogical writings which I
examined earlier. Speaking of their conversion experience[206], which "a plu
à Dieu de nous joindre aussi bien dans son nouveau monde par l'esprit,
comme il avait fait dans le terrestre par la chair",[207] they continue with an
assertion which both places memory on an important spiritual footing and
is strongly coloured by Augustinian terminology:

> Nous te prions qu'il n'y ait point de jour où tu ne le repasses en ta
> mémoire, et de reconnaître souvent la conduite dont Dieu s'est servi
> en cette rencontre, où il ne nous a pas seulement faits frères les uns
> des autres, mais encore enfants d'un même père; car tu sais que mon
> père nous a tous prévenus et comme conçus dans ce dessein. C'est en
> quoi nous devons admirer que Dieu nous ait donné et la figure et la
> réalité de cette alliance; car, comme nous avons souvent dit entre
> nous, les choses corporelles ne sont qu'une image des spirituelles, et
> Dieu a représenté les choses invisibles dans les visibles. Cette pensée
> est si générale et si utile qu'on ne doit point laisser passer un espace
> notable de temps sans y songer avec attention. (pp. 581-2)

The act of remembering highlights not only their physical kinship but also
their common relationship with God, which is sealed by
conversion/baptism, defined by Saint-Cyran (and quoted by Pascal), as "le

---

[205] This is the French translation which accompanies Nicole's original Latin in the
Recueil d'Utrecht, p. 337. It is worth noting the close similarity between Nicole's
words and those of Cicero in *De Oratore*, in Cassagne's 1673 translation, from which
I quoted in chapter 1: "la memoire des mots est la moins necessaire à l'Orateur [...].
C'est la memoire des choses dont l'Orateur a particulierement besoin", p. 405.

[206] This is known as Pascal's "first conversion", which took place in 1646 when two
brothers associated with Port-Royal had cared for Pascal's father after he had been
injured.

[207] B.Pascal, *Œuvres complètes*, vol. 2, ed. J. Mesnard (Paris: Desclée de Brouwer,
1970), p. 581. All quotations from Blaise and Jacqueline's letters will be from this
edition.

commencement de la vie".[208] Augustine's influence, even at this early
stage (Pascal was only 25), can be seen in the imagery of the spiritual being
figured in the material. Moreover, as the letter of the 5th November of the
same year (to be discussed later) demonstrates,[209] both Blaise and
Jacqueline had been reading Augustine's letters at that time. Philippe
Sellier identifies the precise reference in this extract to Augustine's letter
(243-38) to Laetus, where the familial and the spiritual are similarly
juxtaposed.[210] Through the memory, therefore, they are able to recall both
God's grace in the world and, as Christian Meurillon puts it, "une
admirable et exceptionnelle leçon divine à réactualiser chaque jour".[211]
Such profound issues, Pascal argues, are indeed difficult to keep away from
the memory. As he reiterates to Gilberte later in the 1st April letter, such a
subject is "trop beau pour ne t'être pas resté dans la mémoire" (p. 582).
Even at this early stage of Pascal's religious writings, the image of the Fall
dominates his thoughts. As he states, "il faut que nous nous servions du lieu
même où nous sommes tombés pour nous relever de notre chute" (p. 582).
It is the memory of the original perfection of humankind which allows the
possibility of escaping from the corruption of the post-lapsarian world. As
we shall see, this theme forms a central role in the *Pensées*. Moreover,
Pascal asserts the pedagogical value of remembering those positive things
which we have lost: "tant d'objets [...] nous servent d'une leçon
continuellement présente" (p. 582).

Whereas the 1st April 1648 letter deals largely with memory on a
spiritual level, the letter of 5th November 1648, again addressed to Gilberte
by both her siblings, concerns memory on a human scale. This dichotomy
between spiritual and human uses of memory can be found throughout
Pascal's writings, as we shall see in the course of this chapter.

---

[208] See *Lettre de Messire Jean Du Verger de Hauranne, abbé de Saint-Cyran, à un
ecclésiastique de ses amis touchant les dispositions à la prestrise* (Paris, 1648), p. 69.

[209] See Pascal, *Œuvres complètes*, vol. 2, p. 698: "cette tour mystique, dont tu sais que
saint Augustin parle dans une de ses lettres." This has been identified by Philippe
Sellier in *Pascal et saint Augustin*, p. 160, n.35, as a reference to Augustine's
Epistulae 243-38.

[210] P. Sellier, *Pascal et saint Augustin*, p. 160.

[211] C.Meurillon, "Mémoire et vérité: itinéraire pascalien", in *Revue des Sciences
Humaines* 244 (1996), p. 141. Meurillon's reading of Pascal's use of memory is
perceptive and illuminating. Although he stresses the "effet pédagogique et
thérapeutique" of memory in this letter (p. 141), he does not relate his comments to
the wider context of Port-Royal.

The subject of the letter centres on an unidentified difference of opinion which had resulted between Etienne Pascal and his three children and which Blaise and Jacqueline claim now to have forgotten. However, it seems that Gilberte had declared in a previous letter (now lost) that she was communicating an opinion which her brother had previously relayed to her. Pascal's upbraids her:

> je ne me souviens point de t'en avoir parlé, et si peu que cela m'a été très nouveau. Et de plus, quand cela serait vrai, je craindrais que tu ne l'eusses retenu humainement, si tu n'avais oublié la personne dont tu l'avais appris pour ne te ressouvenir que de Dieu, qui peut seul te l'avoir véritablement enseigné. (p. 695)

What would seem to be a minor question of remembering or forgetting becomes an involved analysis of the function of memory in a human and divine context. According to Pascal, the kind of teaching which God provides through the memory is different from the type of "reconnaissance" which is entirely human.[212] In keeping with the pedagogical aims of the Port-Royal schools, Pascal asserts the educational value of memory but perceives it to be of a significantly lower order:

> Ce n'est pas que nous ne devions reconnaître et nous ressouvenir des personnes dont nous tenons quelques instructions, quand ces personnes ont droit de les faire, comme les pères, les évêques et les directeurs, parce qu'ils sont les maîtres dont les autres sont les disciples. Mais quant à nous, il n'en est pas de même [...]. (p. 696)

A similar distinction can be made with respect to the daily education of pupils at Port-Royal: memorizing secular texts is of an entirely different order to the value of memory within prayer, as we saw in Nicole's *Traité de la Priere*. These are precisely Pascal's preoccupations in the next section of the letter, which merits quotation at length:

> tu dis qu'il n'est pas nécessaire de nous répéter ces choses, puisque nous les savons déjà bien; ce qui nous fait craindre que tu ne mettes pas encore ici assez de différence entre les choses dont tu parles et celles dont le siècle parle, puisqu'il est sans doute qu'il suffit d'avoir appris une fois celles-ci et de les avoir bien retenues pour n'avoir plus besoin d'en être instruit, au lieu qu'il ne suffit pas d'avoir une fois compris celles de l'autre sorte, et de les avoir connues de la bonne manière, c'est-à-dire par le mouvement intérieur de Dieu, pour en

---

[212] See Chapter 4 for my discussion of the link between recognition and memory in Racine's theatre.

conserver la connaissance de la même sorte, quoique l'on en conserve
bien le souvenir. Ce n'est pas qu'on ne s'en puisse souvenir, et qu'on
ne retienne aussi facilement une épître de saint Paul qu'un livre de
Virgile; mais les connaissances que nous acquérons de cette façon
aussi bien que leur continuation ne sont qu'un effet de mémoire, au
lieu que pour y entendre ce langage secret et étranger à ceux qui le
sont du ciel, il faut que la même grâce, qui peut seule en donner la
première intelligence, la continue et la rende toujours présente en la
retraçant sans cesse dans le coeur des fidèles pour la faire toujours
vivre, [...]. (p. 696)

The implication in the final lines of this extract that memory by itself is
inadequate corresponds to the pedagogical theories of Port-Royal, where it
is stressed that the memory should be cultivated along with the mind and
heart, and is developed by Pascal in the same letter (and indeed in the
Pensées). God's grace alone, placed within the heart, can allow one to
understand the "langage secret et étranger" of which Pascal speaks and
which forms such an important part of his discussion of figurative language
in the *Pensées*. As he and Jacqueline confirm to Gilberte, "c'est pourquoi
tu ne dois pas craindre de nous remettre devant les yeux les choses que
nous avons dans la mémoire, et qu'il faut faire rentrer dans le cœur" (p.
697). Just as Coustel and Nicole accentuate the value of memorizing
appropriate holy maxims and sayings, so too does Pascal:

> C'est ainsi qu'on ne doit jamais refuser de lire ni d'ouïr les choses
> saintes, si communes et si connues qu'elles soient; car notre mémoire,
> aussi bien que les instructions qu'elle retient, n'est qu'un corps
> inanimé et judaïque sans l'esprit qui les doit vivifier. (p. 697)

The choice of the word "judaïque" to describe the memory when it is not
used in conjunction with *esprit* or *cœur* is significant, because it can be
related to Pascal's later discussion in the *Pensées* of ways of reading the
Old and New Testaments. According to Pascal, the Jewish people belonged
to the material order in that they were unable to discern the spiritual or
figural significance of their prophets' predictions. In this context, memory
alone is incapable of comprehending the spiritual value of grace.[213]

---

[213] I shall discuss memory within the context of the Bible at a later stage in this chapter.
For a more detailed analysis of figures in Pascal, see P. Force, *Le Problème
herméneutique chez Pascal* (Paris: J.Vrin, 1989), pp. 87-163.

I. *Les Lettres Provinciales*: memory games

Pascal first became directly involved in the defence of the Jansenists at Port-Royal, from 1656 to 1657, with the publication of the *Lettres Provinciales*. Various manifestations of memory inform the depiction of the polemical debate between the Jansenists and Jesuits in the *Provinciales*. Just as we saw with teaching methods at Port-Royal, a discussion of the pedagogical use and abuse of memory plays a crucial role in a number of the letters.

From the outset, unthinking memorization (so important to Jesuit teaching practices[214]) is strongly implied to be useless. As Montalte, the naïve narrator, on being given the definition of the term *pouvoir prochain* by a Jesuit, exclaims in the very first letter,

> Je chargeai ma mémoire de ce terme; car mon intelligence n'y avait aucune part. Et, de peur de l'oublier, je fus promptement retrouver mon Janséniste,[...].[215]

Memory and failure of memory underpin the ongoing debate between Montalte and the Jesuit priest, forming an essential part of the satirical depiction of the Jesuits. The Jesuit priest is portrayed as out of touch with reality, forgetting the true value of Christian doctrine and remembering only the dubious sayings of his superiors. Just as Montalte has difficulty understanding the definition of *pouvoir prochain*, so too does he exploit the Jesuits' use of the term *grâce suffisante*, explicitly equating their obscure application of the term with the failure to remember the real world:

> C'est-à-dire, lui dis-je, que tous ont assez de grâce, et que tous n'en ont pas assez; c'est-à-dire qu'elle est suffisante de nom, et insuffisante en effet. En bonne foi, mon Père, cette doctrine est bien subtile. Avez-vous oublié, en quittant le monde, ce que le mot de *suffisant* y signifie? Ne vous souvient-il pas qu'il enferme tout ce qui est

---

[214] See, for example, Jonathan Spence's *The Memory Palace of Matteo Ricci* (London, Boston, 1984), pp. 5, 15, 135, where he discusses the literal way in which Jesuit teachers took up Ignatius of Loyola's advice to students to commit to memory all they had learned. See also my discussion of Jesuit education in chapter 2.

[215] Pascal, *Œuvres complètes* (Paris, 1963), ed. L.Lafuma, letter 1, p. 373. All quotations from the *Provinciales* will be from this edition.

nécessaire pour agir? Mais vous n'en avez pas perdu la mémoire;...
(2, p. 376).[216]

In the last chapter, it was shown how educational theorists like
Coustel stress the need for children to memorize "les plus excellentes
choses qui sont dans les bons Auteurs",[217] most particularly the thoughts
("maximes") of ancient Church fathers.[218] One of the major objections of
those at Port-Royal to the Jesuits was the latter group's reliance on recent
writers sympathetic to them alone. As Pascal's Jesuit priest explains to
Montalte, all the Jesuit-approved authors "citent nos Pères à toute heure,
avec éloge" (5, p. 391). A significant portion of the argument in the
Provinciales is focused on the *maximes* drawn from recent writers and used
by the Jesuits. Just as those at Port-Royal emphasized the importance of
memorizing useful maxims, so too was it deemed dangerous to memorize
potentially harmful maxims. This is precisely the issue at stake in the
Provinciales. At various points, the Jesuit priest in his role of teacher of the
naïve Montalte attempts to drum the thoughts of Jesuit thinkers into
Montalte's memory, at the expense of the assertions of ancient Church
authorities. On one occasion, for example, we find the following exchange:

> - Vous n'avez point de mémoire, dit le Père; ne vous appris-je pas
> l'autre fois *que l'on ne doit pas suivre dans la morale, les anciens
> Pères, mais les nouveaux casuistes,* selon nos Pères Cellot et
> Reginaldus?
> Je m'en souviens bien, lui répondis-je. Mais il y a plus ici. Car il y a
> les lois de l'Eglise. (6, p. 395)

However, Montalte proves to be a less than perfect pupil. As the Jesuit
exclaims in a later letter,

> - Cela est bien vrai, dit le Père, à l'égard de certaines gens: mais ne
> savez-vous pas que nous nous accommodons à toute sorte de
> personnes? Il semble que vous ayez perdu la mémoire de ce que je
> vous ai dit si souvent sur ce sujet. Je veux donc vous en entretenir la
> première fois à loisir, en différant pour cela notre entretien des

---

[216] *Cf.* Letter 6, where again it is implied that the Jesuit priest, through the failure of
memory, is cut off from reality: "- Quel Jean d'Alba? dit le Père. Que voulez-vous
dire? - Quoi! Mon Père, ne vous souvenez plus de ce qui se passa en l'année 1647? Et
où étiez-vous donc alors?" (p. 396).

[217] P. Coustel, *Regles de l'Education des Enfans*, vol. 2, p. 55.

[218] "quelque sentence de l'Ecriture, ou quelque belle maxime de morale, dont ils puissent
ressouvenir toute leur vie"; Coustel, vol. 2, p. 24.

adoucissements de la confession. Je vous le ferai si bien entendre, que
vous ne l'oublierez jamais. (9, p. 413).

The Jesuit's confidence in his pedagogical skills evaporates as Montalte,
increasingly combative, uses his memory to counter and indeed overturn
what he views as the biased ideas of the Jesuits. As early as the third letter,
Montalte exhorts his provincial correspondent, using several terms
traditionally associated with memory ("ressouvenir", "impressions",
"rappeler", "mémoire"), to remember the distorted image bestowed by the
Jesuits on the Jansenists:

> Pour l'entendre avec plaisir, ressouvenez-vous, je vous prie, des
> étranges impressions qu'on nous donne depuis si longtemps des
> Jansénistes. Rappelez dans votre mémoire les cabales, les factions, les
> erreurs, les schismes, les attentats, qu'on leur reproche depuis si
> longtemps; (3, p. 379)

Progressively, Montalte uses his memory of what the Jesuit has taught him
in order to contradict him. In Letter 9, for instance, as the Jesuit attempts to
argue with him about the issue of killing, Montalte responds by stating, "je
me souviens sur cela de vos autres définitions de l'assassinat" (p. 410). In
the same letter, he even has the temerity to quote from the Latin poet
Catullus, explaining that "je me souvins sur cela d'un passage d'un poète
païen, qui a été meilleur casuiste que ces Pères" (pp. 411-412).

Soon afterwards, by the beginning of Letter 11, all pretence of a
fictional exchange has been dropped. Not only did the Jesuit counter-
polemic force Pascal to change his line of attack to a more direct assault on
the Jesuits as a whole but also within the fictional scenario there was no
further need to continue the master-pupil exchange. The naïve narrator's
replacement by a knowing polemicist coincides with Montalte's attainment
of a memory independent of the Jesuit's teachings.[219]

---

[219] One later reference to memory is made in the *Provinciales*, where the polemicist
responds to the Jesuits' accusation that the writer known as Petrus Aurelius (correctly
attributed by the Jesuits to Saint-Cyran) denied the permanence of the order of the
priesthood. On the contrary, the polemicist claims, Saint-Cyran has reaffirmed the
perpetuity of the priesthood in his discussion of those priests or bishops who are
excommunicated by the Church: "Pour rendre calviniste feu M. de Saint-Cyran, à qui
vous attribuez le livre de *Petrus Aurelius*, vous vous servez d'un passage où Aurelius
explique, page 89, de quelle manière l'Eglise se conduit à l'égard des prêtres et même
des évêques qu'elle veut déposer ou dégrader. *L'Eglise*, dit-il, *ne pouvant pas leur
ôter la puissance de l'ordre, parce que le caractère est ineffaçable, elle fait ce qui est
en elle; elle ôte de sa mémoire ce caractère qu'elle ne peut ôter de l'âme de ceux qui*

II. The *Pensées*: memory lapses

Many issues of memory, raised both in Port-Royal pedagogical writings and in Pascal's earlier work, are explored and developed in the *Pensées*, to such an extent, I would argue, that they are fundamental to both the composition and the persuasive process of the work.

From the moment that the first Port-Royal editors wrestled with the manuscript of the *Pensées*, critics have been divided about the form and purpose of the work. In his *Discours sur les Pensées de Monsieur Pascal* (initially intended as a preface to the first edition), Filleau de la Chaise expresses his hope that readers will not be too surprised to find a work (which everyone had expected to be near completion) in such a fragmentary state:

> Car quoy que Monsieur Pascal n'eust encore rien écrit sur ce sujet que quelques pensées detachées, qui auroient pû trouver leur place dans l'ouvrage qu'il meditoit, mais qui n'en avoient fait qu'une tres-petite partie, et qui n'en sçauroient donner qu'une idée fort imparfaite, on peut dire neanmoins qu'on n'a encore rien veu d'approchant sur cette matiere. Cependant on ne sçauroit presque prévoir de quelle maniere les precieux restes de ce grand dessein seront reçûs dans le monde. Quantité de gens seront sans doute choqués d'y touver si peu d'ordre, de ce que tout y est imparfait, et de ce qu'il y a mesme quantité de Pensées sans suite ny liaison, et dont on ne voit point où elles tendent.[220]

Significantly, Etienne Périer, who wrote the eventual preface to the first edition in 1670, attributes the fragmentariness of the *Pensées* to his uncle's very good memory. Initially, as Périer explains, "comme il avait une mémoire excellente, et qu'on peut dire même prodigieuse",[221] Pascal did not feel the need to write down all his thoughts, having also (according to Périer) a clear idea of the ordering of the work. However, as Pascal's health began to fail him, when trying to organize his thoughts,

---

l'ont reçu." 16, p. 449. It is possible for the Church to banish such renegade priests from its collective memory, but the sacred character of the order can never be effaced from the "âme" of its priests. As with other Port-Royal writings on memory, Saint-Cyran here shows that, even within the context of the Church, memory on its own is malleable.

[220] F. de la Chaise, *Discours sur les Pensées de Monsieur Pascal* (Paris, 1672), p. 6.

[221] *Œuvres complètes*, (Paris: Seuil, 1963), p. 495.

comme il n'était pas alors en état de s'y appliquer aussi fortement
qu'il faisait quand il se portait bien, ni de les imprimer dans son esprit
et dans sa mémoire, il aimait mieux en mettre quelque chose par écrit
pour ne le pas oublier; et pour cela il prenait le premier morceau de
papier qu'il trouvait sous sa main, sur lequel il mettait sa pensée en
peu de mots, et fort souvent même seulement à demi-mot; car il ne
l'écrivait que pour lui; et c'est pourquoi il se contentait de le faire fort
légèrement, pour ne pas se fatiguer l'esprit, et d'y mettre seulement
les choses qui étaient nécessaires pour le faire ressouvenir des vues et
des idées qu'il avait.[222]

It is important to bear in mind the context of Périer's remarks here, for they
obscure issues as much as they illuminate them. He is attempting to explain
to a baffled public, about to read the work for the first time, why many
fragments "semblent assez imparfaits, trop courts et trop peu expliqués".[223]
As I hope to show in the remainder of this chapter, the fragmentary nature
of the text would seem to be less an accident than a deliberate ploy on
Pascal's part. However, Périer's comments are perhaps most revealing in
the role which he attributes to Pascal's memory and failure of memory. I
would argue that Pascal's preoccupation with memory, at a time when his
health was particularly bad, is central to how we may most usefully read
the *Pensées*, for he was able to incorporate these ideas into the very fabric
of the text. But first, a consideration of the ways in which various editors
have treated the fragmentary text is necessary.

The first 1670 Port-Royal edition is instructive in many ways of the
ethos at Port-Royal, for the editors tried to resolve the difficulties of the
text by subscribing to the vogue for the maxim which we have already seen
to be so important to educational methods at Port-Royal. Antony McKenna
has convincingly shown that the order in which the fragments were found
was abandoned by the Port-Royal editors in order to fit in with the
popularity in the 1670s for collections of such sayings: "L'édition des
Pensées participe à la fois au genre des sentences chrétiennes et à celui de
la maxime moraliste: dans les deux cas la référence à la doctrine
augustinienne caractérisait le milieu des amis de Port-Royal".[224]

---

[222] *Ibid.*, p. 497.

[223] *Ibid.*, p. 497.

[224] A.McKenna, *De Pascal à Voltaire* (Oxford: Voltaire Foundation, 1990) 2 vols, vol. 1,
     p. 103. See also pp. 99-103.

In the centuries since the 1670 Port-Royal edition, editors have tended to smooth over the open-endedness of the text as much as possible, incorporating the fragments into arbitrary thematic chapters, none more so than in the editions of Léon Brunschvicg and Jacques Chevalier which were used by scholars for much of the twentieth century.[225] Even as recently as 1992, Emmanuel Martineau in his edition embarked on the foolhardy task of eliminating fragmentation altogether by incorporating many of the shorter passages into longer discourses.[226] By following original manuscript copies of the *Pensées*, the editions by Louis Lafuma (1963) and Philippe Sellier (1976), and, to a lesser extent, Michel Le Guern's 1977 edition, have preserved as much as possible the order in which the fragments were found.[227] Pol Ernst's painstaking research into the original paper on which those surviving fragments were written has given us invaluable insight into the chronology of the fragments, research which is certainly more objective and of greater use than those subjective categories which earlier editors imposed on readers of the *Pensées*.[228] Moreover, his findings would seem to contradict Périer's assertion (quoted above) that Pascal used to write his thoughts on the nearest scrap of paper to hand, as there is considerable evidence that Pascal wrote his thoughts on larger pieces of paper, some of which he himself subsequently cut up into smaller pieces.[229]

Not only has the form of the *Pensées* continued to exercise the brains of scholars but the purpose of the projected book has proved to be of similar complexity. Although the work is generally considered to contain a large amount of material for a religious apology, certain aspects, like its unconventional format, the depiction of the human condition, the coexistence of many competing voices within the text, and the presence of several fragments with no apologetic dimension (such as the passage known as "Le Mystère de Jésus", L919/S749-51[230], and the fragments

---

[225] *Pensées*, ed. L. Brunschvicg , 3 volumes (Paris, 1904); *Pensées*, ed. J. Chevalier (Paris, 1954).

[226] *Discours sur la religion et sur quelques autres sujets*, ed. E. Martineau (Paris, 1992).

[227] *Pensées*, ed. L. Lafuma (Paris, 1963); *Pensées*, ed. P. Sellier (Paris, 1976 and 1991); *Pensées*, ed. M. Le Guern (Paris, 1977).

[228] P. Ernst, L*es Pensées de Pascal: géologie et stratigraphie* (Paris, 1996).

[229] See Ernst, pp. 128-143.

[230] All references to the *Pensées* will include the Lafuma (L) and Sellier (S) numberings.

devoted to miracles), indicate a more broad-ranging work than simply a defence of the Christian religion.[231]

It is my contention that an examination of memory in the *Pensées* can offer vital clues to solving the puzzle of the form and purpose of the work.

Three critics in particular have produced illuminating work on memory in the *Pensées*: Philippe Sellier, Pierre Force and Christian Meurillon. Sellier, in the introduction to his 1991 edition of the *Pensées*, which itself is partly a reworking of an earlier article,[232] concentrates largely on *memoria* as the fourth part of rhetoric. He asserts that "Pascal a métamorphosé le champ de la *memoria*", adding that for Pascal "la *memoria* pénètre ainsi jusqu'au plus intime de l'écriture littéraire."[233] Sellier's discussion of memory is suggestive rather than a fully evolved analysis of memory in the *Pensées*. Force, in his article, 'Invention, disposition et mémoire dans les *Pensées* de Pascal',[234] develops Sellier's exploration of Pascal and rhetorical memory, showing how Quintilian's use of *dispositio* as a subdivision of *inventio*, and his use of *memoria* as a subdivision of *elocutio* are transformed by Pascal from their originally oral application to the demands of the written form. According to Force, "redéfinissant et simplifiant les catégories de la rhétorique ancienne, Pascal fonde l'invention sur la disposition, et l'élocution sur la mémoire" (p. 761). Indeed, he views the art of writing for Pascal as intertwined with the art of reading. Meurillon's 'Mémoire et Vérité: itinéraire pascalien', which I have mentioned already in this chapter, includes an analysis of memory as related particularly to the concepts of *sentiment, raison* and *le moi*. Meurillon concludes that, although individual memory as consciousness of the self is an important element in the *Pensées*, "conception épistémologique et projet apologétique amènent Pascal à privilégier une mémoire qui dépasse le sujet connaissant: de même que la vérité, la mémoire sera générale" (p. 156). In a more recent article, 'Oubli de soi, oubli de Dieu: écriture et oubli chez Pascal',[235] Meurillon considers the

---

[231] See my *Playing with truth*, pp. 3-10, for a fuller examination of this question.

[232] P. Sellier, 'Imaginaire et rhétorique dans les *Pensées*', in *Pascal thématique des Pensées*, ed. L.M. Heller and I.M. Richmond (Paris, 1988) 115-135.

[233] Introduction to 1991 Sellier edition (Classiques Garnier), p. 77.

[234] *XVIIe siècle* 181 (oct-déc 1993) 757-772.

[235] In *Revue des Sciences humaines* 252/4 (oct-dec 1998) 23-36.

failure of memory, particularly with reference to the function of original sin in the *Pensées*. All four articles are influential in my analysis of memory. However, my reading differs from theirs in two main areas: (1) they do not examine a number of significant fragments which will be central to my argument; (2) they do not make the crucial link between educational theory and practice at Port-Royal and Pascal's use of memory.[236]

In the *Pensées*, Pascal's discussion of memory tends to be divided between its private function as part of the perception of self and its place within the wider Christian tradition. Both these features, as we shall see, are essential to the persuasive mechanisms of the work.

a) Memory and Self

Pascal is one of the first writers to conceive of what might be termed a modern sense of self. Certainly he speaks of "le moi" in a way that not even Montaigne considers. In questioning the exact nature of the self, he is reacting against both Montaigne's reliance on a "moi" which Pascal deems "haïssable" (L597/S494) and Descartes's confidence in man's ability to achieve the sovereign good through his own powers.[237] In L688/S567, which commences with the question, "qu'est-ce que le moi?", memory and judgement are deemed not to be an intrinsic part of one's self but rather "qualités" which can disappear while the self remains:

> Et si on m'aime pour mon jugement, pour ma mémoire, m'aime-t-on? *Moi*? Non, car je puis perdre ces qualités sans me perdre moi-même. Où est donc ce *moi*, s'il n'est ni dans le corps, ni dans l'âme? Et comment aimer le corps ou l'âme, sinon pour ces qualités, qui ne sont point ce qui fait le moi, puisqu'elles sont périssables? Car aimerait-on la substance de l'âme d'une personne, abstraitement, et quelques qualités qui y fussent? Cela ne se peut, et serait injuste. On

---

[236] Yvan Bamps' article, 'Trace d'ombre: Pascal, Montaigne et la mémoire', in *Les lieux de mémoire et la fabrique de l'œuvre*, ed. V.Kapp (Paris, Seattle, Tübingen, 1993) 267-276, focuses on Pascal's *De l'esprit géométrique* as opposed to the *Pensées* and will be discussed later in this chapter.

[237] For a stimulating analysis of the self in early modern thinking, see C.Taylor, *Sources of the Self* (Cambridge, 1994), especially pp. 356-7.

n'aime donc jamais personne, mais seulement des qualités.
(L688/S567)[238]

This statement demonstrates at the same time both the weakness and the
strength of memory. Like the Port-Royal pedagogues who stressed that
memory should not be used separately from other faculties (such as
judgement), here memory on its own is viewed as "périssable". Our
individual memory may fade while our individuality, or sense of self,
remains. Yet it is also implied that memory can induce the admiration and
love of others, which in itself is very much in keeping with the high regard
for memory traditionally held not only by writers on rhetoric such as
Quintilian and Cicero but also in subsequent ages.[239] It is clear that Pascal
too is fascinated by the possibilities of the workings of memory and its
connection with reason. As he stresses, "la mémoire est nécessaire pour
toutes les opérations de la raison" (L651/S536). As with Pascal's analysis
of so many key concepts, this statement is deceptively simple, especially
given the context of memory in L688/S567. Unlike Descartes's belief in
the solidity of reason, here reason is shown to be dependent on memory,
which was described as "périssable" in L688/S567. Reason is therefore not
only just as corruptible as memory but also subservient to the vagaries of
memory. Yet, just as "pensée fait la grandeur de l'homme" (L759/S628),
memory, in its close association with reason, must show us our potential
for greatness. Even so, as we have seen repeatedly in the Port-Royal
pedagogical writings, aspects such as mind, memory and judgement cannot
be considered in isolation from each other. It is illuminating to know, for

---

[238] In two other fragments, L587/S486 and L647/S532, which concern questions of
honnêteté, Pascal makes an indirect link between "qualités" and remembering.
Interestingly, as in L688/S567 where memory as a single quality is deemed of less use
than the combined qualities which make up the self, he praises the idea of a "qualité
universelle": "Les gens universels ne sont appelés ni poètes, ni géomètres, etc. Mais
ils sont tout cela et juges de tous ceux-là. On ne les devine point et parleront de ce
qu'on parlait quand ils sont entrés. On ne s'aperçoit point en eux d'une qualité plutôt
que d'une autre, hors de la nécessité de la mettre en usage, mais alors on s'en
souvient. Car il est également de ce caractère qu'on ne dise point d'eux qu'ils parlent
bien quand il en est question." (L587/S486); "*Honnête homme.* Il faut qu'on n'en
puisse (dire) ni il est mathématicien, ni prédicateur, ni éloquent mais il est honnête
homme. Cette qualité universelle me plaît seule. Quand en voyant un homme on se
souvient de son livre c'est mauvais signe. Je voudrais qu'on ne s'aperçut d'aucune
qualité que par la rencontre et l'occasion d'en user, *ne quid nimis*, de peur qu'une
qualité ne l'emporte et ne fasse baptiser; qu'on ne songe point qu'il parle bien, sinon
quand il s'agit de bien parler, mais qu'on y songe alors." (L647/S532).

[239] See J.Coleman and M.Carruthers. *Cf.* Coustel, p. 54.

example, that the fragment just quoted (L759/S628) was written on the same manuscript page as L513,[240] for the juxtaposition of these fragments can help us to gain a new perspective on the question of persuasive strategies within the *Pensées*:

> Géométrie. Finesse.
> La vraie éloquence se moque de l'éloquence, la vraie morale se moque de la morale. C'est-à-dire que la morale du jugement se moque de la morale de l'esprit qui est sans règles.
> Car le jugement est celui à qui appartient le sentiment, comme les sciences appartiennent à l'esprit. La finesse est la part du jugement, la géométrie est celle de l'esprit. (L513/S671)

When it comes to rhetorical effectiveness ("éloquence"), Pascal sees a kind of natural eloquence as more successful than eloquence which is both contrived and (as is implied) governed only by reason. One's judgement, on the other hand, belongs to quite another order, that of "sentiment", and is clearly perceived to be more effective than reason in the realm of persuasion. In this case, "sentiment" would seem to be akin to intuition, but it is worth bearing in mind that the term is notoriously complex in the *Pensées*, for it can have a variety of different meanings. As Buford Norman puts it,

> *Sentiment* […] refers to an operation and to the product of that operation. It is an operation that involves the reception of sensual stimuli and of intellectual impressions, and the formation of impressions and opinions about them. It also receives divine stimuli, and forms impressions and opinions about them.[241]

L513/671 also helps to clarify another fragment where memory and reason feature prominently, for memory is determined to be, like judgement, associated with non-discursive reasoning or intuition ("sentiment"). As we saw in Norman's comment above, "sentiment" (and by extension "mémoire") can be linked to the reception of divine stimuli:

> *Sentiment.* La mémoire, la joie sont des sentiments et même les propositions géométriques deviennent sentiments, car la raison rend

---

[240] See P. Ernst, *Les Pensées de Pascal: géologie et stratigraphie*. The thesis on which the book is based (Université de Paris IV, 1990) has a more complete album with reconstituted pages.

[241] B.Norman, *Portraits of thought* (Columbus: Ohio State University Press, 1988), p. 15. See pp. 3-17 for analysis of the different meanings of *sentiment*.

les sentiments naturels et les sentiments naturels s'effacent par la
raison. (L646/S531)

It is significant that reason in this fragment is linked to a verb often used to
denote forgetfulness – "s'effacer" – for if reason predominates, especially
in persuasive discourse, other more intuitive features will disappear and be
forgotten. Jacques Sojcher, discussing another section of the *Pensées*, helps
to elucidate, I believe, the inadequacy of reason as opposed to memory in
this context:

> Mémoire et puissance révélatrices de notre dignité, elle [la raison]
> reste en fait sans véritable objet, et, par l'orgueil qui la soustrait à
> Dieu et la concupiscence qui l'attache, avec la volonté et les sens, à la
> terre, elle se cache le vide et travaille contre ce savoir. Oubliant sa
> limite (qui renvoie à l'illimitation, c'est-à-dire à l'ordre de la
> soumission), elle mésuse de son pouvoir et maintient l'homme dans le
> milieu de la 'pure ignorance' et de 'l'ignorance savante' où sa
> suffisance trouble le monde et juge mal de tout.[242]

It should be added that the two terms defined as "sentiments" in L646/S531
– *joie* and *mémoire* – reappear together at the end of that most personal of
documents, appropriately known as the *Mémorial*, the record of Pascal's
definitive conversion experience on 23 November 1654. Discursive reason
has no part to play here, for the joy felt at the conversion experience and
the remembrance of God's word can only be encapsulated in the idea of
"sentiment" as non-discursive reasoning or intuition:

> Eternellement en joie pour un jour d'exercice sur la terre.
> *Non obliviscar sermones tuos. Amen.* (L913/S742)[243]

When it comes to persuasion, therefore, memory is deemed to be
closely linked to intuition rather than reason alone.[244]

---

[242] 'Portrait de l'oublieux', *Europe* 597-8 (1979) 14-29, p. 23.

[243] "I will not forget your words". The quotation is from Psalm 118, v.16.

[244] In Pascal's *Préface sur le traité du vide*, another distinction between memory and
reason is made, where historical truths are compared with scientific truths: "il faut
considérer que les unes dépendent seulement de la mémoire et sont purement
historiques, n'ayant pour objet que de savoir ce que les auteurs ont écrit; les autres
dépendent seulement du raisonnement, et sont entièrement dogmatiques, ayant pour
objet de chercher et découvrir les vérités cachées." *Œuvres complètes*, vol. 2, pp. 777-
8.

b) Persuading (or educating) the Self

In the difficult task of persuading the reader of the necessity of religion, Pascal (or rather the speaker – the dialectician – of the *Pensées*) locates memory as an essential component of that persuasive process.

Many of the elements which make up those fragments concerned with memory and the self, such as the relationship between memory, reason and the heart or the role played by "sentiments naturels", attain even greater force in those passages which deal directly with the art of persuasion. The paragraph which immediately followed L651 – "la mémoire est nécessaire pour toutes les opérations de la raison" – on the manuscript page (numbered by Lafuma as L652/S536 but construed by Sellier as part of the same fragment) only makes sense in conjunction with what precedes it when considered in this light:

> Quand un discours naturel peint une passion ou un effet, on trouve dans soi-même la vérité de ce qu'on entend, laquelle on ne savait pas qu'elle y fût, de sorte qu'on est porté à aimer celui qui nous la fait sentir, car il ne nous a point fait montre de son bien, mais du nôtre. Et ainsi ce bien fait nous le rend aimable, outre que cette communauté d'intelligence que nous avons avec lui incline nécessairement le cœur à l'aimer. (L652/S536)

I have discussed elsewhere how the way in which we read the text and are forced to make sense of it for ourselves is central to the persuasive process of the *Pensées*.[245] The fragmentary nature, or open-endedness, of the text is deemed to be more effective as a persuasive tool, because the reader, far from being fed truths or being told what to believe by someone else, is encouraged to search or fill in the gaps for him or herself. As Pascal stresses in another fragment, "on se persuade mieux pour l'ordinaire par les raisons qu'on a soi-même trouvées que par celles qui sont venues dans l'esprit des autres" (L737/S617). Here the reader's own memory must be used to grasp intuitively ("sentir") a truth. Just as those pupils at Port-Royal were encouraged to make active use of their memories, here the reader is engaged in a similar task of learning in a positive way.

Indeed, the reader's memory plays a crucial role in the dialectician's persuasive design, for he is seeking to write in a way which will be remembered most effectively by his reader. One fragment in particular

---

[245] See my *Playing with Truth*, pp. 50-78.

brings together many of the elements discussed thus far, where the styles of the two most influential worldly writers (as named by Pascal in his *Entretien avec M. de Sacy*) – Montaigne and Epictetus – and of himself, hidden under the pseudonym Salomon de Tultie (which is itself an anagram of two previous pseudonyms which Pascal used, Amos Dettonville and Louis de Montalte), are singled out as particularly memorable:

> La manière d'écrire d'Epictète, de Montaigne et de Salomon de Tultie est la plus d'usage qui s'insinue le mieux, qui demeure plus dans la mémoire et qui se fait le plus citer, parce qu'elle est née sur les entretiens ordinaires de la vie, ... (L745/S618)

Pierre Force has shown brilliantly how traditional rhetoric is here inverted by Pascal: *elocutio* ("la manière d'écrire") becomes subservient to *memoria*, reshaped to accommodate written ("art d'écrire") rather than oral ("art de dire") discourse. As Force puts it, "la mémoire dont il s'agit n'est plus celle de l'orateur, mais celle du lecteur. Si la manière d'écrire de Salomon de Tultie [...] consiste à faire en sorte que le lecteur retienne ce qu'on écrit, alors on peut soutenir que pour Pascal, l'élocution (l'art de la phrase) est toute contenue dans la mémoire ainsi définie."[246] Pascal adds that he, Montaigne and Epictetus are more easily memorable as writers because they draw their style from "les entretiens ordinaires de la vie". On one level, this is very much in keeping with the "discours naturel" which Pascal praises in L652/S536.[247] On another level, knowledge of Port-Royal educational practice can again throw light on the importance which Pascal attaches to "entretiens". As I discussed in the previous chapter, small-group teaching, based on conversation, was deemed to be the most effective way of learning and remembering ("en conferant avec les vivans", as Coustel describes it[248]). For Pascal, this useful effect of conversation is recreated in the *Pensées*, not only through a natural style but also through the use of

---

[246] P. Force, 'Invention, Disposition, Mémoire dans les *Pensées* de Pascal', art.cit., p. 761. *Cf.* B.Lamy, whose *La Rhétorique ou l'art de parler* (1675) was strongly influenced by Port-Royal, also sees *elocutio* as a subdivision of *memoria* in Book IV, chapter 2, entitled "Les qualités du style de chaque auteur dépendent de celles de son imagination, de sa mémoire et de son esprit": "les expressions heureuses et justes sont l'effet d'une bonne mémoire", ed. B.Timmermans (Paris: PUF, 1998), p. 359.

[247] *Cf.* L675/S554: "Quand on voit le style naturel on est tout étonné et ravi, car on s'attendait de voir un auteur et on trouve un homme."

[248] *Regles de l'Education des Enfans*, p. 213.

dialogue.[249] Indeed, many of the fragments are inhabited by unattributed fragmentary voices. The fact that this memorable style "se fait le plus citer" is once more supported by the Port-Royal schools' preference for memorizing only those passages which are most useful.

The text of the *Pensées*, in its memorability, can therefore be viewed in this context as an educational self-help manual where the reader learns about himself or herself in the process. But, more than that, not only is the style of the fragments themselves striking, but the text is peppered with maxims and quotations from other writers, which provide the same purpose as those extracts used for the children at Port-Royal.

c) *Les plus excellentes choses qui sont dans les bons Auteurs*

One of the most valuable texts which contains Pascal's own ideas on the reading of secular writers comes, appropriately given the teaching methods at Port-Royal, in the form of a conversation between Pascal (soon after his second conversion) and his spiritual director, Isaac Le Maistre de Sacy, which took place at Port-Royal des Champs: the *Entretien avec M. de Sacy*.

Jean Mesnard, in countering Henri Gouhier's assertion that the *Entretien* is primarily an apologetic piece, makes the crucial point that it should be viewed instead as "un écrit à visée *pédagogique*".[250] Indeed, a number of factors help to reinforce the link between the text and educational practices at Port-Royal. The *Entretien* was recorded by Sacy's secretary, Nicolas Fontaine, who himself was a teacher at the Port-Royal petites écoles, possibly at the very time that Pascal and Sacy met.[251] Moreover, if Mesnard's dating of the conversation held between Sacy and Pascal is to be followed as during 1655,[252] it is perhaps significant that it

---

[249] For a subtle and interesting analysis of conversation in the *Pensées*, see G. Magniont, *Traces de la voix pascalienne* (Lyon: Presses Universitaires de Lyon, 2003), pp. 185-196.

[250] J.Mesnard in Pascal, *Œuvres complètes*, vol. 3, p. 117. He is referring to Gouhier's argument in *Blaise Pascal: Commentaires* (Paris, 1966). Page references to the *Entretien* are from Mesnard's edition.

[251] F.Delforge argues convincingly that Fontaine was a teacher at Port-Royal "probablement avant 1656"; he adds that as an educator Fontaine placed himself firmly "dans le sillage de Sacy", *Les petites écoles de Port-Royal*, p. 185.

[252] Mesnard in Pascal, *Œuvres complètes*, vol. 3, p. 120.

was in the same year that Pascal developed his reading method which was to be used in the petites écoles.

Sacy, to whom Pascal had come for instruction, spoke to Pascal about his reading of philosophers. However, far from finding a humble supplicant to whom he could teach the value of reading the Bible and Church fathers such as Augustine, Sacy was faced with a young man who passionately espoused reading the secular writers, Montaigne and Epictetus. Sacy, who, according to Fontaine, "avait toujours cru devoir peu lire ces auteurs" (p.130), appears in the text somewhat surprised by Pascal's vehemence. Moreover, Pascal seems to usurp Sacy's role as teacher as he stresses "l'utilité de ces lectures" (p.156). After Pascal's initial comments about Montaigne, for example, Sacy confirms the pedagogical success of his interlocutor: "je suis sûr que si j'avais longtemps lu Montaigne, je ne le connaîtrais pas autant que je fais depuis cet entretien que je viens d'avoir avec vous" (p. 144). At a later stage in their conversation, after Sacy has attempted to reassert his authority by insisting on the need to read only religious writers, Pascal, while paying lip service to Sacy's position as his spiritual director, again takes on the mantle of instructor:

> Il est vrai, Monsieur, que vous venez de me faire voir admirablement le peu d'utilité que les chrétiens peuvent faire de ces lectures philosophiques. Je ne laisserai pas, néanmoins, avec votre permission, de vous en dire encore ma pensée, prêt néanmoins de renoncer à toutes les lumières qui ne viendront point de vous. (p. 152)

Far from imbibing only the insight that comes from his spiritual director, Pascal reasserts his pedagogical theme by stressing the potential usefulness of reading such secular authors. But, just as the Port-Royal teachers must have, in Coustel's words, "prudence pour pouvoir regler les mœurs",[253] Pascal insists:

> C'est pourquoi ces lectures doivent être réglées avec beaucoup de soin, de discrétion et d'égard à la condition et aux mœurs de ceux à qui on les conseille. (pp. 156-7)

Perhaps the most striking proof of Pascal's success in reversing the teacher-pupil dynamic can be found in a comment reportedly made by Sacy himself and recorded in the *Recueil de choses diverses*, the collection which I

---

[253] P. Coustel, *Les Regles de l'education des enfans*, vol. 1, p. 134.

discussed in chapter 2: "M. Paschal estoit l'homme du monde le plus propre pour former un esprit".[254]

i. Montaigne

Pascal's readings of Montaigne play a crucial role in the *Pensées*, not only on a thematic or stylistic level but also with respect to the disorder of the text. As we saw in L745/S618, the style of his writing, along with that of Epictetus, remains "plus dans la mémoire", but also, as can be found in L780/S644, Montaigne's "confusion" is partially praised, because "il avait bien senti le défaut d'une droite méthode".[255] Yet, as Pascal notes elsewhere, he will not be following the "confusion sans dessein" (L532/S457) which he associates with Montaigne. It will be carefully regulated to communicate the disorder of his fallen human subject matter: "je ferais trop d'honneur à mon sujet si je le traitais avec ordre puisque je veux montrer qu'il en est incapable" (L532/S457).

The piece of writing which combines most directly discussion of Montaigne with an evocation of memory is the section of Pascal's *De l'esprit géométrique*, entitled 'De l'art de persuader'. Given the importance of conversation to Pascal's style and apologetic/pedagogic design, it is significant that he refers here directly to Montaigne's *De l'Art de conférer*, for this chapter of the *Essais* celebrates conversation as "le plus fructueux et naturel exercice de nostre esprit".[256] Moreover, the likelihood that Pascal was influenced by Montaigne in his choice of title only serves to show again the close link which he makes between conversation or discussion (*conférer*) and persuasive techniques (*persuader*). Just as the *Entretien avec M. de Sacy* concerns the pedagogical usefulness of reading, so too in 'De l'art de persuader' Pascal analyses different ways of reading (and, significantly, of memorizing) books. A section from *De l'Art de conférer*,

---

[254] *Recueil de choses diverses*, 148v, p. 373.

[255] See also H.Phillips, 'The inheritance of Montaigne and Descartes', in *The Cambridge Companion to Pascal*, ed. N.Hammond (Cambridge: Cambridge University Press, 2003), pp. 23-30, especially p. 29.

[256] Montaigne, *Essais*, ed. M.Rat (Paris: Pléiade, 1962), III, viii, p. 900. Yvan Bamps gives a different reading of memory in *De l'esprit géométrique* from my own in 'Trace d'ombre: Pascal, Montaigne et la mémoire', in *Les lieux de mémoire et la fabrique de l'œuvre*. His discussion of Pascal's assimilation of Montaigne and Descartes into the text is particularly illuminating. See also L.Thirouin, 'Pascal et *L'Art de conférer*', in *Cahiers internationaux d'étude française* 48 (1988) 199-218.

where Montaigne criticizes those who use only their memorization of books as proof of knowledge, acts as one possible source:

> J'ayme et honore le sçavoir autant que ceux qui l'ont; et, en son vray usage, c'est le plus noble et puissant acquest des hommes. Mais en ceux là (et il en est un nombre infiny de ce genre) qui en establissent leur fondamentale suffisance et valeur, qui se raportent de leur entendement à leur memoire, [...] et ne peuvent rien que par livre, je le hay, si je l'ose dire, un peu plus que la bestise.[257]

Pascal reappropriates Montaigne's thoughts in a fascinating way, because these ideas can once more be related to the Port-Royal pedagogical practice of praising the active and positive use of memory as opposed to the potentially dangerous passive use of memory:

> Ceux qui ont l'esprit de discernement savent combien il y a de différence entre deux mots semblables, selon les lieux et les circonstances qui les accompagnent. Croira-t-on, en vérité, que deux personnes qui ont lu et appris par coeur le même livre le sachent également, si l'un le comprend en sorte qu'il en sache tous les principes, la force des conséquences, les réponses aux objections qu'on y peut faire, et toute l'économie de l'ouvrage; au lieu qu'en l'autre ce seraient des paroles mortes, et des semences qui, quoique pareilles à celles qui ont produit des arbres si fertiles, sont demeurées sèches et infructueuses dans l'esprit stérile qui les a reçues en vain?[258]

At this point, Pascal mentions Montaigne by name, emphasizing the need to delve below the surface of assertions, which anticipates to a large extent Pascal's perception of *raison des effets* in the *Pensées*:

> Tous ceux qui disent les mêmes choses ne les possèdent pas de la même sorte: et c'est pourquoi l'incomparable auteur de *l'Art de conférer* s'arrête avec tant de soin à faire entendre qu'il ne faut pas juger de la capacité d'un homme par l'excellence d'un bon mot qu'on lui entend dire; mais, au lieu d'étendre l'admiration d'un bon discours à la personne, qu'on pénètre, dit-il, l'esprit d'où il sort; qu'on tente s'il le tient de sa mémoire ou d'un heureux hasard; qu'on le reçoive avec

---

[257] Montaigne, *Essais*, III, viii, p. 905. See also III, viii, p. 919, where Montaigne evokes the different parts of rhetoric by asking how one can discern "la force et beauté" of "un homme sçavant et memorieux", and to what extent the "chois, disposition, ornement et langage" are his alone or simply borrowed from others.

[258] Pascal, *Œuvres complètes*, vol. 3, pp. 422-3. All other references to *De l'esprit géométrique* will be taken from this edition.

froideur et avec mépris, afin de voir s'il ressentira qu'on ne donne pas
à ce qu'il dit l'estime que son prix mérite. On verra le plus souvent
qu'on le leur fera désavouer sur l'heure, et qu'on les tirera bien loin de
cette pensée meilleure qu'ils ne croient, pour les jeter dans une autre
toute basse et ridicule. Il faut donc sonder comme cette pensée est
logée en son auteur; comment, par où, jusqu'où il la possède.
Autrement, le jugement précipité sera jugé téméraire. (p. 423)

Montaigne himself writes widely on memory in the *Essais*. Although
it is clearly beyond the remit of this study to discuss Montaigne's use of
memory at length,[259] there are certain mentions of memory in the *Essais*
which have a particular bearing on the *Pensées* and which merit
examination. Michel Beaujour summarizes the two main types of remarks
on memory to be found at first glance in the *Essais*: "les uns déplorent, ou
du moins affirment, l'exceptionnelle amnésie de l'autoportraitiste, tandis
que d'autres opposent brutalement deux *facultés* qui, à la Renaissance,
étaient habituellement envisagées dans une relation de complémentarité: le
jugement et la *mémoire*".[260] The question of forgetfulness will recur in my
discussion of failure of memory in the *Pensées*. Judgement and memory, in
the *Pensées* and at Port-Royal, as we have seen, conform more closely to
the Renaissance idea of complementarity than to Montaigne's placing the
two in conflict with each other. As Raymond La Charité sees it, with few
exceptions, for Montaigne "judgement is an active faculty which is
fashioned by exercise, whereas memory, which is passive in nature, can
only receive and retain".[261] On the other hand, as far as the field of
education is concerned, Jean Chateau makes the pertinent observation that
"on dit trop de la pédagogie de Montaigne que c'est une pédagogie du

---

[259] Several critics have examined memory in Montaigne. See, for example, M.Beaujour,
Miroirs d'encre (Paris, 1980); J. Holyoake, 'Montaigne's attitude towards memory',
in *French Studies* XXV no.3 (July 1971) 257-270; D. Ménager, 'Improvisation et
mémoire dans les *Essais*', in *Bulletin de la Société des amis de Montaigne* VII no.1-2
(July-December 1985) 101-110. Angelica Goodden's brief examination in *The
Backward Look* of Montaigne and memory within the context of what she terms the
writing self is particularly stimulating: "In language that captures the flow of
experience, Montaigne gives notice that he is both a remembered and a created being,
and so puts a doubly substantial life into what might otherwise have seemed the
echoing halls of the self", p. 18.

[260] *Miroirs d'encre*, p. 113.

[261] R.C. La Charité, *The Concept of Judgment in Montaigne* (The Hague, 1968), p. 15.
Cf. D. Ménager's comment about memory, in 'Improvisation et mémoire dans les
Essais', that "au lieu de l'envisager comme une force de proposition, il la voit comme
un poids mort, un lourd passé s'opposant au bel aujourd'hui", p. 104.

jugement: c'est oublier que le jugement naît lui-même en bonne part de la mémoire bien conduite".[262] In addition to *De l'Art de conférer*, one chapter in the *Essais* is particularly useful for my discussion of memory and education in the *Pensées*: *De l'Institution des enfans* (I,xxvi).

Montaigne himself received an education which emanated from the Renaissance inheritance of the Socratic tradition, based on a dialogic conception of learning.[263] This was indeed the basic method which educators at Port-Royal took up and adapted for their purposes. Pascal was well aware of Montaigne's musings on education in *De l'Institution des enfans*, for the first lines of the chapter find a clear echo in the *Pensées*. Montaigne writes:

> Aussi moy, je voy, mieux que tout autre, que ce ne sont icy que resveries d'homme qui n'a gousté des sciences que la crouste premiere, en son enfance, et n'en a retenu qu'un general et informe visage: un peu de chaque chose, et rien du tout, à la Françoise. (I,xxvi, p. 144)

Montaigne's thoughts are transformed into what looks very much like prescriptive pedagogical ideas in a fragment (crossed out by Pascal) from the *Pensées*:

> (Peu de tout). Puisqu'on ne peut être universel en sachant tout ce qui se peut savoir sur tout, il faut savoir peu de tout, car il est bien plus beau de savoir quelque chose de tout que de savoir tout d'une chose. Cette universalité est la plus belle. Si on pouvait avoir les deux encore mieux, mais s'il faut choisir il faut choisir celle-là. Et le monde le sait et le fait, car le monde est un bon juge souvent. (L195/S228)

These reflections are very much corroborated by the educational practices at Port-Royal, where the pupils were taught a wide range of disciplines, including languages (both modern and ancient), Geography, History, Mathematics, Rhetoric, Philosophy and Christian Civility.[264]

As far as memory is concerned in *De l'Institution des enfans*, unthinking memorization is deemed to be worthless: "Sçavoir par cœur n'est pas sçavoir: c'est tenir ce qu'on a donné en garde à sa memoire"

---

[262] J. Chateau, *Montaigne psychologue et pédagogue* (Paris, 1964), p. 77.

[263] See S. Rendall, *Distinguo: Reading Montaigne differently* (Oxford, 1992), pp. 64-5.

[264] See F. Delforge, *Les petites écoles de Port-Royal*, pp. 287-320.

(I,xxvi, p. 151). Indeed, forgetfulness of the source of one's opinions is even recommended to the pupil: "qu'il oublie hardiment, s'il veut, d'où il les tient, mais qu'il les sçache approprier" (p. 150). This idea of appropriation is crucial to Montaigne (and, we shall see, to Pascal), for he goes on to assert that "ce n'est pas non plus selon Platon que selon moy, puis que lui et moi l'entendons et voyons de mesme" (p. 150). Terence Cave's discussion of this passage is illuminating, for, as he sees it, Montaigne's version seems to rely on perspectives which are coincidental: "le propos de Platon s'est déplacé vers une nouvelle subjectivité, mais apparemment sans changer de valeur".[265] Pascal's appropriation of Montaigne, on the other hand, is more radical: "Ce n'est pas dans Montaigne mais dans moi que je trouve tout ce que j'y vois" (L689/S568). In Cave's words, "la négation, transférée de Platon à Montaigne, est cette fois plus rigoureuse: le moi pascalien absorbe et efface tout Montaigne pour y substituer son contenu, sa propriété à lui".[266]

Perhaps the most telling link between *De l'Institution des enfans* and the *Pensées* brings us back to Pascal's choice of himself, Montaigne and Epictetus as the most memorable writers because of their assimilation of "les entretiens ordinaires de la vie" (L745/S618) into their writing. Montaigne, in examining the best way to convince a pupil, locates a style which is direct and which, paradoxically, makes one forget the individual components (the words) in order (presumably) to remember more effectively the wider message:

> Je veux que les choses surmontent et qu'elles remplissent de façon l'imagination de celuy qui escoute, qu'il n'aye aucune souvenance des mots. Le parler que j'ayme, c'est un parler simple et naïf, tel sur le papier qu'à la bouche; un parler succulent et nerveux, court et serré. (p. 171)

In *De l'Institution des enfans* as in the *Entretien avec M de Sacy* and the *Pensées*, pedagogical effectiveness and stylistic success are equated in a striking way. Steven Rendall's illuminating comments on Montaigne can easily be applied to Pascal in this regard:

> Montaigne extends the parallel between writing and education in a somewhat different direction by suggesting that the writer plays both

---

[265] T.Cave, *Pré-histoires*, p. 125.

[266] *Ibid.*, p. 125.

> the role of student with respect to antecedent master-texts and that of
> teacher with respect to readers [...].[267]

Yet I would argue that the case is more complex than Rendall suggests, as Pascal in particular plays the role of both pupil and teacher with respect to Montaigne's *Essais* as "antecedent master-text", for at the same time that he acknowledges Montaigne's stylistic success he is able to take issue with many of the ideas which Montaigne proposes and redirect them towards his own persuasive aims.

At times in the *Pensées*, for example, Pascal appears to engage with Montaigne in a way not unlike his conversation with Sacy. As we have seen already, he makes positive use of Montaigne in certain areas (like in applauding the style of writing), but also he criticizes him with a simplicity and directness which, paradoxically, is precisely the style that Montaigne praises in *De l'Institution des enfans*.[268] L525/S454, for example, which is concerned with custom, commences with a bald assertion reminiscent of spoken discourse, "Montaigne a tort", before Pascal specifies and develops his particular objections. In the *Pensées* as a whole, Pascal's quotation of Montaigne is always inventive and always moulded to fit his particular persuasive design. As Bernard Croquette in his study *Pascal et Montaigne* observes, "par un double travail – sur le signifiant et le signifié – Pascal défait le texte de Montaigne. Parfois même il le démantèle totalement: d'un ensemble, il ne garde que quelques éléments isolés dont il fait un usage tout différent".[269] This "usage" is indeed transformed for the "utilité" of his apologetic project.

ii. Epictetus

Pascal's assimilation of Epictetus into the text, although less wide-ranging than that of Montaigne, is nonetheless crucial within the context both of conversation and of memory.[270] It has been established that Pascal used the

---

[267] S.Rendall, p. 64.

[268] See J. Mesnard, 'De la "Diversion" au "Divertissement"', in *Mémorial du premier congrès international des études montaignistes* (Bordeaux, 1964) 123-128: "C'est que l'influence se combine sans cesse à une réaction. Chez Pascal, Montaigne est spontanément combattu en même temps qu'admiré", p. 128.

[269] B.Croquette, *Pascal et Montaigne* (Geneva, 1974), p. 130.

[270] K. Christodoulou in her article, 'Le stoïcisme dans la dialectique apologétique des *Pensées*', in *Méthodes chez Pascal* (Paris, 1979), argues that many fragments, such as

1609 translation by Jean Goulu of the *Entretiens* (then translated as *Propos*) and the *Manuel*.[271] Significantly, Epictetus's writings are essentially dialogic in nature, emanating from his own experience as a teacher in Rome in the first century a.d. Just as Pascal lauds Epictetus for his use of "[les] entretiens ordinaires de la vie" in L745/S618, Epictetus praises Socrates in the *Propos* for his ordinary use of language (II,xii). This combination of pedagogy and conversation seems to be assimilated by Pascal into the *Pensées*, because at almost every point that Epictetus is mentioned, he appears within the context of an imagined dialogue. In L98/S132, for example, Epictetus is introduced as an interlocutor at an important stage to add greater impetus to Pascal's argument:

> D'où vient qu'un boiteux ne nous irrite pas et un esprit boiteux nous irrite? A cause qu'un boiteux reconnaît que nous allons droit et qu'un esprit boiteux dit que c'est nous qui boitons. Sans cela nous en aurions pitié et non colère.
> Epictète demande bien plus fortement: pourquoi ne nous fâchons-nous pas si on dit que nous avons mal à la tête, et que nous nous fâchons de ce qu'on dit que nous raisonnons mal ou que nous choisissons mal. (L98/S132)[272]

The role of dialogue in this fragment is highlighted not only by the presence of Epictetus's name but also by the clear allusion in the first paragraph to a passage from Montaigne's *De l'Art de conférer*: "De vray, pourquoy sans nous esmouvoir rencontrons-nous quelqu'un qui ait le corps tordu et mal basty, et ne pouvons souffrir la rencontre d'un esprit mal rangé sans nous mettre en cholere?"[273]

Elsewhere in the *Pensées*, Epictetus as a spokesman for stoicism is incorporated into a dialogue with sceptical interlocutors:

> 'Haussez la tête, hommes libres', dit Epictète. Et les autres lui disent: 'Baissez vos yeux vers la terre, chétif ver que vous êtes, et regardez les bêtes dont vous êtes le compagnon.' (L430/S683)

---

those on reason and the three orders, "ne semblent être qu'un souvenir vivant de la lecture d'Epictète", p. 422.

[271] This translation was first identified by F.Strowski in *Pascal et son temps* (Paris, 1907-8), 3 volumes, vol. 2, pp. 319-328.

[272] *Cf.* "Quand Epictète aurait vu parfaitement bien le chemin, il dit aux hommes: vous en suivez un faux." (L140/S172)

[273] Montaigne, *Essais*, III, viii, p. 907.

Moreover, as far as memory is concerned, in the *Entretien avec M de Sacy*, Epictetus's exhortation to remember our role as actors on the stage of life is enthusiastically quoted by Pascal:

> 'Souvenez-vous', dit-il ailleurs, 'que vous êtes ici comme un acteur, et que vous jouez le personnage d'une comédie, tel qu'il plaît au maître de vous le donner.'[274]

It would therefore be plausible to see Montaigne and Epictetus as important secular interlocutors within the *Pensées*, forming part of the dialogue which is perceived to be so essential to pedagogical success.[275]

Bearing in mind M de Sacy's insistence in the *Entretien* on the need to read the Church fathers, and indeed the central place accorded to sacred texts in the curriculum at the petites écoles, we should not ignore the very important dialogic role of sacred interlocutors in the *Pensées*. The one Church father who towers above all the others for his presence in the text is, not surprisingly, St Augustine.[276]

---

[274] *Œuvres complètes*, vol. 3, p. 131. See Goulu's translation, p. 654.

[275] Two secular interlocutors, Charron and Descartes, who make an appearance in the *Pensées*, albeit largely from a critical perspective (see L780/S644 and L887/S445), wrote on memory. However, their concerns with memory seem different from those of Pascal and had little direct impact on Pascal's own discussion of it. Charron, using a modified version of the Aristotelian conception of the soul and its faculties, considers primarily the link between the state of the brain and the effectiveness of understanding, imagination and memory. See Charron, *De la sagesse* (Paris, first published 1601), I.13. Moreover, as Christian Belin explains, memory is "toujours suspecte aux yeux de Charron", *L'Œuvre de Pierre Charron (1541-1603)*, p. 198. Descartes writes widely on memory, most notably in his *Méditations*. However, he shows little interest in the traditional practical questions of memory and is more concerned with how memory is stored and its operation as a faculty. Although sceptical doubt in the third *Méditation* involves memory, as Harry Frankfurt sees it, "the problem of the reliability of memory was of only incidental concern", 'Memory and the Cartesian Circle', *The Philosphical Review* LXXI (1962), 504-511, p. 511. *Cf.* Charles Larmore's article on 'Scepticism' in *The Cambridge History of Seventeenth-Century Philosophy*, ed. D.Garber and M.Ayers, (Cambridge, 1998) 2 vols, vol. 2, pp. 1171-2, and Stephen Gaukroger, *Descartes: an intellectual biography* (Oxford, 1995), pp. 273-4. See also my discussion of Descartes in chapter 1.

[276] It is worth pointing out here, within the context of secular writers, that, in the *Entretien*, Sacy uses a common image particularly associated with Augustinian memory, the digestion of food, referring in this instance to the dangerous thought of secular thinkers, where he paraphrases V, 6 of Augustine's *Confessions*: "ces viandes, au lieu de nourrir le cœur, le vident", p. 147.

iii. Augustine

We have seen already in the first two chapters the great influence of Augustine on seventeenth-century thought as a whole and on educational practices at Port-Royal in particular. Moreover, Philippe Sellier's magisterial work *Pascal et saint Augustin*[277] has amply demonstrated Pascal's great debt to Augustine. Given the importance of the *Confessions* to thinkers like Sacy and the centrality of memory in Book X of the *Confessions*, it is surprising that the work plays only a minor role in Pascal's writings.[278] However, in a more recent article, Sellier has provided a convincing explanation of this fact, although, as we saw in Nicole's use of Augustinian memory in the last chapter, it is more equivocal than he suggests:

> L'auteur des *Pensées* se rangerait simplement du côté des théologiens de profession – du Grand Arnauld et de Pierre Nicole – qui eux non plus ne citent guère les *Confessions*. La violence et l'urgence des controverses sur la grâce divine a conduit ces penseurs à mettre au premier plan les dernières œuvres d'Augustin, ses combats contre Pélage (412 à 430).[279]

As might be expected, Augustine is cited for the most part in the *Pensées* as an authority, at times appearing in the guise of an interlocutor, such as in L169/S200 – "Je ne serais pas chrétien sans les miracles, dit saint Augustin", at other times acting as a marker in the text to signal Pascal's source: "Saint Augustin. La raison ne se soumettrait jamais si elle ne jugeait qu'il y a des occasions où elle se doit soumettre" (L174/S205). However, even if the speaker of the *Pensées* mostly places himself *in statu pupilaris* with regard to Augustine, the spirit of interaction between two minds is always maintained, to the extent that, not unlike Pascal's exchanges with Sacy in the *Entretien*, roles are reversed. In L577/S480, for example, Pascal praises Augustine for acknowledging the role of uncertainty in daily life but upbraids him for not seeing "la règle des partis" (defined by Laurent Thirouin as "la possibilité d'un comportement

---

[277] Paris, 1970.

[278] Pierre Courcelle in *Les Confessions de saint Augustin dans la tradition littéraire* (Paris, 1963) locates only three direct references to the *Confessions* in all of Pascal's work.

[279] P. Sellier, 'Des *Confessions* aux *Pensées*: les seuils platoniciens', in *Revue de l'Institut Catholique* 60 (october-december 1996) 21-30, p. 22. *Cf.* N.Fontaine in his *Mémoires*, who consciously attempts to imitate the style of the *Confessions*.

rationnel face au hasard"[280]). In keeping with the idea of dialogue, Pascal
then goes on to refer to *De l'Art de conférer* (the same section which he
discussed in L98/S132), criticizing Montaigne for not delving enough
below the surface:

> Saint Augustin a vu qu'on travaille pour l'incertain sur mer, en
> bataille, etc. – mais il n'a pas vu la règle des partis qui démontre qu'on
> le doit. Montaigne a vu qu'on s'offense d'un esprit boiteux et que la
> coutume peut tout, mais il n'a pas vu la raison de cet effet.
> (L577/S480)

The persuasive process of the *Pensées* relies on this interactive relationship
with master-texts, where the persuader is both teacher and pupil.

From a stylistic point of view, the fact that Augustine is not
mentioned in L745/S618 as an example of memorable writers shows that
he is not perceived by Pascal to capture the modulations of ordinary
conversation which are integral to the stylistic success of Montaigne and
Epictetus. However, we find in the *Pensées* another kind of memorable
style – namely a lyrical mode of discourse – which can be traced to the
influence of Augustine and biblical passages. Pascal's repeated use of
groups of two or three terms is an acknowledged Augustinian device.[281]
Moreover, as Sellier has shown, "l'apologiste recrée un certain nombre de
figures du lyrisme augustinien: non seulement les *énumérations*, mais les
interrogations, les *cris*, les *apostrophes*, et jusqu'à la solennelle
prosopopée."[282]

I shall limit myself to one passage from the *Pensées* which is
strongly coloured by the poetic style of both Psalm 136 (137 in the
Jerusalem Bible) and by Augustine's commentary on the psalm.[283]
Significantly, another function of memory is presented in this fragment
which is not individual but rather part of the wider Jewish and Christian
traditions. In other words, it is a collective memory which signifies
permanence as opposed to the "choses périssables" of the present. Indeed,

---

[280] L.Thirouin, *Le Hasard et les Règles: le modèle du jeu dans la pensée de Pascal* (Paris, 1991), p. 116.

[281] See Sellier, *Pascal et saint Augustin*, p. 566.

[282] *Ibid.*, p. 568.

[283] See Sellier, *Pascal et saint Augustin*, pp 462-3, for a discussion of the borrowings made by Pascal from Augustine's commentary. I shall focus on aspects of memory in the commentary which were not examined by Sellier.

this memory could hardly be more different from the individual memory which was viewed as a "qualité périssable" in L688/S567:

> Tout ce qui est au monde est concupiscence de la chair ou concupiscence des yeux ou orgueil de la vie. *Libido sentiendi, libido sciendi, libido dominandi.* Malheureuse la terre de malédiction que ces trois fleuves de feu embrasent plutôt qu'ils n'arrosent. Heureux ceux qui étant sur ces fleuves, non pas plongés, non pas entraînés, mais immobilement affermis sur ces fleuves, non pas debout, mais assis, dans une assiette basse et sûre, d'où ils ne se relèvent pas avant la lumière, mais après s'y être reposé en paix, tendent la main à celui qui les doit élever pour les faire tenir debout et fermes dans les porches de la sainte Jérusalem où l'orgueil ne pourra plus les combattre et les abattre, et qui cependant pleurent, non pas de voir écouler toutes les choses périssables que ces torrents entraînent, mais dans le souvenir de leur chère patrie de la Jérusalem céleste, dont ils se souviennent sans cesse dans la longueur de leur exil. (L545/S460)

The lyrical quality of Psalm 136, a piece which itself revolves around shared memory and the perils of forgetfulness, is vividly evoked in this fragment. Sacy's translation of the psalm successfully captures these elements:

> 1. Nous nous sommes assis sur le bord des fleuves de Babylone, et là nous avons pleuré en nous souvenant de Sion.
> 2. Nous avons suspendu nos instruments de musique aux saules qui sont au milieu de Babylone.
> 3. Parce que ceux qui nous avaient emmenés captifs nous demandaient de chanter des cantiques.
> 4. Ceux qui nous avaient enlevés nous disaient: Chantez-nous quelqu'un des cantiques de Sion.
> 5. Comment chanterons-nous un cantique au Seigneur dans une terre étrangère?
> 6. Si je t'oublie, ô Jérusalem, que ma main droite soit mise en oubli.
> 7. Que ma langue soit attachée à mon gosier, si je ne me souviens point de toi;
> 8. Si je ne me propose pas Jérusalem comme le principal sujet de ma joie.
> 9. Souvenez-vous, Seigneur, des enfants d'Edom, de ce qu'ils ont fait au jour de la ruine de Jérusalem,
> 10. Lorsqu'ils disaient: Exterminez et abattez jusqu'à ses fondements.
> 11. Malheur à toi, fille de Babylone; heureux celui qui te rendra tous les maux que tu nous as faits.
> 12. Heureux celui qui prendra tes petits enfants et les brisera contre la pierre.

(Psalm 136)

In Augustine's commentary on the psalm, the distinction between permanence and temporality which is so important to Pascal's analysis is repeatedly stressed. As Augustine explains (in Arnauld's translation), of the two cities described in the psalm, "l'une a pour fin une paix eternelle, et se nomme Jerusalem; l'autre trouve sa joye dans une paix temporelle, et se nomme Babylone".[284] Moreover, the emphasis on *concupiscences* in Pascal's discussion finds its root in Augustine's assertion that "la concupiscence de la chair a humilié les uns; le mépris de la concupiscence a elevé les autres" (p. 139). As far as memory is concerned, both Augustine and Pascal point out the necessity for a fallen being who is a believer to remember, for not only is it crucial to be reminded of man's fallen state but also it is through the memory that humans can recall their original perfection. As Augustine states at the beginning of his commentary,

> Vous n'avez pas oublié, mes freres, ce que je vous ay dit, ou plustost ce dont je vous ay fait ressouvenir, que toute personne bien instruite dans l'Eglise doit sçavoir de quelle patrie nous sommes citoyens, quel est le lieu de nostre exil; que le peché est la cause de nostre bannissement, et que la grace qui nous fait retourner dans nôtre bienheureuse patrie est la remission des pechez, et la justification où nous establit la misericorde de Dieu. (pp. 111-2)

However, remembering Jerusalem, Augustine warns us, is not a simple exercise, for even the enemies of Jerusalem are able to remember it:

> C'est donc peu de se souvenir de Jerusalem. Il faut voir de quelle maniere on s'en souvient. Il y a de certaines choses dont nous nous souvenons avec aversion et avec haine. Il y en a d'autres dont nous nous souvenons avec amour. (p. 136)

Pascal takes up precisely this theme in L928/S756, where he warns that "il n'y a rien de si périlleux que ce qui plaît à Dieu et aux hommes", because, citing the parable of the pharisee and publican (Luke 18, 9-14), fallen humans have different criteria, usually governed by worldly glory. As he concludes,

> Que me servirait de m'en souvenir si cela peut également me nuire et me servir, et que tout dépend de la bénédiction de Dieu qu'il ne donne qu'aux choses faites pour lui, et selon ses règles et dans ses voies.

---

[284] Augustine, *Commentaires des Pseaumes*, translated by A.Arnauld (Paris, 1701), vol. 7, p. 112. All other references to this commentary will come from this translation.

La manière étant ainsi aussi importante que la chose, et peut-être plus, puisque Dieu peut du mal tirer du bien, et que sans Dieu on tire le mal du bien. (L928/S756)

iv. The Bible

Fontaine reports in his *Mémoires* that Sacy would often cite a maxim by Jansenius, "qu'il irait jusqu'au bout du monde avec son saint Augustin"; Sacy would then add, "et moi, j'irais avec la Bible".[285] A large proportion of the *Pensées*, as we have seen already, is populated by quotations not only from Augustine but also from liturgical texts and above all the Bible, much of which Pascal had memorized.[286] Pascal's citation of Psalm 136 in L545 is indicative of the central role which the Psalms in particular play in the text. Indeed, the Psalms are quoted by Pascal more than any other biblical text. As with Augustine's poetic mode of discourse, their lyrical nature clearly appealed to Pascal, but also they formed an integral part of his daily worship. As Sellier explains, "les Pseaumes constituent l'essentiel de l'Office et le grand écrivain en récitait plusieurs chaque jour".[287] In other words, they could be interpreted as essential ingredients in "les entretiens ordinaires" of his religious life.

It is not my intention to delve into the many biblical allusions in the *Pensées*, as this area has been comprehensively explored in a number of scholarly works.[288] However, of much greater relevance to this chapter is the biblical influence on Pascal's conception of collective memory in the *Pensées*, because almost all references to this wider application of memory are accompanied by biblical quotation or allusion. The durability of this memory is founded on the ancient status of the Jewish people. As Pascal states,

---

[285] N. Fontaine, *Mémoires*, ed. P. Thouvenin, p. 548.

[286] Nicole in his *éloge* of Pascal writes that "il étoit si assidu à lire l'Ecriture Sainte qu'il la sçavoit presque toute par cœur", in the *Recueil d'Utrecht*, p. 339. *Cf.* P. Sellier, *Pascal et la liturgie* (Paris, 1966): "sa prodigieuse mémoire lui permettait certainement de se rappeler, longtemps après, tel ou tel texte qui l'avait frappé", p. 25. See also D.Wetsel, *L'Ecriture et le Reste* (Ohio, 1981).

[287] See Sellier, *Pascal et la liturgie*, p. 52.

[288] In addition to the Sellier and Wetsel works *op. cit.*, see J.Lhermet, *Pascal et la Bible* (Paris, 1930) and J. Miel, *Pascal and Theology* (Baltimore, 1969).

> Je trouve d'effectif que depuis que la mémoire des hommes dure,
> voici un peuple qui subsiste plus ancien que tout autre peuple.
> (L793/S646)

Moreover, its permanence is dependent on passing the memory from generation to generation. The Book of *Genesis* was widely believed in the seventeenth century to have been written by Moses, who as a direct descendant of Adam was continuing the line from the creation through to the birth of Christ. Adam after all was seen as "le témoin et le dépositaire de la promesse du Sauveur" (L392/S11). Pascal argues that in *Genesis* "les six jours que Moïse représente pour la formation d'Adam ne sont que la peinture des six âges pour former Jésus-Christ et l'église" (L590/S489). Great events occur as a continuous sign of God's power, and for this reason, in a fragment entitled "Preuves de Moïse" (and placed in a *liasse* of the same name), Pascal perceives Moses in *Genesis* to be putting "deux choses les plus mémorables qui ne soient jamais imaginées, savoir la création et le déluge si proches qu'on y touche" (L292/S324). Similarly, in another fragment Pascal outlines the link between Noah and Moses:

> La mémoire du déluge étant encore si fraîche parmi les hommes
> lorsque Noé vivait encore, Dieu fit ses promesses à Abraham et
> lorsque Sem vivait encore Dieu envoya Moïse, etc. (L392/S11)[289]

Continuing the idea of lineage, Pascal refers again to *Genesis* and the chronology of patriarchs (chapters 37 to 50) whom he locates as prefiguring Christ's coming. In L570/S474, entitled "Jésus-Christ figuré par Joseph", Joseph's experience in prison as an innocent man caught between two criminals is interpreted as presaging Christ on the cross between the two thieves. Both Joseph and Christ's plights are associated with the act of remembering:

> Joseph ne fait que prédire, Jésus-Christ fait. Joseph demande à celui
> qui sera sauvé qu'il se souvienne de lui quand il sera venu en sa
> gloire. Et celui que Jésus-Christ sauve lui demande qu'il se souvienne
> de lui quand il sera en son royaume. (L570/S474)

However, the biblical references in the *Pensées* are dominated not only by memory but also by forgetfulness. The starkest warning of the dangers of forgetting God come in a paraphrase of *Deuteronomy* chapter 9:

---

[289] *Cf.* "les miracles de la création et du déluge s'oubliant Dieu envoya la loi et les miracles de Moïse" (L594/S491).

Si vous oubliez Dieu et que vous suivez des dieux étrangers je vous
prédis que vous périrez en la même manière que les nations que Dieu
a exterminées devant vous. (L543)[290]

The importance of forgetfulness is not limited to the Bible alone. It forms a
crucial part of both the *Pensées* and Pascal's other writings.

d) Forgetfulness and Prayer

The biblical references to man's forgetfulness of God find a vivid
parallel in Pascal's examination in his *Ecrits sur la Grâce* of the
Augustinian notion of "double délaissement", where God's abandonment
of man is perceived to follow directly the conscious abandonment of God
by Adam in committing original sin.[291] In other words, fallen human
beings'corrupt state is continually shaped by forgetfulness of God. And, for
the non-believer who consciously chooses not to remember God but who
considers instead "le moi haïssable"(L597/S494), this forgetfulness
becomes, as Meurillon puts it, "le mode de présence paradoxal de Dieu".[292]
For the believer, however, in a reversal of this model, it is God who is
remembered and the self which is forgotten.

It is therefore unsurprising that the appropriately named *Mémorial*,
effectively an *aide-mémoire* which Pascal kept sewn in his garment, is
punctuated by references to memory and forgetfulness. As he reminds
himself, "Oubli du monde et de tout, hormis Dieu" (L913/S742).

---

[290] This fragment does not appear in the Sellier edition. *Cf.* the various quotations from
Isaiah in L489/S735: "Mais perdez la mémoire de ces anciens bienfaits et ne jetez
plus les yeux vers les choses passées. [...] Mais c'est pour moi-même que j'effacerai
vos péchés et que j'oublierai vos crimes, car – pour vous, repassez en votre mémoire
vos ingratitudes, pour voir si vous aurez de quoi vous justifier. [...] Ressouvenez-vous
des premiers siècles et connaissez qu'il n'y a rien de semblable à moi, qui annonce dès
le commencement les choses qui doivent arriver à la fin, et déjà dès l'origine du
monde. [...] les choses passées ne seront plus en mémoire, et ne reviendront plus en la
pensée." *Cf.* also L483, which constitutes a quotation from *Isaiah* 49,14-15: "Et
cependant Sion a osé dire: Le Seigneur m'a abandonnée, et n'a plus mémoire de moi.
Une Mère peut-elle mettre en oubli son enfant, et peut-elle perdre la tendresse pour
celui qu'elle a porté dans son sein? mais, quand elle en serait capable, je ne t'oublierai
pourtant jamais, Sion."

[291] See *Ecrits sur la Grâce*, in *Œuvres complètes*, vol. 3, pp. 669-677. *Cf.* C. Meurillon,
'Oubli de soi, oubli de Dieu', pp. 26-8.

[292] C. Meurillon, 'Oubli de soi, oubli de Dieu', p. 27.

Moreover, the very next line in the document resituates the believer in the pedagogical tradition of the Bible: "Il [God] ne se trouve que par les voies **enseignées** dans l'Evangile" (my emphasis). This pedagogical imperative is reiterated later in the same text, this time with respect to the preservation (or indeed, commemoration) of Christ: "Il [Christ] ne se conserve que par les voies **enseignées** par l'Evangile" (L913/S742). Indeed, Christ's death represents the most powerful sign of the Christian faith, for at the Eucharist, Christ's words at the Last Supper are repeated, exhorting all believers (in Sacy's translation) to commemorate him: "Ceci est mon corps, qui est donné pour vous; faites ceci en mémoire de moi" (Luke 22, 19). Through biblical teaching and through the Eucharist, God and Christ are maintained in the collective memory, an idea which, as we saw earlier, is reinforced in the final line of the *Mémorial* in a quotation from Psalm 118: *Non obliviscar sermones tuos. Amen.* (L913/S742).[293]

The notion of *conservation*, allied with memory and prayer (the *Amen* at the end of the *Mémorial* signalling the text's prayer-like status), recurs in the letters written by Pascal to Mlle de Roannez, the daughter of his friend the Duc de Roannez. These letters, written between September 1656 and February 1657, as Jean Mesnard explains, "nous offrent l'avantage de nous faire assister à la pratique concrète de la direction de conscience".[294] Even more importantly, they show us Pascal in the role of teacher. The fact that their composition coincides with the early stages of Pascal's work on the *Pensées* adds further weight to my hypothesis that the *Pensées* can most usefully be read as a self-education manual.[295] As we saw in the previous chapter with Coustel and Nicole stressing the need to extract useful maxims from religious texts rather than from potentially harmful secular works, Pascal exhorts Mlle Roannez similarly: "car en vérité les préceptes chrétiens sont les plus pleins de consolations: je dis plus que les maximes du monde" (p. 1045). Also, just as the Port-Royal schools founded their daily educative process on biblical readings and prayer, so too does Pascal name them as the basis for his guidance of Mlle de Roannez. In his first letter, for example, he writes,

---

[293] "je n'oublierai point vos paroles" (Sacy translation), Psalm 118, v.16.

[294] J. Mesnard, in Pascal, *Œuvres complètes*, vol. 3, p. 1026. All references to the letters to Mlle de Roannez will be to this edition.

[295] For discussion of the dating of early fragments, see Pol Ernst, *Les Pensées de Pascal: géologie et stratigraphie*, pp. 151-178.

> Ce chapitre de l'Evangile, que je voudrais lire avec vous tout entier, finit par une exhortation à veiller et à prier pour éviter tous ces malheurs, et en effet il est bien juste que la prière soit continuelle, quand le péril est continuel. (p. 1030)

Moreover, the same ideas of biblical grounding, *conservation* and memory recur in letter 6, where Pascal quotes from *Ecclesiasticus*, XI, 27:

> Et ainsi nous devons travailler sans cesse à nous conserver cette joie qui modère notre crainte, et à conserver cette crainte qui conserve notre joie; et selon qu'on se sent trop emporter vers l'un, se pencher vers l'autre pour demeurer debout. *Souvenez-vous des biens dans les jours d'affliction, et souvenez-vous de l'affliction dans les jours de réjouissance*, dit l'Ecriture... (pp. 1041-2)[296]

Memory, like forgetting, seems to act as a catalyst for the antinomies which dominate Pascal's writing. As he states elsewhere in the *Pensées*, using the rhetorical technique of redescription, "à la fin de chaque vérité il faut ajouter qu'on se souvient de la vérité opposée" (L576/S479). We have just seen that memory of self can lead to forgetfulness of God and vice versa. Moreover, as the quotation from *Ecclesiastes* shows, memory dictates that our present emotional, physical or moral state implicitly calls to mind its contrary state.[297]

Just such an opposition is explicitly demonstrated in the above juxtaposition of *crainte* and *joie*, which, within the context of memory and prayer, calls to mind two fragments in the *Pensées* which, as Pol Ernst has shown,[298] were written consecutively on the same piece of paper. The first, L213/S246, consists of a quotation from a Church father favoured by Port-Royal and known for his own writings on memory and forgetfulness, St Bernard of Clairvaux:[299]

---

[296] The Furetière dictionary makes a link between the verb "conserver" and memory under the category of "choses morales et spirituelles".

[297] For a stimulating discussion of the technique of redescription, or paradiastole, see Q.Skinner, *Reason and Rhetoric in the philosophy of Hobbes* (Cambridge: Cambridge University Press, 1996), pp. 142-153, 161-172.

[298] *Les Pensées de Pascal: géologie et stratigraphie*, p. 304.

[299] A number of writers associated with Port-Royal translated St Bernard's works. Sacy, for example, in addition to possessing Bernard's *Opera* (Paris, 1645), also had translations of Bernard by Gabriel de S. Malachie and Antoine Le Maistre. See O.Barenne, *Une grande bibliothèque de Port-Royal: Inventaire inédit de la bibliothèque de Isaac-Louis le Maistre de Sacy* (Paris, 1985), p. 259. Moreover, St

Dignior plagis quam osculis
non timeo quia amo. (L213/S246)
(More deserving of blows than kisses, I am not afraid because I
love)[300]

The following fragment continues the theme of love of God, where prayer
is seen as one particular remedy against human corruption:

La vraie religion doit avoir pour marque d'obliger à aimer son Dieu.
Cela est bien juste et cependant aucune ne l'a ordonné, la nôtre l'a
fait.
Elle doit encore avoir connu la concupiscence et l'impuissance, la
nôtre l'a fait.
Elle doit y avoir apporté des remèdes. L'un est la prière. Nulle religion
n'a demandé à Dieu de l'aimer et de le suivre. (L214/S247)

The origin of these ideas can be found in St Bernard's sermons, where
prayer plays a crucial part in each human's need to "forget" or "remedy"
his/her sins. One sermon in particular, *De Conversione*, which was written
in 1140 for men wishing to enter the Cistercian order, translated (with two
other sermons) into French by Antoine Le Maistre in 1649, is essential.
Bernard uses the familiar trope of the stomach of memory in this sermon,
as indeed he does elsewhere. In a sermon on the solitary life, for example,
Bernard discusses the role of memory in the reading process:

il faut que de la lecture il demeure tous les jours quelque chose dans la
memoire, qui est comme l'estomac de l'ame, et avoir soin de le bien
digerer, le rappellant en la pensée pour le ruminer souvent, afin de
raffermir ainsi nos bonnes resolutions, d'avancer nos saints desirs, et
d'occuper nostre esprit de telle sorte, qu'il ne prenne plus de plaisir
dans les pensées qui le peuvent distraire.[301]

Bernard was associated particularly with Jacqueline Pascal. There exists a St Bernard
text (from his 45th sermon on the *Song of Songs*), once believed to be a reading
suggested by Pascal to his sister but now accepted as from Antoine Arnauld to
Jacqueline. See Pascal, *Œuvres complètes*, ed. Mesnard, vol. 3, p. 1079.

[300] St Bernard, *Sermons on the Canticles*, LXXXIV. Janet Coleman asserts that Bernard's
sermons on the *Song of Songs* "stand as the supreme example of his monastic method
which cauterised the memory and yet stimulated it by replacing private memorials
with scriptural reminiscences, which he saw as the very discipline of a converted life",
Ancient and medieval memories, p. 191.

[301] *De la vie solitaire, Traduction de trois excellens ouvrages de S.Bernard* (Paris, 1649)
tranlation by A. Le Maistre, pp. 217-8.

However, in *De Conversione*, Bernard transforms the trope. As Janet Coleman observes, "Augustine's treasure house of memory has become a sewer for Bernard. The belly of Bernard's memory is congested with filth".[302] Monastic life has the effect of eliminating self-will. Yet, for Bernard, this does not amount to obliteration of the memory (as Coleman seems to suggest), especially within the context of prayer. On the contrary, in Mary Carruthers' words, "a monk who had completely forgotten himself by obliterating his own past would not be able to pray".[303] The "forgetting" which occurs, therefore, is of a different order from complete effacement of self. For Bernard, the memory of one's own past sins can be instructive. As he states (in Le Maistre's translation),

> C'est sa grace [de Dieu] qui efface le peché, non en l'ostant de la memoire, mais en faisant qu'il y demeure sans la gaster et sans la rendre difforme comme auparavant. Nous nous souvenons de plusieurs pechez que nous ou d'autres ont commis, mais il n'y a que les nostres qui nous soüillent, ceux des autres ne nous nuisent point.[304]

Bernard's answer to the problems of memory lies in the question of *conversio*, willed relocation. As Carruthers explains, "the only way to 'forget' one's sins is to ask God's forgiveness and then change one's attitude, one's 'intention', towards them".[305]

e) Forgetfulness and the reading / writing process

For Pascal, both memory and the failure of memory prove to be crucial to his persuasive design. All the major themes related to memory which have recurred in this chapter – education, reading, antinomies – form the basis of Pascal's discussion of forgetfulness in the *Pensées*.

---

[302] *Ancient and medieval memories*, p. 181.

[303] *The Craft of thought*, p. 96. Carruthers makes the point that Coleman's reading of monastic attitudes towards memory "suffers from her disengagement with the praxis of prayer, memory in action", p. 306.

[304] St Bernard, *Traduction de trois excellens ouvrages de S.Bernard*, p. 79. *Cf.* the Port-Royal doctor Jean Hamon's musings on Bernard and forgetfulness in his *Relation de plusieurs circonstances...* (1734): "il faut s'oublier soi-même, comme saint Bernard dit que fait l'Epouse des Cantiques, pour pouvoir posseder Jesus-Christ parfaitement", p. 117. See also pp. 63 and 87-8.

[305] *The Craft of thought*, p. 97.

To a large extent, the memory/forgetfulness matrix governs notions of reading and writing in the *Pensées*. For this reason, it is useful to examine briefly the role of the reader and reading in the *Pensées*. Pascal himself was concerned with the pedagogical role of teaching young children to read, as can be seen in the teaching method which he devised for the children at the Port-Royal schools. Another level of reading is explored in the *Pensées*, where, as I have mentioned already in this chapter, the reader is forced through the fragmentary discourse to make sense of the text for him or herself. Like figurative language, which "porte absence et présence" (L260/S291), and which is dependent precisely on its ambiguity, the lacunae within and outside the text can be as instructive as the text itself. Richard Lockwood's analysis of figurative language is particularly illuminating in this context:

> It is a language where the relation of sign and meaning is precisely always in question – for the reader. For it is the reader, the reader as figured in the text and the reader outside the text, who is left with the problem of ascertaining whether the proper meaning is received, who must discern.[306]

In a world where "un même sens change selon les paroles qui l'expriment" (L789/S645), the reader is continually reminded both of the difficulties of attaining certainty through language alone and of his/her fallibility as a reader. Just as *Ecclesiastes* advises us to remember the antithesis of our present state, so too do individual fragments in the *Pensées* push us either to look beyond the subject-matter contained in the text or to reconsider a statement which might be explicitly negated in the text.

One seemingly insignificant fragment, where the act of reading itself appears to be negated, is potentially instructive in this light:

> Quand notre passion nous porte à faire quelque chose nous oublions notre devoir; comme on aime un livre on le lit lorsqu'on devrait faire autre chose. Mais pour s'en souvenir il faut se proposer de faire quelque chose qu'on hait et lors on s'excuse sur ce qu'on a autre chose à faire et on se souvient de son devoir par ce moyen. (L937/S763)

On one level, this fragment can be seen as a warning not to be seduced by *divertissements*, such as reading a pleasurable book, when one should be

---

[306] R.Lockwood, *The Reader's Figure: epideictic rhetoric in Plato, Aristotle, Bossuet, Racine and Pascal* (Geneva, 1996), pp. 281-2.

focused on serious matters. On another level, however, it constitutes a self-reflexive figure of reading. Just as with the concept of *divertissement*, which Pascal sees both as proof of "le malheur naturel de notre condition faible" (L136/S168) and as a potential pathway towards recognition of the need for God,[307] here the example of reading is signalled as dangerously diverting but also instructive. After all, as we read the fragment, we are being warned of the pitfalls which may mark our very act of reading. If we are lured by the stylistic delights of the text, we may forget our duty. As we are counselled in the fragment, we should think of something hateful to us so that we may become mindful of remembering our duty. Yet the only way that we can learn from this pointer is through reading Pascal's text. The *Pensées* encapsulate the paradox of reading/learning. The pedagogical value of reading is simultaneously denied and affirmed, in a way not unlike Port-Royal's distrust and espousal of the written word in the learning process.

Within the context of memory and forgetfulness, the reading paradox finds its most striking explanation in a crucial fragment on the act of writing. Moreover, it provides perhaps the most convincing support for my argument that the *Pensées* can best be interpreted within a pedagogical context:

> En écrivant ma pensée elle m'échappe quelquefois; mais cela me fait souvenir de ma faiblesse que j'oublie à toute heure, ce qui m'instruit autant que ma pensée oubliée, car je ne tiens qu'à connaître mon néant. (L656/S540)

The apologist/dialectician/pedagogue here accentuates the fact that the content of his thought is of less importance than the significance which he attaches to his forgetfulness of it. In forgetting, he is able to remember something of much greater import. As Christian Meurillon writes of this fragment, "l'oubli est ainsi récupéré par l'apologiste au profit d'une remémoration de la faiblesse humaine, bien nécessaire à qui veut apprécier avec justesse sa condition véritable".[308] I would go even further than Meurillon, because the essential ingredient of the fragment is the educational value which he derives from forgetting ("ce qui m'**instruit** autant…"). Pascal is here rewriting a thought by Montaigne on the value of

---

[307] For a fuller discussion of these different uses of *divertissement*, see my *Playing with truth*.

[308] Meurillon, 'Oubli de soi, oubli de Dieu', p. 24.

one's own experience, taken (appropriately) from 'De l'experience' (III, 13), where the word "instruction" is also central:

> D'apprendre qu'on a dict ou faict une sottise, ce n'est rien que cela; il faut apprendre qu'on n'est qu'un sot, instruction bien plus ample et importante. Les faux pas que ma memoire m'a fait si souvant, lors mesme qu'elle s'asseure le plus de soy, ne sont pas inutilement perduz.[309]

Pascal transforms Montaigne's ideas into an instructive tool, where the paradoxical value of forgetting acts as a continual reminder of human postlapsarian imperfection, redirecting both reader and writer towards recognition of the perfection of God.

III. Conclusion

Memory is therefore integral to Pascal's persuasive purpose, for the reader is continually confronted with ideas of memorability (which themselves involve questions of who and how to read, how to learn most effectively, how to persuade and be persuaded) and forgetfulness (which crucially serves as a reminder of fallibility while at the same time engaging the reader in the persuader's thinking and writing process). In almost all cases, whether in letters or polemical exchanges, conversations or apologetics, in reading secular or sacred writers, remembering and forgetting are used by Pascal as an instructive tool, where the reader becomes as much a teacher of self as a pupil of ancient or modern authorities.

Many of the questions which I have explored in this chapter recur in the plays of the most famous pupil of the Port-Royal schools, Jean Racine. However, far from palely reflecting what he learned at school, Racine vividly transforms traditional theories of memory to fit a specifically theatrical context. That will be the subject of the next chapter.

---

[309] Montaigne, *Essais*, III, 13, p. 1051.

CHAPTER 4

RACINE AND MEMORY

I. Racine and the Petites Ecoles

Racine's connection with the Port-Royal schools lasted for most of his childhood and adolescence. Both his aunt and grandmother were closely linked to the convent, and he moved between Port-Royal in Paris, Port-Royal des Champs and the other Port-Royal schools, such as those at Les Granges, Vaumurier and Le Chesnay. We know that Racine lived at the various petites écoles from at least 1649 (when he was ten), staying there until 1653. He then spent two years at the Collège de Beauvais, which had strong connections with Port-Royal, returning to Port-Royal in October 1655 and remaining there until 1658, when he spent a year at the Collège d'Harcourt.[310]

Especially towards the end of his life, Racine wrote of his schooling. The high quality of the Port-Royal schools receives warm praise, for example, in his *Abrégé de l'Histoire de Port-Royal*.[311] With regard to the teachers (Nicole, Arnauld, Lancelot) and then the pupils (such as de Harlay, de Bagnols and Le Nain de Tillemont) at the schools, he writes:

> Ces maîtres n'étaient pas des hommes ordinaires. Il suffit de dire que l'un d'entre eux était le célèbre M. Nicole. Un autre était ce même M. Lancelot, à qui l'on doit les *Nouvelles Méthodes* grecque et latine, si connues sous le nom de *Méthodes de Port-Royal*. M. Arnauld ne dédaignait pas de travailler lui-même à l'instruction de cette jeunesse par des ouvrages très utiles, et c'est ce qui a donné naissance aux excellents livres de *La Logique*, de *La Géométrie*, et de *La*

---

[310] See Delforge, pp. 257-261.

[311] *Cf.* the Abbé d'Olivet's remark in his *Histoire de l'Académie française* (1729) that "par reconnaissance pour l'éducation qu'il avait reçue à Port-Royal, il [Racine] employa les dernières années de sa vie à écrire l'histoire de cette fameuse abbaye", quoted by Jean Dubu in 'A propos de l'*Abrégé de l'histoire de Port-Royal* de Jean Racine', *Port-Royal et les Mémoires*, p. 278.

Grammaire générale. On peut juger de l'utilité de ces écoles par les hommes de mérite qui s'y sont formés.[312]

Even in his will, Racine mentions "l'excellente éducation que j'ai reçue autrefois dans cette maison".[313]

Racine himself was singled out at the Port-Royal schools for his exceptional abilities as a pupil, particularly for his excellent memory. Racine's son Louis writes, for example, in his *Mémoires sur la vie de Jean Racine* (Lausanne, 1747) that his father "sçavoit presque par cœur" the works of Sophocles and Euripides and that he had "une memoire surprenante" (p. 45). He even recounts an anecdote of how Racine used his extraordinary memory to deceive his teachers at Port-Royal:

> Il trouva par hazard le Roman grec des amours de Théagene et de Cariclée. Il le dévoroit, lorsque le Sacristain Claude Lancelot, qui le surprit dans cette lecture, lui arracha le livre et le jetta au feu. Il trouva moyen d'en avoir un autre exemplaire qui eut le même sort, ce qui l'engagea à en achetter un troisiéme; et pour n'en plus craindre la proscription, il l'apprit par cœur et le porta au Sacristain en lui disant, 'vous pouvez brûler encore celui-ci comme les autres.' (pp. 45-6)

One particularly useful source for our knowledge of Racine's own education and intellectual interests lies in the various notes which Racine himself made either in the form of annotations on the pages of texts or as separate jottings, many of which have been published in Picard's edition of the complete works.[314] The varied annotations pertaining to memory which the young Racine made while still a student at Port-Royal will be my central concern. In addition to notes made on Plutarch's *Lives*, where he writes, amongst other things, that 'on se souvient plutôt des injures que des faveurs'[315], and in which Racine inscribed the date 1655, we can also find his annotations (dating from 1656[316]) in a copy of Plutarch's *Moralia*,

[312] J. Racine, *Abrégé de l'Histoire de Port-Royal*, ed. A. Couprie (Paris: La Table Ronde, 1994), pp. 89-90.

[313] Quoted by J. Rohou in *Jean Racine* (Paris: Fayard, 1992), p. 452.

[314] See J. Racine, *Œuvres complètes*, ed. R. Picard (Paris: Pléiade, 1966), vol. 2. For a discussion of the texts which he studied, see W. McC. Stewart, 'L'Education de Racine', *Cahiers de l'Association internationale des études françaises*, 3 (1953), 55-71.

[315] *Vie d'Artaxerxe*, in Racine, *Œuvres complètes*, ed. R. Picard, vol. 2, p. 933.

[316] See W. McC. Stewart, pp. 58-9.

where his interest in the educational effect of memory is clear. In one annotation, for example, he remarks that 'les enfants [sont] plus faciles à instruire', accompanied by the suggestion that one should 'ne trop charger les enfants',[317] which, as we saw in Chapter 2, were pieces of advice repeatedly stressed in the various Port-Royal pedagogical tracts. Racine's further annotation that 'ceux qui ont de la peine à comprendre retiennent mieux'[318] matches the distinction made by Port-Royal educators between passive or thoughtless memorization, which they abhorred, and active, intelligent use of the memory.

Above all, Racine's notes on memory relate to his training in rhetoric. In his copy of Cicero's *De Oratore*, for example, he summarizes in French the five parts of rhetoric, "trouver, disposer, orner, retenir, prononcer" (ch.xxxi), and also refers to "la mémoire locale" (ch. xxxiv) – the system in which one associates commonplaces with symbols.[319] He also notes from chapter xxv the following "qualités d'esprit": "prompt à imaginer, fécond à expliquer, ferme à se ressouvenir".[320]

However, the most significant notes relating to memory which Racine made as a pupil have never been published: those on Quintilian's *Institutio Oratoria*, the manuscript of which has been preserved, along with extracts taken from Tacitus, at the Bibliothèque Nationale (fonds français 12,888). The following words, believed to be in Louis Racine's hand,[321] are written on the cover of the manuscript: "Extraits ecrits par Jean Racine des auteurs Latins qu'il lisoit à Port-Royal en 1656". Not only did Racine possess a copy of the *Institutio* (published in Lyon in 1665) at the time of his death,[322] but he refers to and quotes Quintilian in his preface to *Iphigénie*. The first scholar to have recognized the full significance of these notes from all books of the *Institutio*, Michael Hawcroft, devotes four

---

[317] J. Racine, *Œuvres complètes*, ed. R. Picard, vol. 2, p. 938.

[318] *Ibid.*, p. 940.

[319] *Ibid.*, p. 978.

[320] *Ibid.*, p. 973.

[321] See C. Fierville's edition of Quintilian, *De Institutione Oratoria liber primus* (Paris, 1890), p. xxxviii n. 5.

[322] See R. Picard's list of the books in Racine's library in *Nouveau Corpus Racianum*, pp. 446-451.

pages of his *Word as Action* to them.[323] In keeping with the subject of his book, Hawcroft chooses to concentrate on those notes which relate to *inventio, dispositio* and *actio*, but he does not discuss the many sections on memory which Racine copied in his notes.

These notes are fascinating not only because of the information they provide of Racine's reading at school but also because the primary focus of the *Institutio Oratoria*, very much reflected in Racine's notes, is educational. As Quintilian writes in the preface to Book I, copied by Racine, "oratorem autem instituimus illum perfectum" (my aim then is the education of the perfect orator).[324] Indeed, in his transcriptions from Books I and II, Racine seems particularly interested in those sections which concern how a teacher may most effectively teach a child. In I,i,1, for example, Quintilian's statements that reasoning is a natural gift which man possesses and that unteachable pupils are few and far between are faithfully copied by the Port-Royal pupil. Moreover, he writes down at length the advice that children should be taught in varied ways in order to refresh their minds (I,xii,4-5).

Memory forms a major part of the learning process for Quintilian. Indeed, many of his precepts were undoubtedly taken into account by the Port-Royal educators, especially the emphasis placed on nurturing the child's memory from an early age:

> Non ergo perdamus primum statim tempus, atque eo minus, quod initia litterarum sola memoria constant, quae non modo iam est in parvis sed etiam tenacissima est. (Let us not therefore waste the earliest years: there is all the less excuse for this, since the elements of literary training are solely a question of memory, which not only exists even in small children, but is specially retentive at that age.) I,i,19

This point is reiterated at a later stage in Book I, when memory is perceived to be the only faculty which can usefully be developed in a young child:

---

[323] M. Hawcroft, *Word as Action: Racine, Rhetoric and theatrical language* (Oxford: The Clarendon Press, 1992), pp. 30-4. I am grateful to Michael Hawcroft for allowing me to consult his transcription of Racine's notes on Quintilian.

[324] *Institutio Oratoria.* I, preface, 9. I shall use the translation and chapter numbering by H. E. Butler in the Loeb edition. However, I have maintained the Latin version transcribed by Racine, which includes a few, mainly minor, variations from the Loeb edition. At a later stage of the work, Quintilian even goes so far as to assert that the whole of our education depends on memory (XI,ii,1).

[…] maxime necessaria est oratori memoria, et ea praecipue firmatur atque alitur exercitatione, et in iis, de quibus nunc loquimur, aetatibus, quae nihildum ipsae ex se generare queunt, prope sola est, quae iuvari cura docentium possit. (…memory is most necessary to an orator, and there is nothing like practice for strengthening and developing it. And at the tender age of which we are now speaking, when originality is impossible, memory is almost the only faculty which can be developed by the teacher.) I,i,36[325]

In the last chapter, I discussed the close relationship between *memoria* and *elocutio* (style) in the *Pensées*. Quintilian sees memory as a subdivision of *elocutio*. For the diligent pupil and future playwright taking notes from Book II, Quintilian's advice to budding orators concerning memory and style would appear particularly apposite, for not only is memorization of other authors considered beneficial to one's own style but also the significance of those models which one might imitate was to be a central feature in Racine's theatre, especially in the *querelle des anciens et des modernes*, where Racine reiterated the need to bear in mind ancient authorities:[326]

[…] et exercebitur acrius memoria aliena complectendo quam sua; […] et assuescent optimis semperque habebunt intra se, quod imitentur; et iam non sentientes formam orationis illam, quam mente penitus acceperint, expriment. Abundabunt autem copia verborum optimorum ac compositione et figuris iam non quaesitis sed sponte et ex reposito velut thesauro se offerentibus. ([…] it is a better exercise for the memory to learn the words of others than it is to learn one's own […]. Further they will form an intimate acquaintance with the best writings, will carry their models with them and unconsciously reproduce the style of the speech which has been impressed upon the memory. They will have a plentiful and choice vocabulary and a command of artistic structure and a supply of figures which will not have to be hunted for, but will offer themselves spontaneously from the treasure-house, if I may so call it, in which they are stored.) II,vii,3-4.

---

[325] *Cf.* "Ingenii signum in parvis praecipuum memoria est. […] Proximum imitatio." (The surest indication in a child is his power of memory. […] The indication of next importance is the power of imitation.) *Institutio Oratoria*, I,iii,1.

[326] *Cf.* Racine's Préface to *Iphigénie* (in which he quotes Quintilian), where, in contradistinction to the *Modernes*, he writes of one of his sources, Euripides, that "en vérité j'ai trop d'obligation à Euripide, pour ne pas prendre quelque soin de sa mémoire".

Books III to X of the *Institutio* are less concerned with memory in a pedagogical context, but Racine still notes down a number of references to memory: for example, Quintilian urges the orator to remember even the lies which he utters, for a liar needs to have a good memory (IV,ii,91). Racine remains interested in the best methods to memorize speeches, copying a section on partitions of speeches as the greatest assistance to the speaker's memory (IV,iv,3) as well as a short sentence on the necessity of learning short, clear and intelligible verses which can be easily remembered (IX,iv,125). Although Quintilian has reservations about an orator premeditating too greatly the content of his speech, he nonetheless asserts that disasters in speeches can be averted by developing the power of memory (X,vi,6-7). In these books, Racine transcribes sections which relate particularly to the relationship between writing, reading and oral delivery. One paragraph concerns the way in which reading can assist the memory. Quintilian uses a familiar image of eating which, as we saw in Chapter 2, appears regularly in writings on memory:

> Lectio libera est nec actionis impetu transcurrit; sed repetere saepius licet, sive dubites sive memoriae penitus adfigere velis. Repetamus autem et retractemus, et ut cibos mansos ac prope liquefactos demittimus, quo facilius digerantur, ita lectio non cruda, sed multa iteratione mollita et velut confecta, memoriae imitationique tradatur. (Reading, however, is free, and does not hurry past us with the speed of oral delivery; we can reread a passage again and again if we are in doubt about it or wish to fix it in the memory. We must return to what we have read and reconsider it with care, while, just as we do not swallow our food till we have chewed it and reduced it almost to a state of liquefaction to assist the process of digestion, so what we read must not be committed to the memory for subsequent imitation while it is still in a crude state, but must be softened and, if I may use the phrase, reduced to a pulp by frequent re-perusal.) X,i,19[327]

For our purposes, by far the most significant sections of the *Institutio* which Racine transcribes come from the chapter which is devoted

---

[327] *Cf.* Ego autem ne scribendum quidem puto, quod [non] simus memoria persecuturi. Nam hic quoque accidit, ut revocet nos cogitatio ad illa elaborata nec sinat praesentem fortunam experiri. Sic anceps inter utrumque animus aestuat, cum et scripta perdidit et non quaerit nova. (For my own part, I think that we should never write out anything which we do not intend to commit to memory. For if we do, our thoughts will run back to what we have elaborated in writing and will not permit us to try the fortune of the moment. Consequently, the mind will waver in doubt between the two alternatives, having forgotten what was committed to writing and being unable to think of anything fresh to say.) X,vii,32-3.

specifically to rhetorical memory, XI,ii. Toward the beginning of the chapter, Quintilian's praise of memory as the most powerful component of effective oratory is the first paragraph noted down by Racine:

> Quid? Non haec varietas mira est, excidere proxima, vetera inhaerere? Hesternorum immemores acta pueritiae recordari? Quid quod quaedam requisita se occultant et eadem forte succurrunt? Nec manet semper memoria, sed aliquando etiam redit? Nesciretur tamen, quanta vis esset eius, quanta divinitas illa, nisi in hoc lumen orandi vim extulisset. (Again, is it not an extraordinary inconsistency that we forget recent and remember distant events, that we cannot recall what happened yesterday and yet retain a vivid impression of the acts of our childhood? And what, again, shall we say of the fact that the things we search for occur to us by chance, or that memory does not always remain with us, but will even sometimes return to us after it has been lost? But we should never have realised the fullness of its power nor its supernatural capacities, but for the fact that it is memory which has brought oratory to its present position of glory.) XI,ii,6-7[328]

In many ways what Racine omits as well as what he puts in proves instructive. Racine, like the educators at Port-Royal, seems to take a minimal interest in the art of memory; Quintilian's account in XI,xi of

---

[328] Quintilian and Racine seem very interested in the role that time plays in the workings of the memory. Racine copied another later section from the *Institutio* where the Latin author wonders about the way in which the memory paradoxically can be strengthened by the passage of time: "Mirum dictu est nec in promtu ratio, quantum nox interposita afferat firmitatis, sive quiescit labor ille, cuius sibi ipsa fatigatio obstat, sive matuatur atque concoquitur, quae firmissima eius pars est, recordatio; quae statim referri non poterant, contexuntur postera die, confirmatque memoriam idem illud tempus, quod esse in causa solet oblivionis. Etiam illa praevelox fere cito effluit, et, velut praesenti officio functa nihil in posterum debeat, tanquam dimissa discedit. Nec est mirum, magis haerere animo quae diutius adfixa sint.

(It is a curious fact, of which the reason is not obvious, that the interval of a single night will greatly increase the strength of the memory, whether this be due to the fact that it has rested from the labour, the fatigue of which constituted the obstacle to success, or whether it be that the power of recollection, which is the most important element of memory, undergoes a process of ripening and maturing during the time which intervenes. Whatever the cause, things which could not be recalled on the spot are easily co-ordinated the next day, and time itself, which is generally accounted one of the causes of forgetfulness, actually serves to strengthen the memory. On the other hand, the abnormally rapid memory fails as a rule to last and takes its leave as though, its immediate task accomplished, it had no further duties to perform. And indeed there is nothing surprising in the fact that things which have been implanted in the memory for some time should have a greater tendency to stay there.), XI,ii,43-4.

Simonides' discovery of the art of memory, for example, is not copied by
the young Racine. Instead, he takes again a particular interest in the
practicality of learning by heart and in the importance of the spectator or
listener's memory.

As far as learning by heart is concerned, Racine takes note of a
number of methods to remember more easily. At one point, for instance,
Quintilian suggests:

> Si longior complectenda memoria fuerit oratio, proderit per partes
> ediscere; laborat enim maxime onere; et hae partes non sint
> perexiguae, alioqui rursus multae erunt et eam distinguent atque
> concident. (If a speech of some length has to be committed to
> memory, it will be well to learn it piecemeal, since there is nothing so
> bad for the memory as being overburdened. But the sections into
> which we divide it for this purpose should not be very short: otherwise
> they will be too many in number, and will break up and distract the
> memory.) XI,ii,27

At another juncture, a link is made between the writing down of a passage
and committing it to memory:

> Illud neminem non iuvabit, iisdem quibus scripserit ceris ediscere.
> Sequitur enim vestigiis quibusdam memoriam, et velut oculis intuetur
> non paginas modo, sed versus prope psos, qui tum dicit similis legenti.
> Iam vero si litura aut adiecto aliqua atque mutatio interveniat, signa
> sunt quaedam, quae sequentes errare non possumus. (There is one
> thing which will be of assistance to everyone, namely, to learn a
> passage by heart from the same tablets on which he has committed it
> to writing. For he will have certain tracks to guide him in his pursuit
> of memory, and the mind's eye will be fixed not merely on the pages
> on which the words were written, but on individual lines, and at times
> he will speak as though he were reading aloud. Further, if the writing
> should be interrupted by some erasure, addition or alteration, there are
> certain symbols available, the sight of which will prevent us from
> wandering from the track.) XI,ii,32

Artistic structure in both prose and poetry is also considered vital for the
effective memorization of a passage (as found in XI,ii,39, for example).

Quintilian's statement (copied by Racine) that "in longissimis
actionibus prius audiendi patientia quam memoriae fides deficit" (even in
the longest pleadings the patience of the audience flags long before the
memory of the speaker", XI,ii,8) is certainly one which he bore in mind in

his theatre and which was a major preoccupation of theorists like D'Aubignac in his *Pratique du Théâtre* (1657), a copy of which Racine possessed at the time of his death.[329] D'Aubignac repeatedly stresses that the spectator's memory should not be overburdened. In IV,iii of the *Pratique*, for example, he claims that *récits* or *narrations* should not contain too many disparate pieces of information which are difficult for the spectator to remember, because, as in the case of a narration at the beginning of a play, "le Spectateur qui se persuade que tout ce récit est nécessaire pour l'intelligence de la Piéce, s'efforce de tout retenir, et se sentant la memoire accablée de tant de choses et l'imagination confuse, il se fâche contre soy-méme, et ensuitte contre le Poëte, et enfin il abandonne tout sans plus écouter".[330]

Above all, and of particular use to the hard-working Port-Royal schoolboy, is Quintilian's declaration that regular exercise of the memory is of utmost importance. Indeed, he even compares such practice to the exercise of muscles by athletes (XI,ii,42). Quintilian in his role as educator comes to the fore in XI,ii,40:

> Si quis tamen unam maximamque a me artem memoriae quaerat, exercitatio est et labor; multa ediscere, multa cogitare, et si fieri potest cotidie, potentissimum est. Nihil aeque vel augetur cura vel negligentia intercidit.
>
> (However, if anyone asks me what is the one supreme method of memory, I shall reply, practice and industry. The most important thing is to learn much by heart and to think much, and, if possible, to do this daily, since there is nothing that is more increased by practice or impaired by neglect than memory.) XI,ii,40

*
* *

Although it is tempting to apply these jottings on memory by the young Racine to all his plays, inevitably this would lead to the too easy conflation of Racine's early Port-Royal career with the content of his secular plays. Happily, the traditional interpretation of Racine as a card-carrying Jansenist in all his plays is now more often rejected than

---

[329] See Picard, *Nouveau Corpus Racianum*, pp. 446-451.

[330] F. D'Aubignac, *La Pratique du Théâtre* (Geneva: Slatkine Reprints, 1996), ed. P. Martino IV,iii, p. 291.

accepted.[331] All the tragedies, up to and including *Phèdre*, are necessarily belittled and emprisoned by such a narrow reading; but his two final plays, *Esther* and *Athalie*, are very different, in that their inspiration is not only religious but also educational. For this reason, these two plays will form the principal focus of the latter part of this chapter.

II. Memory in Racine's secular theatre

However, three phenomena in Racine's earlier theatre are worthy of brief examination first, in order to highlight the role of education and memory in the final two plays: (a) theatrical, or rhetorical, memory, (b) the significance of teacher figures in the plays,[332] and (c) tragedy as instruction.

a) theatrical memory

Les Plaideurs, Racine's only comedy, provides the most direct evidence of the way in which Quintilian's educational manual for the prospective orator made an impact upon Racine's theatre. Memory as a part of rhetoric appears most prominently in the trial scene of *Les Plaideurs* (III,3), where Petit-Jean, the porter of the judge Dandin, is designated as the lawyer in the trial of a dog which has eaten a chicken. The appearance of a prompter in this scene affords the dramatist the opportunity to parody the actor's craft and to give theatrical life to *memoria*. As the prompter explains to Dandin, "je viens secourir leur mémoire troublée" (691). Of the various parts of rhetoric which are parodied in the course of the scene,

---

[331] For a recent rejection of the interpretation of Racine as Augustinian, see J. Campbell, 'Racine and the Augustinian inheritance: the case of *Andromaque*', *French Studies* 53 (1999), pp. 279-291. For a view which still adheres to Augustinian readings of the plays, see J. Rohou, *Jean Racine* (Paris: Fayard, 1992).

[332] Both these first two categories are dominated by characters involved in an instructive or educational role, *confident(e)s* in the former, *gouverneurs* in the latter. Far from giving a comprehensive survey of all *confidents* and *gouverneurs* in Racine's theatre, which would belong to a different study altogether, I intend solely to offer a few examples of such figures in order to throw light on the two plays which were written specifically for educational purposes, *Esther* and *Athalie*. Valerie Worth-Stylianou, in *Confidential Strategies: the confident in French Tragic Drama* (Geneva: Droz, 1999), justifiably chooses to categorize both *gouverneur* and *confident*, along with other designations like *ami*, *suivante* and *dame d'honneur*, as *confident* figures, pp. 14-15. However, within an educational context, a distinction needs to be made; as I shall show, whereas the *gouverneur* is explicitly a pedagogue, the *confident* acts more in a prompting capacity.

memoria is accorded significant status in that the prompter is the only character to appear uniquely in the context of the trial scene. All other characters play different parts in the rest of the play. As a result, although in this scene the other characters are either consciously playing a role or (as in the case of the Dandin) continuing their public profession, the prompter belongs to a world where distinctions between real and imaginary are dissolved. Indeed, the comic effect of this scene is largely derived from the blurring of these boundaries. The prompter makes his first intervention when Petit-Jean, who has "perdu la parole" (716), is unable to remember his lines, but the scene continues with an exchange of insults between Petit-Jean and the prompter. It might be noted that such confrontations between actors and prompters were not unknown in the seventeenth-century theatre. Samuel Chappuzeau, whose *Théâtre françois* was first published in 1674, writes that he has witnessed actors "crier au Soufleur trop pront, de se taire, soit pour n'avoir pas besoin de son secours, soit pour faire voir qu'ils sont seurs de leur memoire, quoy qu'elle pust leur manquer".[333] The example of *Les Plaideurs* shows how Racine derives maximum comic impact from such a use of *memoria* within the context of rhetoric and theatrical action. But can such a use of memory be extended to his tragedies? I would argue that the *confident* figure allows for just such an interpretation.

If we consider *memoria* in the tragedies from a purely theatrical standpoint, it is possible to equate the *confident(e)*'s role with that of the prompter. Often the *confident(e)* attempts to help revive the protagonist's memory of an event in order to understand the situation better, such as Phénice's exhortations to her mistress in *Bérénice*. At the end of Act II, scene 4, Titus leaves Bérénice hastily without giving any reason for his departure. In the next scene, Phénice tries to elicit from Bérénice the possible reason for this sudden exit. The reiteration of words relating to memory gives the sense of Phénice acting as a supplementary memory for her mistress:

> BERENICE:
> Quoi me quitter si tôt, et ne me dire rien?
> Chère Phénice, hélas! Quel funeste entretien!
> Qu'ai-je fait? Que veut-il? Et que dit ce silence?
> PHENICE:
> Madame, je me perds d'autant plus que j'y pense.
> Mais ne s'offre-t-il rien à votre souvenir
> Qui contre vous, Madame, ait pu le prévenir?

---

[333] S. Chappuzeau, *Le Théâtre françois*, ed. G. Monval (Paris, 1876), pp. 145-6.

Voyez, examinez.
BERENICE:
                      Hélas, tu peux m'en croire;
Plus je veux du passé rappeler la mémoire,
Du jour que je le vis, jusqu'à ce triste jour,
Plus je vois qu'on me peut reprocher trop d'amour.
(625-634)

The most interesting and complex example of *confidente* as exponent of theatrical memory is undoubtedly Œnone in *Phèdre*. Phèdre's obsession with the distant past of her ancestors and her less sure grasp of her immediate past and of her present surroundings conform largely to Quintilian's question, quoted earlier, that, "is it not an extraordinary inconsistency that we forget recent and remember distant events, that we cannot recall what happened yesterday and yet retain a vivid impression of the acts of our childhood?" (XI,ii,7). One of Œnone's earliest actions, just before Phèdre admits to Œnone that she loves Hippolyte, consists in her attempting to suppress her mistress's memory of the past (I,3):

PHEDRE:
O haine de Vénus! O fatale colère!
Dans quels égarements l'amour jeta ma Mère!
ŒNONE:
Oublions-les, Madame. Et qu'à tout l'avenir
Un silence éternel cache ce souvenir. (249-252)

This exhortation to forget returns to haunt Œnone later in the play when Phèdre accuses her *confidente* of making her forget her duty: "Tes prières m'ont fait oublier mon devoir" (IV,6,1311).

Once Phèdre has articulated her secret love, Œnone's role changes. Thinking Thésée to be dead, she encourages Phèdre to continue living and to pursue Hippolyte. At the beginning of the scene of the *aveu* (II,5), there is a moment of metatheatricality which recalls the prompter's role in *Les Plaideurs*. On seeing Hippolyte, Phèdre forgets the lines which clearly she has rehearsed. Œnone, performing the function of prompter, reminds her of her words:

PHEDRE:
J'oublie, en le voyant, ce que je viens lui dire.
ŒNONE:
Souvenez-vous d'un Fils qui n'espère qu'en vous. (582-3)

As Phèdre begins to declare her love, Hippolyte appears to take over the prompter's role, by trying to force her to recall the words which she should be uttering as wife of Thésée. Phèdre's response on one level calls to mind Chappuzeau's example of actors attempting to prove to the prompter the sureness of their memory but on another level shows how she is once more confronted by the very memories which Œnone has been trying to make her forget:

> HIPPOLYTE:
> Dieux! Qu'est-ce que j'entends? Madame, oubliez-vous
> Que Thésée est mon Père, et qu'il est votre Epoux?
> PHEDRE:
> Et sur quoi jugez-vous que j'en perds la mémoire,
> Prince? Aurais-je perdu tout le soin de ma gloire? (663-6)

It is perhaps no coincidence in Racine's theatre that the word "mémoire" appears almost always as the rhyme word (41 out of 46 times). Significantly, on 30 of these 41 occurrences, "mémoire" rhymes with "gloire", with another important rhyme word being "histoire". For Racine's characters, memory is almost always closely connected to an impossible ideal of glory or to the glorious example of their ancestors, corresponding to memory in the sense of the Latin term *reminiscentia*.

Until Act IV, Œnone limits herself to prompting Phèdre, but in Act IV, scene 1, she turns her attention towards prompting Thésée, this time in a deliberately misleading way. As Barthes observes, "la ruse d'Œnone consiste précisément, non pas à *reprendre* l'aveu de Phèdre, à l'annuler, ce qui est impossible, mais à le retourner".[334] Whereas earlier she had told Phèdre, "Souvenez-vous d'un fils qui n'espère qu'en vous", here she prompts Thésée with the words,

> Seigneur, souvenez-vous des plaintes de la Reine.
> Un amour criminel causa toute sa haine. (1029-30)

Œnone's reference to Phèdre's distress and the ambiguity of her statement imply that Hippolyte rather than Phèdre is guilty, provoking Thésée's curse of his son which in turn leads to Hippolyte's death. In the scene of the curse, IV,2, it is telling that Thésée seems to inscribe the idea of Hippolyte's death into his own memory before he has even uttered the

---

[334] R. Barthes, *Sur Racine* (Paris: Seuil, 1963), p. 119.

curse. In one strangely prophetic moment, memory and its link with the past dissolve into a future event:[335]

> C'est bien assez pour moi de l'opprobre éternel
> D'avoir pu mettre au jour un Fils si criminel,
> Sans que ta mort encor honteuse à ma Mémoire
> De mes nobles travaux vienne souiller la gloire.
> (1055-8)

I shall return to the significance of memory in *Phèdre* in section c, on tragedy as instruction.

b) teachers, pupils and memory

Of those words used by Racine to describe his secondary characters, *gouverneur* is the term most directly related to pedagogy. As the Académie Dictionary of 1694 defines it, 'Gouverneur' is "celuy qui est commis pour avoir soin de l'education et de l'institution d'un jeune Seigneur, d'un jeune Prince". In his annotations on Sophocles' *Electra*, Racine shows particular interest in Orestes' teacher, whom he calls "gouverneur", and discusses the greater sagacity of the old man as opposed to the younger characters.[336] In Racine's theatre, we find three plays where characters are explicitly designated as *gouverneurs*: Phœnix in *Andromaque*, Burrhus and Narcisse in *Britannicus*, and Théramène in *Phèdre*.

As the *gouverneur* of Pyrrhus, Phœnix's role in *Andromaque* is negligible. The reason for this must stem mainly from the fact that Pyrrhus is already king and is less in need of advice from his teacher than a young prince might be.[337] To a large extent, Phœnix represents the king's past, a

---

[335] G. Forestier in his edition of Racine's theatre attempts to explain "ma Mémoire" in line 1057 as meaning "le souvenir que je laisserai de moi", p. 1654. However, this conflation of past and future memory seems to me more complex.

[336] Racine, *Œuvres complètes*, ed. R. Picard vol. 2, pp. 842-50. *Cf.* his comments on line 1326, in which he discusses Oreste's teacher: "le gouverneur d'Oreste leur reproche leur imprudence, et leur dit qu'on les aurait surpris sans lui. – Sophocle a voulu marquer l'imprudence des jeunes gens, qui ne peuvent se contenir dans leurs passions, et afin que le spectateur ne trouve point étrange qu'on ne les a point entendus de la maison, il fait que ce vieillard, plus sage qu'eux, a fait sentinelle à la porte", pp. 848-9.

[337] Worth-Stylianou gives two slightly different reasons for the under-exposure of the Pyrrhus-Phœnix dynamic; firstly, his position as king affords him the opportunity to speak openly to the three other main protagonists; secondly, he is the most "transparent" of the main characters, p. 95.

past in which the teacher remains entrenched. Not only is he designated by Racine as "gouverneur d'Achille, et ensuite de Pyrrhus" but also his major response on hearing in II,5 that Pyrrhus has overcome his passion for Andromaque is to compare his two star pupils, father and son:

> C'est Pyrrhus. C'est le Fils, et le Rival d'Achille,
> Que la Gloire à la fin ramène sous ses lois,
> Qui triomphe de Troie une seconde fois. (634-6)

However, the very ineffectual nature of Phœnix (accentuated by his fragmentary utterances) plays an important structural role in *Andromaque*, for at the beginning and end of the play, his words are interrupted by Pyrrhus in a way which shows the pupil's autonomy. In Act I, scene 3, Phœnix's objections are swept aside by Pyrrhus at the arrival of Andromaque:

> PHŒNIX:
> Seigneur...
> PYRRHUS:
>   Une autre fois je t'ouvrirai mon Ame,
> Andromaque paraît. (257-8)

Similarly, and fatally, Pyrrhus's final words involve the interruption of his teacher, at the end of Act IV:

> PHŒNIX:
> Oreste l'aime encore. Et peut-être à ce prix...
> PYRRHUS:
> Andromaque m'attend. Phœnix, garde son Fils. (1399-1400)

Théramène's role in *Phèdre* is more central, precisely because Hippolyte is still a young prince and dependent on his tutor's advice. The close kinship between the two men is stressed by Hippolyte in the very first scene in his acknowledgement to the older man, "Toi qui connais mon cœur depuis que je respire" (66). Moreover, when Théramène recites tales of Thésée's brave deeds, Hippolyte responds not only to the stories themselves but also to the teacher recounting them. As Hippolyte tells Théramène,

> Tu sais combien mon âme attentive à ta voix
> S'échauffait au récit de ses nobles exploits; (75-6)

Yet, Théramène knows the limits of his function as Hippolyte's *gouverneur*, for, unlike Œnone who attempts to change the course of events, he does not intervene at crucial moments, such as in II,6, when Hippolyte responds to Phèdre's *aveu*, and III,6, where he witnesses Hippolyte's meeting with his father.[338] In the end, he is unable to prevent his charge's death. It is significant that, just before Théramène's long récit, Thésée draws direct attention to Théramène's role as Hippolyte's mentor. Not only has Théramène been given the duty of educating the young price, but also, as Thésée implies, his role has been to act *in loco parentis*:

> Théramène est-ce toi? Qu'as-tu fait de mon Fils?
> Je te l'ai confié dès l'âge le plus tendre. (V,6,1488-9)

The fact that *Britannicus* features two *gouverneurs* rather than the one in *Andromaque* and *Phèdre* both highlights their presence and brings the role of education to the fore. Of all Racine's plays, *Britannicus* features the most lines spoken by *confident* figures.[339] Much of the play revolves around the instruction of Néron by Burrhus and Narcisse and the dangers involved in teaching a young man who wields considerable power. In many ways, the focus of the play is as much upon the teachers as the pupil. The two central teacher-figures constitute what Barthes calls "la double postulation de Néron".[340] Yet other teacher/*conseiller* characters form part of the backdrop of the main action. Sénèque, for example, who, we are told, is "occupé loin de Rome" (808) is referred to as another tutor figure for Néron.[341] From the very beginning of the play, in a speech to Burrhus, before Narcisse is identified as a rival tutor, Agrippine, who almost obsessively refers to the different *gouverneur* figures in charge of her son, accuses both Sénèque and Burrhus of trying to erase her from Néron's memory:

> Entre Sénèque et vous disputez-vous la gloire
> A qui m'effacera plus tôt de sa mémoire?
> Vous l'ai-je confié pour en faire un ingrat? (I,2,147-9)[342]

---

[338] Worth-Stylianou discusses these two scenes, p. 211.

[339] See Worth-Stylianou's appendix, p. 224. 30.38% of lines in *Britannicus* are spoken by *confident* figures, compared with 27.93% in *Phèdre*, 17.51% in *Andromaque*, 17.12% in *Bérénice*, 12.93% in *Mithridate* and 9.42% in *Iphigénie*.

[340] R. Barthes, *Sur Racine*, p. 87.

[341] *Cf.* lines 184, 1165.

[342] For an illuminating discussion of the different characters in *Britannicus*, see V. Schröder, *La Tragédie du sang d'Auguste: politique et intertextualité dans Britannicus* (Tübingen: Narr, 1999).

Agrippine wavers between wishing to give to others the authority to instruct Néron and attempting to maintain pedagogical authority herself. As she states in the same scene,

> Je puis l'instruire au moins, combien sa confidence
> Entre un sujet et lui doit laisser de distance. (167-8)

Burrhus's reply effectively summarizes the various pressures involved in the teaching of Néron, such as the relinquishing of authority by the mother, the need for the *gouverneur* to remember the importance of his task, the conflict between family and state, and the question of how much one should teach the "Maître du monde":

> Vous m'avez de César confié la jeunesse,
> Je l'avoue, et je dois m'en souvenir sans cesse.
> Mais vous avais-je fait serment de le trahir,
> D'en faire un Empereur, qui ne sût qu'obéir?
> Non. Ce n'est plus à vous qu'il faut que j'en réponde.
> Ce n'est plus votre fils. C'est le Maître du monde.
> J'en dois compte, Madame, à l'Empire Romain
> Qui croit voir son salut, ou sa perte en ma main.
> Ah! si dans l'ignorance il le fallait instruire,
> N'avait-on que Sénèque, et moi pour le séduire?
> Pourquoi de sa conduite éloigner les Flatteurs?
> Fallait-il dans l'exil chercher des Corrupteurs? (175-186)

Pallas represents another tutor figure who features prominently in Agrippine's thoughts, especially as he has been banished by her son:

> Hé bien, je me trompais, Burrhus, dans mes soupçons?
> Et vous vous signalez par d'illustres leçons.
> On exile Pallas, dont le crime peut-être
> Est d'avoir à l'Empire élevé votre Maître.
> Vous le savez trop bien. Jamais sans ses avis
> Claude qu'il gouvernait n'eût adopté mon Fils. (III,3,809-814)

The importance of the *gouverneur* figures is highlighted by the fact that both Narcisse and Burrhus are granted monologues in quick succession, II,8 and III,2. Burrhus's monologue is dominated by his worries about his decreasing authority as counsellor to Néron:

> Hé bien, Burrhus, Néron découvre son génie.
> Cette férocité que tu croyais fléchir
> De tes faibles liens est prête à s'affranchir.
> En quels excès peut-être elle va se répandre!

> O dieux! En ce malheur quel conseil dois-je prendre?
> Sénèque, dont les soins me devraient soulager,
> Occupé loin de Rome ignore ce danger. (III,2,800-8)

The struggle between Narcisse and Burrhus is in many ways akin to a struggle over Néron's memory. At several points, both advisers, and Agrippine, refer to words associated with memory and forgetting. Just as Burrhus appeals to Néron to remember his wife,

> Si vous daigniez, Seigneur, rappeler la mémoire
> Des vertus d'Octavie (III,1,784-5),[343]

so too does he try to make him forget his animosity towards Britannicus:

> Appelez votre frère. Oubliez dans ses bras... (IV,3,1385)

In the opposing camp, in the very next scene, Narcisse manages to sway Néron by claiming that his mother has been praising herself for making him forget his previous decisions:

> Qu'elle n'avait qu'à vous voir un moment:
> Qu'à tout ce grand éclat, à ce courroux funeste
> On verrait succéder un silence modeste,
> Que vous-même à la Paix souscririez le premier,
> Heureux que sa bonté daignât tout oublier. (1418-22)

In almost the same breath, he asks Néron, "De vos propres désirs perdrez-vous la mémoire?" (1435). As we know, it is this selfish memory which persists at the end of the play. Burrhus's final wish concerning Néron, "Plût aux Dieux que ce fût le dernier de ses crimes!" (1788), is not fulfilled.

c) tragedy as instruction

Memory also has a role to play within the tragic structure of the plays, especially with respect to the instructive role of tragedy. In this section, I shall consider Aristotle on memory and memory as a part of prudence.

At the end of *Phèdre*, after Hippolyte's death, one of Thésée's first reactions consists in his desire to flee the world and "la sanglante image" (1606) of his son. As he states, he will leave "confus, persécuté d'un mortel

---

[343] *Cf.* Agrippine, who claims that Néron has been led towards "le mépris de sa Mère, et l'oubli de sa Femme!" (820).

souvenir" (1607). The conclusion of the plays leaves us with the strong impression that the memory of Phèdre's deeds will linger long in post-dramatic time and space:

> PANOPE:
> Elle expire, Seigneur.
> THESEE:
>   D'une action si noire
> Que ne peut avec elle expirer la mémoire!
> Allons de mon erreur, hélas! trop éclaircis
> Mêler nos pleurs au sang de mon malheureux Fils. (1645-8)

The inclusiveness of Thésée's words, "nos pleurs", allows not only for the characters on stage but also for the spectators to be moved to pity, one of the tragic emotions so central to the Aristotelian precepts followed closely by Racine and mentioned in the preface to the play. Moreover, Racine concludes the same preface by naming Aristotle, Sophocles and Euripides, adding that

> Il serait à souhaiter que nos Ouvrages fussent aussi solides et aussi pleins d'utiles instructions que ceux de ces Poètes. Ce serait peut-être un moyen de réconcilier la Tragédie avec quantité de Personnes célèbres par leur piété et par leur doctrine qui l'ont condamnée dans ces derniers temps, et qui en jugeraient sans doute plus favorablement, si les Auteurs songeaient autant à instruire leurs Spectateurs qu'à les divertir, et s'ils suivaient en cela la véritable intention de la Tragédie.[344]

Tears bear a close relation to the "véritable intention" of tragedy also, for the spectators' tears, "le plaisir de pleurer et d'être attendris", as he puts it in his preface to *Bérénice* (p. 452), are proof of the play's success; after all, as he tells us, *Bérénice* itself was "honorée de tant de larmes" (p. 451). Elsewhere, in the preface to *Iphigénie*, Racine explicitly equates tears with tragic effect:

> Mes Spectateurs ont été émus des mêmes choses qui ont mis autrefois en larmes le plus savant peuple de la Grèce, et qui ont fait dire, qu'entre les Poètes, Euripide était extrêmement tragique [...], c'est-à-dire qu'il savait merveilleusement exciter la compassion et la terreur, qui sont les véritables effets de la Tragédie. (p. 699)

---

[344] Racine, *Œuvres complètes*, vol. 1, ed. G. Forestier, p. 819.

Tears, therefore, are fundamental to what Christian Biet calls "cérémonie de la douleur collective",[345] signifying "fusion des comédiens avec leur rôle, fusion de certains rôles avec d'autres, fusion des spectateurs avec les personnages, fusion des spectateurs avec les comédiens, et fusion des spectateurs entre eux".[346]

In rhetorical terms, the arousal of the spectator's emotions incorporates particularly one of the components of *inventio*, namely *affectus*, the passions. The passions in turn can be linked to memory. Aristotle, who is so often referred to by Racine, makes a distinction between the act of remembering at a particular moment and a disposition or tendency to remember in *De Memoria et Reminiscentia*:

> memory is not perception or conception, but a state (*hexis*) or affection (*pathos*) connected with one of these, when time has elapsed. (449b24)[347]

This disposition to remember comes after perceiving, apprehending, experiencing or learning. As Richard Sorabji puts it,

> The *affection* (450a26; 30; 450b5; 12; 18) turns out to be a sort of imprint stamped in to a bodily organ. […] In addition to the affection (i.e. the quasi-imprint), there is needed a certain *state*. And the state turns out to be (452a10-11) the ability to excite the quasi-imprint and the corresponding mental image.[348]

For Aristotle, then, there is a correspondence between the memory and emotional response.

If we apply Aristotle's ideas on memory to Racinian tragedy, the emotional reaction of the spectators comes precisely from the fact that their memory has assimilated the tragic import of the play. When, as we saw, Racine describes the "plaisir" of weeping, it can be compared to Aristotle's belief that, in Janet Coleman's words, "pleasure, which consists in the sensation of an emotion, attends remembering, and rhetoricians are aware

---

[345] C. Biet, *Racine* (Paris: Hachette, 1996), p. 126.

[346] *Ibid.*, p. 125.

[347] Translation by Richard Sorabji in his *Aristotle on Memory* (London: Duckworth, 1972).

[348] Sorabji, p. 2. See also Janet Coleman, p. 16.

of inducing pleasure by inducing remembering".[349] The need to "plaire" is of course accompanied by the need to "toucher", as Racine accentuates in the preface to *Bérénice* (p. 452), and that emotional response can be instructive.

In this respect, another function of ancient and medieval memory, as a part of prudence, can be brought to the fore. In the context of *prudentia*, *memoria* is the faculty which presents or re-presents experience, the foundation on which moral judgements are established.[350] The representation of experience produces an emotional response. And this response is an *affectio* which is no less authentic than the original experience which engendered it. This link between *memoria* and *affectio* seems to me to illuminate Racine's conception of tragedy, for the plays themselves are representations which evoke in spectators an authentic emotional response. If the dramatist succeeds in motivating the spectator's memory, it then follows that the spectator will have an individual perception of the tragedy which itself will produce a moral judgement.

III. *Esther* and *Athalie*

Many studies of Racine's theatre tend to concentrate primarily on his secular plays, relegating the final two religious dramas, *Esther* and *Athalie*, to a brief postscript. These two plays, however, will form the focus of the remainder of this chapter, not only because they coincide with Racine's reconciliation with Port-Royal, but also because their fundamental purpose was educational.

After having renounced the theatre in the years following *Phèdre*, Racine was named, along with Boileau, as the historiographer of Louis XIV. It was while he was in this post that he was called upon by Mme de Maintenon to review and correct the constitutions (drawn up by Mme de Brinon) of the newly formed school for girls at Saint-Cyr. Although it would be wrong to discern too many similarities between Saint-Cyr and Racine's own education at Port-Royal, as the two institutions were in most ways very different from each other, some comparisons can usefully be made. Firstly, given the fact that Racine found himself involved once more in an educational establishment, it is inevitable that he would be reminded of his schooling. Indeed, as we saw at the beginning of the chapter, the

---

[349] J. Coleman, p. 37.

[350] See M. Carruthers, *The Book of Memory*, pp. 68-9.

number of references which he made during the later years of his life to his
education would corroborate this view.

Moreover, given Mme de Maintenon's wish to maintain simplicity
within the school, Saint-Cyr, like the Port-Royal schools, was being formed
in contradistinction to the practice of many of the Jesuit colleges.[351] Again,
as we saw in chapter 2, the dominance of Jesuit educational establishments
made it inevitable that new institutions would either model themselves on
or shape themselves in opposition to the Jesuit schools. Although the
staging of drama in schools brings Saint-Cyr much closer to the Jesuit
colleges than to the anti-theatre Port-Royalists, it is interesting to consider
the roots of dramas staged at Saint-Cyr, for Mme de Maintenon herself
wrote a series of Conversations on moral topics for the girls to declaim,
dating from May or June of 1687.[352] We have seen how important a role
conversation played in the daily education of the Port-Royal pupils. Mme
de Maintenon's quasi-staging of conversations seems to represent one step
further in the pedagogical process. Mme de Maintenon's mentor, Fénelon,
who published his *Traité de l'éducation des filles* in the same year that
Mme de Maintenon was writing her conversations, explicitly counsels the
staging of moral stories or episodes from history, because of, amongst other
things, their memorability:

> Si vous avez plusieurs enfants, accoutumez-les peu à peu à représenter
> les personnages des histoires qu'ils ont apprises [...]. Ces
> représentations les charmeront plus que d'autres jeux, les
> accoutumeront à penser et à dire des choses sérieuses avec plaisir, et
> rendront ces histoires ineffaçables dans leur mémoire.[353]

As the girls at Saint-Cyr began to stage dramas, many written by Mme de
Brinon, contemporary accounts bear witness to the positive effect which

---

[351] See A. Piéjus, *Le Théâtre des Demoiselles: tragédie et musique à Saint-Cyr à la fin du grand siècle* (Paris: Société Française de Musicologie, 2000): "par ce vœu d'humilité, Saint-Cyr se distinguait des collèges de jésuites, dont les recteurs se faisaient une fierté d'accueillir les hauts rangs de la noblesse, et dont la vaisselle était souvent en argent", p. 35, n. 4. See also the section in the same book, entitled "Les modèles, ou l'impossible référence aux jésuites", pp. 43-5.

[352] See Piéjus, *Le Théâtre des Demoiselles*, n. 14, p. 99.

[353] Fénelon, *De l'éducation des filles* (Paris: Pléiade, 1983), p. 120. For a useful recent piece on Fénelon's role as an educator, see E. Bury, 'Fénelon pédagogue', in *XVIIe siècle* 206 (2000), pp. 47-57.

appropriately moral dramas would have on the girls' memories. Mme de Maintenon herself, in a letter reported by Mme du Pérou, states this:

> j'ai voulu en divertissant ceux de St.-Cyr remplir leur esprit de belles choses, leur donner de grandes idées de la religion, élever leur cœur aux sentiments de la vertu, orner et cultiver leur mémoire de choses dont elles ne seront point honteuses dans le monde [...].[354]

With Mme de Brinon's efforts at writing dramas for the girls being generally derided,[355] and with the successful staging by the girls of *Cinna* and *Andromaque* in particular, Mme de Maintenon then wrote to Racine to ask him to compose a new work appropriate for Saint-Cyr. One of the girls at Saint-Cyr, Mlle de Caylus, gives the background to this episode in her *Souvenirs*, underlining again the way in which Mme de Maintenon perceived the educative role of memory in staging dramas:

> comme elle [Mme de Maintenon] étoit persuadée que ces sortes d'amusemens sont bons à la jeunesse, qu'ils donnent de la grâce, apprennent à mieux prononcer, et cultivent la mémoire (car elle n'oublioit rien de tout ce qui peut contribuer à l'éducation de ces demoiselles, dont elle se croyait avec raison particulièrement chargée), elle écrivit à M. Racine.[356]

It is perhaps inevitable that the religious subject matter of *Esther* and *Athalie* and Racine's reconciliation with Port-Royal a few years earlier would lead to both plays being interpreted in a Jansenist light. *Esther*, as Jürgen Grimm puts it,

> a servi à une lecture qu'on pourrait qualifier de "jansénisante". Qu'il suffise de rappeler la dissolution de la congrégation des *Filles de l'Enfance* de Toulouse en 1686 sur ordre de Louis XIV, qui fléchit

---

[354] Quoted by Piéjus, p. 96. Given both Fénelon and Mme de Maintenon's comments about the educational value of drama, it is difficult to agree with Jürgen Grimm that "on ne trouve, dans les écrits 'pédagogiques' de Madame de Maintenon, aucune réflexion qui concernerait la valeur intrinsèquement pédagogique de l'art dramatique", '*Esther, Athalie* et le double échec de l'éducation théâtrale', *Autour de Françoise d'Aubigné Marquise de Maintenon*, ed. A. Niderst (Niort: Cahiers d'Aubigné, 1999) 2 volumes, vol. 2, 447-455, p. 447. See also in the same volume C. Strosetzki, 'Madame de Maintenon et la tradition humaniste dans l'éducation des demoiselles de Saint-Cyr', 425-446, and R. McBride, 'Mme de Maintenon – pédagogue chrétienne et raisonnable', 411-424.

[355] See Piéjus, pp. 94-7, for a discussion of this.

[356] Quoted by Piéjus, p. 97.

aux pressions des jésuites, et notamment du Père de La Chaise.
Arnauld avait publié, l'année suivante, *L'innocence opprimée par la
calomnie* où il expliquait qu'on avait trompé le Roi. Le livre
d'Arnauld eut un grand succès et l'on peut être sûr que Racine le
connaissait bien.[357]

The reference in the prologue to *Esther* to "ce lieu par la grâce habité" has
also been widely interpreted as an allusion to Port-Royal. Moreover, the
election of Racine's aunt Mère Agnès de Sainte-Thècle as abbess at Port-
Royal des Champs in 1690, at the very time that he was writing *Athalie*,
would at the very least have had an effect on him. *Athalie*, in Raymond
Picard's words, "(dont la réception janséniste est effectivement attestée)
toutefois a certainement présenté une signification particulière pour
quelques-uns des contemporains de Racine".[358] Certainly Pasquier
Quesnel's remark in a letter dating from 1691 to Vuillart (both of whom
were close to Port-Royal) that in *Athalie* "il y a des portraits où l'on n'a pas
besoin de dire à qui ils ressemblent"[359] is testimony to this. However, an
attempt to decode every reference in the two plays would clearly be a
fruitless task. Other contrary readings can often be equally persuasive.[360]
Of greater importance is the fact that the plays were interpreted by some
readers and spectators at the time in this light. I shall limit myself as much
as possible to evidence which is substantiated either by Racine's own
words or by his sources.

One connection made by Racine between Port-Royal des Champs
and the insecure situation of the Jewish people, which so dominates the
action of *Esther* and *Athalie*, is worthy of comment. In his *Abrégé de
l'histoire de Port-Royal*, composed in the years following *Athalie*'s first
performance, he writes with reference to the schoolgirls at Port-Royal,

> On sait avec quels sentiments d'admiration et de reconnaissance elles
> ont toujours parlé de l'éducation qu'elles y avaient reçue; et il y en a
> encore qui conservent au milieu du monde et de la cour, pour les

---

[357] J. Grimm, '*Esther, Athalie* et le double échec de l'éducation théâtrale', p. 453.

[358] R. Picard, *La Carrière de Racine*, p. 429. See also J. Orcibal, *La genèse d'Esther et
d'Athalie*, pp. 81-3.

[359] Quoted in R. Picard, *Nouveau Corpus Racinianum* (Paris: Centre National de la
Recherche Scientifique, 1976), p. 273.

[360] See, for example, J. Rohou, *Jean Racine*, who rehearses both the Jansenist and other
interpretations, pp. 394ff; see also A. Viala, *Racine: la stratégie du caméléon* (Paris:
Seghers, 1990), who prefers to see Racine as a cynical courtier and convert.

restes de cette maison affligée, le même amour que les anciens Juifs conservaient, dans leur captivité, pour les ruines de Jérusalem.[361]

Albeit retrospectively, Racine would seem to be inviting comparison between the plight of the Jewish people, played by schoolgirls at Saint-Cyr, and the children at Port-Royal.

My analysis will focus on the centrality of different kinds of memory in the two plays, particularly within the contexts of history and of education.

a) *Esther* and the fragility of memory

The link between Racine's choice of Esther as the subject for his first play written for Saint-Cyr and Mme de Maintenon herself can be found, perhaps surprisingly, in literature associated with Port-Royal, for in Brienne le Jeune's *Mémoires*, which were written between 1683 and 1684, and which were circulated in Port-Royal circles, Brienne explicitly equates Mme de Maintenon with Esther. As he writes, Louis XIV "a rencontré une seconde Esther, qui l'a sauvé du naufrage. Elle est digne, cette Esther, de toute louange".[362]

However much credence may be given to the idea of *Esther* functioning allegorically, its biblical subject-matter can certainly be related to a project of Port-Royal, namely Louis-Isaac Lemaître de Sacy's translation of the Bible. The publication in 1688 in a single volume of Sacy's translation of the Books of Tobiah, Judith and Esther could hardly have escaped Racine's attention. Sacy had died four years previously, so it is very likely that Racine had access to the manuscript before its publication. Above all, the large number of textual and lexical borrowings indicates that Sacy's translation of the Book of Esther was Racine's principal source.[363] Moreover, Sacy's assertion in his accompanying commentary that the figures of Esther and Mardochée were "deux modèles d'une piété très pure au milieu de la corruption de la Cour d'un très

---

[361] J. Racine, *Abrégé de l'histoire de Port-Royal*, p. 77.

[362] *Mémoires inédits de Louis-Henri de Loménie, Comte de Brienne, secrétaire d'état sous Louis XIV*, ed. F. Barrière (Paris: Ponthiu, 1828) 2 vols, vol. 2, p. 248.

[363] For a discussion of these borrowings, see Forestier's commentary in his Pléiade edition of Racine's theatre, pp. 1682-3. I shall refer to the Sacy translation in the course of my discussion of *Esther*.

puissant Prince et très généreux au milieu des périls" must surely have appealed to Racine when he was choosing an appropriate subject to be performed by schoolgirls in an institution which was so closely associated with the royal court of the day.

The preface which Racine wrote for the 1689 first edition of *Esther* situates the play very firmly in its pedagogical context, using many of the terms which we have already seen both to be traditionally associated with memory and used by Fénelon and Mme de Maintenon herself. Initially, Racine summarizes the education which the girls at Saint-Cyr had been receiving since its foundation, stressing that "on n'y a rien oublié de tout ce qui pouvait contribuer à les rendre capables de servir Dieu dans les différents états où il lui plaira de les appeler". Moreover, as he states, "en leur montrant les choses essentielles et nécessaires, on ne néglige pas de leur apprendre celles qui peuvent servir à leur polir l'esprit, et à leur former le jugement". Various methods which "les instruisent en les divertissant" are then listed: for example, they are encouraged to discuss "les histoires qu'on leur a lues" and "on leur fait réciter par cœur et déclamer les plus beaux endroits des meilleurs Poètes". This active use of the memory is perceived by Racine as highly beneficial to the pupils. However, as was frequently reiterated in the Port-Royal educational treatises, learning profane material is deemed to be potentially harmful on impressionable young minds. For this reason, Racine declares that he was asked by those at Saint-Cyr to "faire sur quelque sujet de piété et de morale une espèce de Poème, où le chant fût mêlé avec le récit". Even more importantly, the purpose of combining these different elements is not to overburden the children's memories; rather, he depicts "le tout lié par une action qui rendît la chose plus vive et moins capable d'ennuyer". Even in his sacred dramas, Racine reiterates the need to maintain the attention of both spectator and actor.

In Racine's biblical source, the strength of memory acts as a powerful leit-motif during the course of the tale, a strength which is rendered much more precarious in Racine's version, as we shall see. Above all in the biblical version, it is the memory of the Jewish religion which is constantly restated, with the figure of Mardochée acting as an important cipher for this memory. In chapter IX, for example, a Jewish festival is set up in order to preserve the memory of Mardochée and Esther's actions:

> 27. Les Juifs donc, en mémoire de ce qui avait été arrêté contre eux et
> de ce grand changement qui était arrivé ensuite, s'obligèrent, eux et
> leurs enfants, et tous ceux qui voudraient se joindre à leur religion,

> d'en faire en ces deux jours une fête solennelle, sans que personne
> s'en pût dispenser, selon qu'il est marqué dans cet écrit, et ce qui
> s'observe exactement chaque année aux jours destinés à cette fête.
> 28. Ce sont ces jours qui ne seront jamais effacés de la mémoire des
> hommes, et que toutes les provinces d'âge en âge célébreront par toute
> la terre. Et il n'y a point de ville en laquelle les jours du Phurim, c'est-
> à-dire les jours des sorts, ne soient observés par les Juifs et par leurs
> enfants qui sont obligés de pratiquer ces cérémonies.

Through the commemoration of these past events, the Jewish line will be
maintained in the future. At all points Mardochée is at hand, either in his
role as historiographer, literally preserving the memory himself by writing
down what has occurred ("Mardochée le mit aussi par écrit pour en
conserver la mémoire", XII,4), or acting as the ideal memory of the Jewish
people in remembering God ("Mardochée alla prier le Seigneur, se
souvenant de toutes les œuvres merveilleuses qu'il avait faites", XIII,8), or
indeed calling upon his people to remember these events (such as in his
exhortation to Esther, "Souvenez-vous […] des jours de votre abaissement,
et de quelle sorte vous avez été nourrie", XV,2).

Racine's *Esther* is placed under the ensign of memory from the very
beginning. In the Prologue, La Piété makes a claim for the play's
immortality by calling out, "Grand Dieu, que cet ouvrage ait place en ta
mémoire!" (15) On a human level, in the first scene, Esther herself recalls
the rigours and suffering of her upbringing within the Jewish faith by
asserting, "Combien ce temps encore est cher à ma mémoire! (I,i,7). Just as
we saw in chapter 2 the importance of the tradition of self-forgetfulness in
prayer, in this play not only is there one scene (I,iv) devoted entirely to
Esther's prayer (and very largely taken from the biblical version) but also
the clearly articulated wish to forget herself before God is made by Esther
in this first scene:

> Aux pieds de l'Eternel je viens m'humilier,
> Et goûter le plaisir de me faire oublier. (109-110)

Yet the certainty which is expressed in the biblical version that the events
described will never be "effacés" becomes noticeably more shaky in a
Racinian context. Indeed, even if the memory of Zion is preserved, what
will be the status of that memory? The words of an isolated Israelite
woman in the next scene underline the emptiness of such a memory if the
Jewish nation is non-existent:

> Déplorable Sion, qu'as-tu fait de ta gloire?

> Tout l'Univers admirait ta splendeur.
> Tu n'es plus que poussière, et de cette grandeur
> Il ne nous reste plus que la triste mémoire. (1,ii,132-135)

The rhyme of "gloire" with "mémoire" serves to associate the marvels of Zion with a past which is becoming increasingly intangible. Much of the play's future action will hinge on the fragility of this memory.

Although memory of the Jewish people remains a central concern of Racine's version, another important element of the dramatic tension revolves around the effectiveness or possible failure of the Persian king Assuérus's memory of Mardochée's faithful deed in uncovering a plot against the king. This is important, because by remembering Mardochée, it is hoped also that Assuérus will remember the plight of the Jewish people. Act II, scene iii, is pivotal in this regard. Together with his officer Asaph, the king enters, pondering an account/history of the previous assassination attempt by two traitors. As he admits,

> De ce couple perfide
> J'avais presque oublié l'attentat parricide.
> Et j'ai pâli deux fois au terrible récit
> Qui vient d'en retracer l'image à mon esprit. (529-32)

Significantly, this "récit" has been written by Mardochée in his role as historian, and it is an account which reminds Assuérus of how his reign was preserved.[364] Unaware of the identity of the person who saved him, Assuérus can only lament such forgetfulness: "O d'un si grand service oubli trop condamnable!" (541). The pressing concerns of the present and anxiety about the future, as well as the selfish demands of others, are recognized by Assuérus as having had a greater influence on him than the memory of past good deeds:

> L'avenir l'inquiète, et le présent le frappe.
> Mais plus prompt que l'éclair le passé nous échappe.
> Et de tant de mortels à toute heure empressés
> A nous faire valoir leurs soins intéressés,
> Il ne s'en trouve point, qui touchés d'un vrai zèle
> Prennent à notre gloire un intérêt fidèle;
> Du mérite oublié nous fassent souvenir;
> Trop prompts à nous parler de ce qu'il faut punir! (547-552)

---

[364] For a cogent analysis of this scene and the role of history in both *Esther* and *Athalie*, see F. Jaouen, '*Esther/Athalie*: histoire sacrée, histoire exemplaire', *Seventeenth-Century French Studies* 21 (1999), pp. 123-131.

This interplay between past, present and future is one which brings to mind Certeau's analysis of the writing of history, which I discussed in chapter 1. Whereas Assuérus turns his attention away from the present and future and towards the past in reading the "récit", Mardochée's purpose is different. Mardochée as historian in this case has written an account which on one level is a "discours sur le passé" but on another much more pivotal level is "un langage entre le narrateur et ses lecteurs, c'est-à-dire entre des présents".[365] Assuérus's present role as reader will have a crucial effect on future events, for, as the audience is aware, this historical account is less about the past and present than the future of the Jewish race.

Racine very deftly delays the revelation of the identity of the man who has saved Assuérus until the end of the scene, for Mardochée's name is mentioned simultaneously with the fact that he is a Jew. The recollection of this name and its juxtaposition with the idea of Virtue cannot fail to be impressed upon the spectator's mind:

> ASSUERUS:
> Et je dois d'autant moins oublier la Vertu,
> Qu'elle-même s'oublie. Il se nomme, dis-tu?
> ASAPH:
> Mardochée est le nom que je viens de vous lire. (563-5)

In Act II, scene iv, Assuérus is therefore able to announce to Aman, the character who represents the greatest threat to the Jewish people, that "la Vertu dans l'oubli ne sera plus cachée" (617). It is especially significant that the triumph of a Jew, Mardochée, is represented by his arch enemy Aman in terms relating to memory and forgetfulness, but for Aman it is "honte" (rather than virtue) "qui jamais ne peut être effacée" (845). Aman himself is an interesting figure in that his role as Assuérus's *favori* is quasi-pedagogical; he is the *mauvais conseiller* who attempts to steer the king away from the influence of the Jews. One might even view him as a variation on the Narcisse *gouverneur* figure.[366]

Although the ultimate survival of the memory of the Jewish people is certainly the overwhelming force at the end of the play, this does not preclude competing memories with possibly more human motives from

---

[365] Certeau, *L'écriture de l'histoire*, p. 60.

[366] *Cf.* V. Worth-Stylianou, who argues that "in *Esther*, the fall of the *mauvais conseiller* is the centrepiece of the drama, but Aman is a main protagonist in his own right, not to be compared with Burrhus or Narcisse", *Confidential Strategies*, pp. 144-5.

entering the fray. In the biblical version, the future commemoration of the events contains no direct reference either to memory or to any human figure to be singled out: "C'est pourquoi nous voulons que vous mettiez aussi ce jour au rang des jours de fête, et que vous le célébriez avec toutes sortes de réjouissances, afin que l'on sache à l'avenir" (XVI,22). In Racine's version, on the other hand, Assuérus appears to make a pitch for personal immortality by stressing that his name be remembered:

> Rebâtissez son Temple, et peuplez vos Cités.
> Que vos heureux Enfants dans leurs solennités,
> Consacrent de ce jour le triomphe et la gloire,
> Et qu'à jamais mon nom vive dans leur mémoire. (1186-9)

Although such human motives at the end of the play are little more than a suggestion within the overall context of the preservation of the Jewish people, in Racine's next and final play, conflicting ideologies become more overtly threatening in a power struggle dominated by competing memories.

b) Educating Joas: competing memories in *Athalie*

Apart from the fact that *Athalie* was intended for performance at Saint-Cyr, there are other convincing arguments which highlight its pedagogical pedigree. Not only did the sole theatrical precedents of the story of Athalie appear in two relatively obscure college plays from 1658 and 1683,[367] the primary purpose of both plays being educational, but also, as preparation for his version, Racine reread the great royal pedagogue Bossuet's *Discours sur l'histoire universelle* (1681), which itself had been written for the instruction of the Dauphin. The term "mémoire" in *Athalie* also attains a greater prominence than in all the previous plays, with the highest number of occurrences of the word itself (9).

Joas, whose education underpins the whole of *Athalie*, is chosen by Racine to be between nine and ten years old, precisely, as he states in the Préface, "pour le mettre déjà en état de répondre aux questions qu'on lui fait". This is very much consistent with theories of teaching at Port-Royal. According to theorists like Coustel, as we saw in chapter 2, "les premiers commencemens des études" of children under the age of nine, and particularly those under seven, "n'ont particulierement besoin que de

---

[367] See J. Racine, *Œuvres complètes*, ed. G. Forestier, p. 1710.

memoire, qui excelle d'ordinaire dans cet âge".[368] It is only after this age
that the memory is used in conjunction with other faculties. As Coustel
states, "il faut bien distinguer dans les enfans la memoire d'avec l'esprit, et
le jugement; qui sont trois qualitez differentes qu'un Maistre doit bien
cultiver".[369] The young Joas is posited by Racine as no different from other
children in his ability to nurture these qualities. As he tells us in the préface
to *Athalie*, "je crois ne lui avoir rien fait dire qui soit au-dessus de la portée
d'un enfant de cet âge, qui a de l'esprit et de la mémoire". What makes him
"tout extraordinaire", according to Racine, is the special education which
he receives from a very early age in his capacity as "l'unique espérance de
sa nation". The obligation of Jewish children to write out the Book of Law
and for Jewish kings in particular to write it out twice and to have it
"continuellement devant les yeux", thereby keeping it continually within
their memory, is seen by Racine as crucial to Joas's exceptional
intelligence. Again, as we saw earlier in this book, Port-Royal's education
policies focused very much on similar methods, relying on the
memorization of books or extracts which were considered educationally
and morally beneficial. Racine's subsequent comparison, in the preface, of
Joas to the eight-year-old Duc de Bourgogne, Louis XIV's grandson, might
smack of toadying, but here again he attributes the boy's gifts to "un
heureux naturel aidé d'une excellente éducation".

Joas's voice as an essential part of the play subscribes to a number of
seventeenth-century theories on "la qualité quasiment magique de la voix
enfantine", convincingly explored by Philippe-Joseph Salazar, and
mentioned briefly in Part II of Chapter 2. [370] Going beyond Salazar's
analysis, this magical, incantatory quality only serves to accentuate the
deep disappointment which will be felt in post-dramatic time, as I shall
discuss later in this section.

The combination of memory and the Law is integral to the education
of Joas in *Athalie*. Racine is insistent on choosing Pentecost as the time to
portray Joas's unveiling as the new King of the Jews, because, as he
explains in the preface, "on y célébrait la mémoire de la publication de la
Loi sur le mont de Sinaï". Joas himself explicitly links learning to read and
write to the Law:

---

[368] Coustel, *Regles de l'education des enfans*, vol. 2, p. 17,

[369] Coustel, vol. 1, p. 111.

[370] P. -J. Salazar, *Le Culte de la Voix au XVIIe siècle*, p. 268. See pp. 251-285 for what he
calls "Variations de la Voix Mystique".

> J'adore le Seigneur. On m'explique sa Loi.
> Dans son Livre divin on m'apprend à la lire,
> Et déjà de ma main je commence à l'écrire. (662-4)

Throughout the play, all major characters seem to concern themselves with the effectiveness of Joas's education. Even Athalie remarks to Josabet, "J'aime à voir comme vous l'instruisez" (690). Members of the chorus offer an ongoing commentary on the divine foundation of his education. In Act II, scene ix, for example, we find one girl's comment:

> O bienheureux mille fois
> L'enfant que le Seigneur aime,
> Qui de bonne heure entend sa voix,
> Et que ce Dieu daigne instruire lui-même! (768-771)

This hymn of praise is then taken up by the whole Chorus, the members of which act as continuous agents of prayer and memory in the play:

> Heureuse, heureuse l'enfance
> Que le Seigneur instruit et prend sous sa défense! (776-7)

Joad is the character to assume principal responsibility for Joas's education, reminding him particularly of his important historical status. In IV, ii, for example, he stresses that

> Il faut que vous soyez instruit, même avant tous,
> Des grands desseins de Dieu sur son peuple et sur vous. (1267-8)

Moreover, in his educative role, he must test his young pupil's memory of Jewish history, as we see in the same scene:

> On vous a lu souvent l'histoire de nos rois.
> Vous souvient-il, mon fils, quelles étroites lois
> Doit s'imposer un roi digne du diadème? (1275-7)

The association of history and memory is of central significance to the play, as Harriet Stone's article, 'Marking time: memorializing history in *Athalie*',[371] has so convincingly shown. She argues that the setting of the play – the Jewish temple – serves as a vivid *lieu de mémoire*, "linking the Jews in the present to their past" (p. 97). While the Jews' murder of Athalie preserves the memory of their sacred past, Stone makes the point that "this memory is preserved as the result of the Jews' historic choice to ignore, if

---

[371] *L'Esprit Créateur* 38/2 (1998), pp. 95-104.

not to forget, the past that identifies them with Athalie" (p. 100). This idea of forgetfulness is crucial to the unfolding of dramatic and post-dramatic time in the play, and will form a central part of the remainder of this chapter, highlighted particularly by the role played by educational memory, which Stone does not examine in her article.

I have mentioned already the role of the chorus in the play. With reference to the build-up to the eventual recognition scene, Terence Cave sees it as one of the functions of the chorus "to comment on and enhance the gradual emergence of hidden knowledge from the sidelines".[372] Memory, I would argue, is essential to this emergence. The chorus continually calls upon God and the Jewish people to remember, no more vividly than in the scene of Joad's vision, III, vii, where the chorus chants,

> Dieu de Sion, rappelle,
> Rappelle en sa faveur tes antiques bontés. (1157-8)

Even more tellingly, those characters who adhere to pagan gods, such as Athalie and Mathan, retain an inkling of the true import of the future unveiling of Joas as King of the Jews. Athalie describes her proleptic dream in terms of memory:

> Moi-même quelque temps honteuse de ma peur
> Je l'ai pris pour l'effet d'une sombre vapeur.
> Mais de ce souvenir mon âme possédée
> A deux fois en dormant revu la même idée. (517-520)

Similarly, Mathan is unable to erase from his soul the trace of the Jewish God, again expressed through memory:

> Toutefois, je l'avoue, en ce comble de gloire
> Du Dieu que j'ai quitté l'importune mémoire
> Jette encore en mon âme un reste de terreur. (955-7)

This represents an interesting reworking of the familiar Augustinian image of God remaining in the memory. In the *Confessions*, Augustine writes (in the Port-Royal translation),

> Aussitôt que j'ai trouvé la vérité, j'ai trouvé mon Dieu qui est la vérité
> même, laquelle je n'ai point oubliée depuis qu'une fois que je l'ai
> connue. Ainsi depuis ce moment que je vous ai connu, mon Dieu,

---

[372] T. Cave, *Recognitions: a study in poetics* (Oxford: Clarendon, 1990, first published 1988), p. 360.

vous êtes toujours demeuré dans ma mémoire où je vous retrouve lorsque je me souviens de vous, et trouve en vous ma consolation et ma joie. (X,xxiv)[373]

To a large extent, Athalie's (and indeed the spectator's) recognition of Joas at the end of the play is simply a way of finding or rediscovering something already couched in the memory.

Yet we ourselves should not forget the crucial role that forgetfulness plays in the drama. From the outset, the play's action hovers between forgetfulness, which characterizes those who have abandoned the Jewish God, and memory, which is exemplified by that same God's continual remembrance of his people. As Abner tells us in the first scene, apart from a few "adorateurs zélés", "le reste pour son Dieu montre un oubli fatal" (17). By contrast, in Joad's words from the same scene, God's people "est toujours présent à sa mémoire" (128). For this reason, Joad sees it as his pedagogical task to make the anointed king remember his historical status and to maintain that memory through the ages. We might usefully be reminded here of the innovative methods of teaching history, particularly ecclesiastical history, at the Port-Royal schools, where the teachers made use of cards to memorize important figures and dates; these cards acted as a *point de départ* for the pupils to discuss amongst themselves the significance of these events, in a way not unlike the constant retelling of Jewish history by Joad and Joas. Joad sees it very clearly as his and Josabet's duty in the education of Joas to recall the significance of that history:

> Il faut que sur le trône un roi soit élevé,
> Qui se souvienne un jour qu'au rang de ses ancêtres,
> Dieu l'a fait remonter par la main de ses prêtres,
> L'a tiré par leur main de l'oubli du tombeau,
> Et de David éteint rallumé le flambeau. (278-282)

However, the difficulty of this task is shown by the people's expression of wavering faith in God's memory, which punctuates the action, no more so than in the concluding scenes of Act IV, where both Josabet tells Joas that "Dieu ne se souvient plus de David votre père" (1433) and a voice in the Chorus laments that "il ne reste plus de mémoire" (1484) of God's name and renown.

---

[373] Augustine, *Confessions*, translated by Robert Arnauld d'Andilly, ed. P. Sellier.

Act II, scene vii, from which I have already quoted, revolves most tellingly around the teaching of Jewish history. Athalie's invitation to Joas to enter her temple and to see her worldly *gloire* is perceived by the young boy as an attempt to induce forgetfulness of God, which is akin to stifling prayer[374]:

> JOAS:
> Moi des bienfaits de Dieu je perdrais la mémoire?
> ATHALIE:
> Non, je ne vous veux pas contraindre à l'oublier.
> JOAS:
> Vous ne le priez point.
> ATHALIE:
> Vous pourrez le prier. (680-2)

Joas's reluctance to follow Athalie results in a squabble between Athalie and Josabet about the pedagogical methods used to educate Joas. Athalie somewhat sourly notes the imprint of Joad and Josabet's teaching on the boy's mind, as she remarks to Josabet:

> Sa mémoire est fidèle, et dans tout ce qu'il dit
> De vous et de Joad je reconnais l'esprit.
> Voilà comme infectant cette simple jeunesse
> Vous employez tous deux le calme où je vous laisse.
> Vous cultivez déjà leur haine et leur fureur.
> Vous ne leur prononcez mon nom qu'avec horreur. (701-6)

Josabet's reply at first seemingly points to the incorruptibility of their shared history but is immediately undermined by her argument that Athalie has made full use of that same history for her own persuasive ends:

> Peut-on de nos malheurs leur dérober l'histoire?
> Tout l'univers les sait. Vous-même en faites gloire. (707-8)

In this context, the question must be asked: how effective is Joad as teacher of Joas? As we have seen, the adult protagonists of *Athalie* are all equally anxious about the pedagogical effect that each of them may have on Joas. Whereas Josabet accuses Athalie of using their common history to

---

[374] This idea, as we saw previously, is a familiar trope in writings associated with Port-Royal; *cf.* Nicole's *Traité de la Priere*, relying strongly on Augustine's writings on memory and prayer, who explicitly states that "pour empêcher que les affaires et les soins du monde ne vous la fissent oublier, et n'effaçassent ainsi ces veritez de notre esprit, on destinât chaque jour un certain temps à cet exercise", p. 269.

achieve personal glory, the same accusation can justifiably be leveled at Joad. Harriet Stone observes, for instance, that "memory, as represented by the Jews, is less authentic than arbitrary, a past chiseled out of history to meet the Jews' own ideological demands" (p. 103). To a large extent, as John Campbell has shown,[375] Joad and Athalie use their surprisingly similar image of their respective gods as weapons to assert political and personal power over each other. Joad may be temporarily victorious at the end of the play's action, but his obsession with vengeance and his bloodthirsty delight at Athalie's demise ("Grand Dieu, voici ton heure, on t'amène ta proie", 1668) suggest that his concerns as a teacher of the future king might not be entirely selfless or directed solely toward the divine.

And, of course, these possible failings as a pedagogue are borne out by the events of post-dramatic time, namely the murder of Zacharie by Joas. The star pupil turns out to be somewhat less stellar than expected. Most significantly, the boy whose memory is so integral to his excellent education, chooses to forget the spiritual duties which have so painstakingly been instilled in him. His final prayer to his God, which turns out to be less effectual than Athalie's curse, is sealed by a plea to remember God throughout his life. It is a prayer which remains fragmentary because of its lack of fulfilment. Yet, for the boy with the superlative memory, it is crushingly ironic that his last word should denote forgetfulness:

> Dieu, qui voyez mon trouble et mon affliction,
> Détournez loin de moi sa malédiction,
> Et ne souffrez jamais qu'elle soit accomplie.
> Faites que Joas meure, avant qu'il vous oublie. (1797-1800)

The final lines of the play, spoken by Joad, cannot be divorced from their pedagogical context, for Joad the teacher is attempting to point out the educational value of Athalie's "fin terrible" to his pupil:

> Par cette fin terrible, et due à ses forfaits,
> Apprenez, roi des Juifs, et n'oubliez jamais,
> Que les rois dans le ciel ont un juge sévère,
> L'innocence un vengeur, et l'orphelin un père. (1813-6)

The two imperatives of line 1814 conclude the play with the dual theme which has been so predominant: education ("apprenez") and memory ("n'oubliez jamais"). But we the audience know already that this final lesson will not be heeded by Joas. Joad himself appears subconsciously to

---

[375] J. Campbell, 'The God of *Athalie*', *French Studies* 43 (1989), pp. 385-404.

anticipate Joas's future deeds by concentrating on the verb "oublier" as part of a negative clause rather than the more positive "Souvenez-vous".

It is perhaps fitting to conclude this analysis of *Athalie* with Racine's source, Bossuet, who provides the most stark and chilling account of what will occur in post-dramatic time, reversing Joad's "n'oubliez jamais" with another negative phrase, but this time accompanying a verb depicting memory itself. Joas will indeed forget his spiritual duties:

> Tant que Joïada vécut, Joas fit garder la loi de Moïse. Après la mort de ce saint pontife, corrompu par les flatteries de ses courtisans, il s'abandonna avec eux à l'idolâtrie. Le pontife Zacharie, fils de Joïada, voulut les reprendre; et Joas, sans se souvenir de ce qu'il devoit à son père, le fit lapider.[376]

IV. Conclusion: Racine as historiographer

I introduced the first chapter of this book with a brief reference to the paradoxical status of Louis XIV's projected *Mémoires*: a supposedly intimate memoir addressed to his son in fact had been written by others and was therefore aimed presumably at a larger readership, transforming a memoir into history or hagiography. I shall conclude this final chapter with a work which evokes paradoxes of its own, again involving the powerful figure of the King, Racine's *Abrégé de l'histoire de Port-Royal*.[377]

How, for instance, could the official historiographer of the King write an intimate history of an institution which the King was instrumental in destroying? Sainte-Beuve poetically sums up this division:

> Louis XIV et Port-Royal, voilà les deux grands derniers mobiles de l'âme de Racine, les deux personnages rivaux en lutte dans ce cœur qui les voudrait concilier et qu'ils mettent au partage.[378]

It is difficult to follow the critical line that Racine's conversion was simply an act of political expediency, given the cloak of piety which had

---

[376] Bossuet, *Discours sur l'histoire universelle* (Paris, 1826, first published 1681) 6 volumes, vol. 1, p. 34.

[377] All page references are to the edition by Alain Couprie (Paris: Editions de la Table Ronde, 1994).

[378] Sainte-Beuve, *Port-Royal*, vol. 3, p. 577.

descended upon the court at the behest of Mme de Maintenon.[379] Even if
Racine's profession of faith did help his advancement in court (which it
surely must have), it would have been in his best interests to write a history
of the Jesuits rather than Port-Royal. The secrecy with which the *Abrégé*
was composed testifies to the potential danger of writing such a work.[380] It
would seem more likely, then, that the composition of the work reflects his
reconciliation and close family ties with Port-Royal.[381]

Nevertheless, Racine still faced the difficult task of writing about a
king who had consistently persecuted the community which he was
attempting to restore through the *Abrégé*, a king who was soon to destroy
that community completely, and a king who also happened to be primarily
responsible for Racine's current worldly success. Whether one views
Racine as merely opportunistic or sincerely devoted to his employer, his
strategy is ingenious. Firstly, he shows how members of the royal family
were favourably disposed towards Port-Royal. The Queen Mother, for
example, is depicted as a "sage princesse" who "commença à juger plus
favorablement" the innocence of the nuns (p. 123). Secondly, concerning
the various arguments given over the condemnation of Jansenius's five
propositions, Louis himself, "à qui ses grands emplois ne laissaient pas le
temps de lire leurs nombreuses justifications" (p. 154), is depicted as
having been misled. Racine concentrates instead his attack exclusively on
the Jesuits, arguing how they distorted the facts ("cette affaire fut rapportée
au Roi d'une manière si odieuse", p. 158), repressed all opposition and
deliberately deceived the King. As Jacques Bersani puts it, neatly evoking
Act III, scene 7 of *Esther*, "Louis XIV est en proie, comme Assuérus, 'aux
conseils des méchants'".[382]

Another problem concerning the *Abrégé* is whether it should be read
as history, hagiography or memoir. We are told in the *Recueil de choses
diverses*, for instance, that the former Port-Royal teacher Jean Bourgeois
"n'estime pas qu'on doive lire les abbregés d'histoires, car on n'y trouve
pas a faire des reflections. Les abbregés ne sont que des memoires pour

---

[379] For a summary of these points of view, see A. Couprie's preface to his edition of the
Abrégé, pp. 12-14.

[380] See Couprie, *ibid.*, pp. 7-8.

[381] Sainte-Beuve even goes so far as to call *Esther* and *Athalie* "la commémoration
secrète" of the *Abrégé*, *Port-Royal*, vol. 3, p. 583.

[382] J. Bersani, '*L'Abrégé de Port-Royal, ou Racine évangéliste*', in *Chroniques de Port-
Royal* 17-18 (1969), p. 11.

ceux qui scavent les choses".[383] In its unfinished state, and comprising as it does two discrete fragments, the *Abrégé* can hardly claim to be an *abrégé* at all, for in attempting to summarize a larger history, it surely must be complete in itself. Like so many of the memoirs which were discussed in chapter 1, or like Pascal's *Pensées*, its fragmentary state can only point towards the possibility of a whole.

Nor can we view the work simply as hagiography. Although it paints a positive portrait of Port-Royal, Racine is careful, in Bersani's words, "de ne jamais donner de Port-Royal l'image d'un parti, d'un groupe ou d'un corps constitué".[384] Moreover, so much of the text is aimed at discrediting the Jesuits that it cannot simply be viewed as focusing entirely on Port-Royal.

If we were to class the work as a memoir, it would be useful to consider the status of the narrator within the text. Although, as we saw in chapter 1, the narrator finds him/herself in an ambiguous position, not wishing to claim too great a prominence, the "je" almost always has a role to play as eye-witness. Given the number of times that Racine praises the education at Port-Royal, as I have already quoted in both chapter 2 and this chapter, it is plausible to view the work in some way as a memoir to his upbringing and the people involved in that. Indeed, the abbé d'Olivet, writing in his *Histoire de l'Académie française* in 1729, thirteen years before the first part of the *Abrégé* was even published, states of Racine that "par reconnaissance pour l'éducation qu'il avait reçue à Port-Royal, il employa les dernières années de sa vie à écrire l'histoire de cette fameuse abbaye".[385] Yet, the "je" of the *Abrégé* does not interpose himself as someone who has experienced that education or been a part of the persecution. Instead, the only times that the "je" appears are exclusively within the context of the act of narrating (for example, speaking of Marguerite Périer, "elle est encore vivante au moment que j'écris ceci"), and, above all, within the context of the digressions in the narrative. Indeed, almost every digression in the text[386] is scrupulously commented upon by the narrator: "pour prendre le fil de mon discours" (p. 100), "j'en

---

[383] *Recueil de choses diverses*, f122v.

[384] Bersani, *op. cit.*, p. 9.

[385] Quoted by J. Dubu, in 'A propos de l'*Abrégé de l'histoire de Port-Royal* de Jean Racine', in *Chroniques de Port-Royal* 48 (1999), pp. 277-300.

[386] Bersani counts about ten such digressions, pp. 6-7.

rapporterai ici un exemple" (p. 101), "c'est ce qui m'oblige à en rapporter ici" (p. 114), "oserais-je parler ici de..." (p. 132), "je ne saurais mieux finir cette longue digression que par..." (p. 133), "mais pour reprendre le fil de notre narration" (p. 133), "revenons maintenant à..." (p. 173), "le serment dont j'ai parlé" (p. 222), "avant que de passer plus loin, il est bon de dire ici..." (p. 222). The "plus loin" of which he speaks in the final example never occurs, for very soon after this point, the narrative ends abruptly, in mid-digression. Like the fragments of the text, the voice itself is fragmentary.

In this way, the text is self-consciously aleatory, mapping out the wanderings of memory. For this reason, rather than calling the *Abrégé* a memoir, I would suggest instead a memory; for, through its emphasis on the excellence of Port-Royal and, in particular, its education, we find Racine at the end of his life casting his mind back to his days as a schoolboy, where memory played such an important part. Yet, instead of concentrating on personal reminiscences, he seems to focus on the workings of the memory itself.

It is perhaps appropriate, therefore, that this chapter should conclude with one passage (not yet quoted) from Quintilian concerning memory which Racine copied down while a pupil at the petites écoles:

> [...] ii quoque versus, qui ad imitationem scribendi proponentur, non otiosas velim sententias habeant sed honestum aliquid monentes. Prosequitur haec memoria in senectutem et impressa animo rudi usque ad mores senectutem et impressa animo rudi usque ad mores proficiet. (I would urge that the lines, which he is set to copy, should not express thoughts of no significance, but convey some sound moral lesson. He will remember such aphorisms even when he is an old man, and the impression made upon his uninformed mind will contribute to the formation of his character.) (*Institutio Oratoria*, I,i,35)

CONCLUSION

The dual theme of memory and education is one which can be applied to a number of texts in the seventeenth century.

The role of instruction in sermons, to take one important seventeenth-century genre, is one which I have not considered in this study but which can readily be linked to memory. Bossuet's great funeral orations, for example, concentrate largely on the memory of the person who has recently died and on the lessons which can be drawn from that death. In the most famous oration of all, that delivered upon the death of Henriette d'Angleterre, Bossuet encourages his congregation to use their own memories as more effective tools than his own words:

> Souvenez-vous donc, Messieurs, de l'admiration que la princesse d'Angleterre donnait à toute la cour. Votre mémoire vous la peindra mieux avec tous ses traits et son incomparable douceur que ne pourront jamais faire toutes mes paroles.[387]

Like the positive interaction between pupil and teacher at Port-Royal, Bossuet in his quasi-pedagogical role calls for the participation of his congregation. Moreover, Madame's death is seen primarily as being a sacrifice made by God for "l'instruction du reste des hommes" (p. 76). As Bossuet goes on to say, "Dieu la sauve par le même coup qui nous instruit" (p. 76). At the end of his oration on the Princesse Palatine's death, Bossuet again values the instructive role of his subject's life, leaving his congregation with "le souvenir de ses instructions, l'image de ses vertus et les exemples de sa vie" (p. 141).[388]

Memory of death and instruction figure prominently in the work of another writer who moved in circles close to Port-Royal, Mme de La Fayette's *Princesse de Clèves*. The story of a young and innocent girl introduced to the life of the court is one which lends itself well to a

---

[387] Bossuet, *Oraison funèbre d'Henriette-Anne d'Angleterre, duchesse d'Orléans*, ed. P. Sellier (Paris: Larousse, 1974), p. 70. Other page references to Bossuet will be made in the text to this same edition.

[388] *Cf.* the peroration of Bossuet's final funeral oration, in 1687, on Condé's death: "vous vivrez éternellement dans ma mémoire; votre image y sera tracé", p. 149.

pedagogical reading. Much of the text is focused upon the princesse's education as she tries to learn from the conflicting advice contained in the various conversations and stories which she hears at court, whether told by her mother, husband or other protagonists. Her mother, Mme de Chartres, was responsible for her education before they first appeared together on the public stage of the court, and for the first part of the text, she continues to act as her daughter's teacher. After Mme de Chartres's death, the Prince de Clèves seems to assume her mantle as principal educator of Mme de Clèves. However, it is only after the death of each character that the memory of their words appears to have the most lasting effect on the princesse. Significantly, the final words of both Mme de Chartres and M de Clèves contain the exhortation to remember: "Souvenez-vous, si vous pouvez, de tout ce que je viens de vous dire" (Mme de Chartres);[389] "Je vous prie que je puisse encore avoir la consolation de croire que ma mémoire vous sera chère" (Clèves).[390] Similarly, when the princesse herself is about to die, we are told that

> Les pensées de la mort lui avaient rapproché la mémoire de M. de Clèves. Ce souvenir, qui s'accordait à son devoir, s'imprima fortement dans son cœur. [391]

La Rochefoucauld, who moved in the same circles as Mme de Lafayette, can also be considered from the perspective of memory and education, for not only does he show himself to be interested in the capriciousness of memory,[392] but also the very form of the maxim is crucial to the memorability of its content, for its pithiness and the symmetry of central concepts make those ideas both seemingly authoritative and easily memorable. Yet, although some of the perceptions of humanity contained in the maxims can be compared to much Port-Royal thought, the pedagogical impact of the maxim is very different, for it relies largely on surprise: the reader's expectations are often reversed by the unusual

---

[389] Mme de Lafayette, *La Princesse de Clèves* (Paris: Livre de Poche, 1972), ed. B. Didier, p. 67.

[390] *Ibid.*, p. 237.

[391] *Ibid.*, p. 267.

[392] See, for example, maxim 313: "Pourquoi faut-il que nous ayons assez de mémoire pour retenir jusqu'aux moindres particularités de ce qui nous est arrivé, et que nous n'en ayons pas assez pour nous souvenir combien de fois nous les avons contées à une même personne?" *Cf.* maxim 89, where he revisits the familiar juxtaposition of memory and judgement: "Tout le monde se plaint de sa mémoire, et personne ne se plaint de son jugement."

juxtaposition of key concepts. Writing on education, for example, La Rochefoucauld combines the word "éducation" with the less expected term "amour-propre": "L'éducation que l'on donne d'ordinaire aux jeunes gens est un second amour-propre qu'on leur inspire" (m261).

Given the fact that memory and education are relevant to other areas of thought, why is it that this dual theme is so important, as I have argued over the course of the book, in defining and encapsulating the schools, teachers, memoir-writers and thinkers attached to Port-Royal?

One possible answer lies in the role played by fragmentation. All the documents which have been discussed in the course of this book are in effect fragmentary voices, forming part of what was hoped would eventually be a harmonious whole. As we have seen, Port-Royal writers seemed painfully aware of the fragmentary status of their works, featuring as isolated voices in a conversation which was destined never to be completed. The comment in the *Recueil de choses diverses* that those attached to Port-Royal "ont fait peu de livres achevés"[393] is remarkably accurate when we consider, for example, the various Port-Royal memoirs, published in the eighteenth century in truncated form, or Pascal's *Pensées*, fragmentary and unfinished, or Racine's *Abrégé de l'histoire de Port-Royal*, incomplete and consisting of two fragments. On a symbolic level, the way in which these works resist closure mirrors the increasingly futile attempts of Port-Royal itself during the second half of the seventeenth century to stave off complete destruction. On another level, fragmentation is inherent to the Port-Royal philosophy of human fallibility: true wholeness can only be achieved by and in God. On yet another, pedagogical, level, we find such incompleteness reflected in the emphasis by Port-Royal teachers on the memorization of selected truncated passages rather than whole books and on conversation, rather than complete texts, as most effective in the learning process.

But it is ultimately the memory of Port-Royal and the instruction derived from that memory which remain at the core of the diverse texts studied during this book. Fontaine, in discussing the destruction of the buildings of Port-Royal, likens those nuns who died during the persecution to "pierres vivantes" moving upwards towards God.[394] And he concludes

---

[393] *Recueil de choses diverses*, f196.

[394] Fontaine, *Mémoires*, p. 989.

with an evocation of memory and its lasting impact on those remaining on earth:

> Le souvenir de ce que nous y avons vu et des vertus dont nous avons été témoins ne partira jamais de notre esprit. Il y vivra toujours et nous consacrons ce qui nous reste de vie à nous tenir entre les vivants et les morts, tenant un de nos yeux sur les uns, et l'autre sur les autres, mais réunissant nos cœurs pour leur rendre à tous un profond respect et une charité sincère.[395]

---

[395] *Ibid.*, p. 990.

BIBLIOGRAPHY

Primary Texts:

Aristotle, *Rhetorique*, trans. F.Cassandre (Paris: D. Thierry, 1654)

A. Arnauld, P. Nicole, *La Logique ou l'art de penser* (Paris: J. Vrin, 1981)

A. Arnauld, abbé de Chaumes, *Mémoires de M. l'Abbé Arnauld, contenant quelques anecdotes de la Cour de France depuis MDCXXXIV jusqu'à MDCLXXV* (Amsterdam: Jean Néaulme, 1756)

R. Arnauld d'Andilly, *Memoires de Messire Robert Arnauld d'Andilly écrits par lui-même* (Hamburg: Van den Hoeck, 1734)

F. D'Aubignac, *La Pratique du Théâtre*, ed. P. Martino (Geneva: Slatkine Reprints, 1996)

Augustine, *Confessions*, trans. R. Arnauld d'Andilly, ed. P. Sellier (Paris: Folio, 1993)

Augustine, *Commentaires des Pseaumes*, trans. A. Arnauld (Paris: F and P. Delaulne, 1701) 7 volumes

Bernard de Clairvaux, *Traduction de trois excellens ouvrages de S. Bernard: de la conversion des mœurs, de la vie solitaire, des commandemens, et des dispenses*, trans. A. Le Maistre (Paris: A. Vitré, 1649)

Brienne, comte de, *Mémoires inédits de Louis-Henri de Loménie, Comte de Brienne, secrétaire d'état sous Louis XIV*, ed. F. Barrière (Paris: Ponthiu, 1828) 2 volumes

S. Chappuzeau, *Le Théâtre françois*, ed. G. Monval (Paris: J. Bonnassin, 1876)

P. Charron, *De la sagesse* (Bordeaux: S. Millanges, 1601)

Cicero, *La Rhetorique de Ciceron ou les trois livres du dialogue de l'Orateur*, trans. J. Cassagnes (Paris: Barbin, 1673)

Les Constitutions du Monastere de Port-Royal du S. Sacrement (Mons: aux dépens de la Compagnie, 1665)

P. Coustel, *Les Regles de l'Education des Enfans* (Paris: Estienne Michallet, 1687) 2 volumes

R. Descartes, *Œuvres complètes*, ed. Adam and Tannery (Paris: J. Vrin, 1996), 11 volumes

Dictionnaire de l'Academie françoise (Paris: Veuve J. -B. Coignard, 1694) 2 volumes

P. T. Du Fossé, *Memoires pour servir à l'histoire de Port-Royal* (Cologne: aux dépens de la Compagnie, 1739)

P. T. Du Fossé, *Memoires*, ed. F. Bouquet (Rouen: Ch. Métérie, 1876, Geneva: Slatkine Reprints, 1976) 4 volumes

P. T. Du Fossé, *Memoires du Sieur Pontis, qui a servi dans les Armées cinquante-six ans, sous les Rois Henry IV, Louis XIII et Louis XIV* (Paris: Compagnie des Libraires Associez, 1715, first published 1676 and 1678), 2 volumes

J. Du Vergier de Hauranne (abbé de Saint-Cyran), *Theologie familiere* (Paris: J. Le Mire 1639)

J. Du Vergier de Hauranne (abbé de Saint-Cyran), *Lettre de Messire Jean Du Verger de Hauranne, abbé de Saint-Cyran, à un ecclésiastique de ses amis touchant les dispositions à la prestrise* (Paris: no named publisher, 1648)

F. de S. Fénelon, *De l'éducation des filles* (Paris: Pléiade, 1983)

C. Fleury, *Discours sur l'Histoire Ecclésiastique* (Paris: J-T. Hérissant, 1763)

N. Fontaine, *Memoires pour servir à l'Histoire de Port-Royal* (Utrecht: aux dépens de la Compagnie, 1736) 2 volumes

N. Fontaine, *Mémoires ou histoire des Solitaires de Port-Royal*, ed. P. Thouvenin (Paris: Honoré Champion, 2001)

A. Furetière, *Dictionnaire universel* (The Hague: A. and R. Leers, 1690) 3 volumes

Abbé Goujet, *Discours sur le renouvellement des études*, in C. Fleury, *Discours sur l'Histoire Ecclésiastique* (Paris: J-T. Hérissant, 1763)

T. Guyot, *Billets que Ciceron a ecrits tant à ses amis communs qu'à Attique* (Paris: C. Thiboust, 1666)

J. Hamon, *Relation de plusieurs circonstances de la vie de Monsieur Hamon, faite par lui-meme sur le modèle des Confessions de S. Augustin* (no place or editor, 1734)

Le Journal de l'Abbaye de Port-Royal, unpublished manuscript P. R. 64, Bibliothèque de la Société de Port-Royal

F. de la Chaise, *Discours sur les Pensées de Monsieur Pascal* (Paris: G. Desprez, 1672)

B. Lamy, *La Rhétorique ou l'art de parler*, ed. B. Timmermans (Paris: P.U.F., 1998, first published 1675)

C. Lancelot, *Memoires touchant la vie de Monsieur de S. Cyran pour servir d'éclaircissement à l'histoire de Port-Royal* (Cologne: aux dépens de la Compagnie, 1738) 2 vols

P. Le Moyne, *De l'Histoire* (Paris: Thomas Jolly, 1670)

Mémoires pour servir à l'Histoire de Port-Royal, et à la vie de la Reverende Mere Marie Angelique de Sainte Magdeleine Arnauld Reformatrice de ce Monastere (Utrecht: aux dépens de la Compagnie, 1742) 3 volumes, known also as *Mémoires d'Utrecht*

F. E. Mézeray, *Histoire de France depuis Pharamond jusqu'à maintenant* (Paris: Mathieu Guillemot, 1643)

M. de Montaigne, *Essais*, ed. M. Rat (Paris: Pléiade, 1962)

Nécrologe de l'Abbaye de Notre-Dame de Port-Royal des Champs (Amsterdam: N. Potgieter, 1723)

P. Nicole, *De l'Education d'un Prince* (Paris: veuve Charles Savreux, 1670)

P. Nicole, *Traité de la Priere* (Paris: E. Josset, 1695)

P. Nicole, *Essais de Morale* (Paris: Desprez, 1715) 13 volumes

P. Nicole, *Essais de Morale: choix d'essais*, ed. L. Thirouin (Paris: P.U.F., 1999)

A. de Paris, *La Veritable Maniere de prescher selon l'esprit de l'Evangile* (Paris: Couterot, 1691)

B. Pascal, *Œuvres complètes*, ed. M. Le Guern (Paris: Pléiade, 1998-9) 2 volumes

B. Pascal, *Œuvres complètes*, ed. J. Mesnard (Paris: Desclée de Brouwer, 1970-1994) 4 volumes

B. Pascal, *Œuvres complètes*, ed. L. Lafuma (Paris: Seuil, 1963)

B. Pascal, *Œuvres complètes*, ed. M. Le Guern (Paris: Pléiade, 1998-2000) 2 volumes

B. Pascal, *Pensées*, ed. L. Brunschvicg (Paris: Hachette et Cie, 1904) 3 volumes

B. Pascal, *Pensées*, ed. J. Chevalier (Paris: Pléiade, 1954)

B. Pascal, *Discours sur la religion et sur quelques autres sujets*, ed. E. Martineau (Paris: Fayard, 1992)

B. Pascal, *Pensées*, ed. P. Sellier (Paris: Classiques Garnier, 1991)

B. Pascal, *Pensées*, ed. G. Ferreyrolles and P. Sellier (Paris: Livre de Poche, 2000)

B. Pascal, *Pensées*, ed. M. Le Guern (Paris: Folio, 1977)

J. Pascal, *Reglement pour les enfans*, in *Les Constitutions du monastere de Port-Royal du S. Sacrement* (Mons: aux dépens de la Compagnie, 1665)

Pontis, *Mémoires*: see Du Fossé

Quintilian, *De Institutione Oratoria liber primus*, ed. C. Fierville (Paris: Firmin-Didot, 1890)

Quintilian, *Institutio Oratoria*, trans. H. E. Butler (London: Lœb, 1920-53) 4 volumes

J. Racine, *Œuvres complètes*, ed. R. Picard (Paris: Pléiade, 1966) 2 volumes

J. Racine, *Œuvres complètes*, ed. G. Forestier (Paris: Pléiade, 1999) vol. 1

J. Racine, *Abrégé de l'Histoire de Port-Royal*, ed. A. Couprie (Paris: La Table Ronde, 1994)

R. Rapin, *Instructions pour l'Histoire* (Paris: Sébastien Mabre-Cramoisy, 1677)

Ratio Studiorum, presented by A. Demoustier and D. Julia, translated by L. Albrieux and D. Pralon-Julia, annotations and commentary by M. -M. Compère (Paris: Belin, 1997)

Recueil de choses diverses, ed. J. Lesaulnier (Paris: Klincksieck, 1992)

Recueil de plusieurs pièces pour servir à l'histoire de Port-Royal (Utrecht: aux dépens de la Compagnie, 1740), known as the *Recueil d'Utrecht*

P. Richelet, *Dictionnaire françois* (Geneva: J. -H. Widerhold, 1680)

Sully, *Mémoires des sages et royales œconomies d'estat domestiques, politiques et militaires d'Henri le Grand* (no place: imprimés au chateau, 1638)

Supplément au Nécrologe de l'Abbaie de Notre-Dame de Port-Royal des Champs (Utrecht: no named publisher, 1735)

J. -M. Tronchay, *La Vie et l'Esprit de Monsieur le Nain de Tillemont* (Cologne: no named publisher, 1713)

Vie des amis de Port-Royal (Utrecht: aux dépens de la Compagnie, 1751)

Secondary Texts:

G. Antoni, *La Prière chez saint Augustin* (Paris: J. Vrin, 1998)

Y. Bamps, 'Trace d'ombre: Pascal, Montaigne et la mémoire', in *Les Lieux de mémoire et la fabrique de l'œuvre*, ed. V. Kapp (Paris, Seattle, Tübingen: Biblio 17, 80, 1993) 267-276

O. Barenne, *Une grande bibliothèque de Port-Royal: inventaire inédit de la bibliothèque de Isaac-Louis Le Maistre de Sacy* (Paris: Etudes augustiniennes, 1985)

H. C. Barnard, *Madame de Maintenon and Saint-Cyr* (Menston: Scolar Press, 1971, first published 1934)

H. C. Barnard, *The French Tradition in Education* (Cambridge: Cambridge University Press, 1970, first published 1922)

R. Barthes, *Sur Racine* (Paris: Seuil, 1963)

R. Barthes, *Le Bruissement de la Langue: Essais critiques IV* (Paris: Seuil, 1984)

F. E. Beasley, *Revising Memory: women's fiction and memoirs in seventeenth-century France* (New Brunswick and London: Rutgers University Press, 1990)

M. Beaujour, *Miroirs d'encre* (Paris: Seuil, 1980)

C. Belin, *L'Œuvre de Pierre Charron (1541-1603)* (Paris: Champion, 1995)

J. Bersani, 'L'Abrégé de Port-Royal ou Racine évangéliste', *Chroniques de Port-Royal* 17-18 (1969) 5-20

B. Beugnot, *La mémoire du texte: essais de poétique classique* (Paris: Champion, 1994)

B. Beugnot, *Les Muses classiques: essai de bibliographie rhétorique et poétique (1610-1716)* (Paris: Klincksieck, 1996)

C. Biet, *Racine* (Paris: Hachette, 1996)

F. Bluche, ed., *Dictionnaire du Grand Siècle* (Paris: Fayard, 1990)

P. Bourgeaud, ed., *La Mémoire des Religions* (Geneva: Labor et Fides, 1988)

B. Bray and C. Strosetzki, eds, *Art de la lettre, art de la conversation* (Paris: Klincksieck, 1995)

T. Breyfogle, 'Memory and Imagination in Augustine's *Confessions*', *Literary Imagination, ancient and modern*, ed. T. Breyfogle (Chicago: University of Chicago Press, 1999) 139-154

P. Burke, *The Fabrication of Louis XIV* (New Haven: Yale University Press, 1992)

E. Bury, 'Fénélon pédagogue', *XVIIe siècle* 206 (January-March 2000), 47-57

J. Campbell, 'The God of *Athalie*', *French Studies* 43 (1989) 385-404

J. Campbell, 'Racine and the Augustinian inheritance: the case of *Andromaque*', *French Studies* 53 (1999) 279-291

I. Carré, *Les Pédagogues de Port-Royal* (Geneva: Slatkine Reprints, 1971, first published 1887)

M. Carruthers, *The Book of Memory: a study of memory in medieval culture* (Cambridge: Cambridge University Press, 1990)

M. Carruthers, *The Craft of Thought: meditation, rhetoric, and the making of images, 400-1200* (Cambridge: Cambridge University Press, 1998)

T. Cave, *Recognitions: a study in poetics* (Oxford: Oxford University Press, 1988)

T. Cave, *Pré-histoires: textes troublés au seuil de la modernité* (Geneva: Droz, 1999)

M. de Certeau, *L'Ecriture de l'histoire* (Paris: Gallimard, 1975)

F. Charbonneau, 'Le théâtre d'ombres de Nicolas Fontaine: augustinisme, platonisme, mémoire', *Chroniques de Port-Royal* 48 (1999) 171-182

J. Chateau, *Montaigne psychologue et pédagogue* (Paris: J. Vrin, 1964)

B. Chédozeau, 'Les jésuites et l'histoire au XVIIe siècle', in *L'Histoire au XVIIe siècle, Littératures Classiques* 30 (1997) 9-19

B. Chédozeau, 'Situation de l'Histoire en France au XVIIe Siècle', *Chroniques de Port-Royal* 46 (1997) 7-14

K. Christodoulou, 'Le stoïcisme dans la dialectique apologétique des *Pensées*', *Méthodes chez Pascal* (Paris: P.U.F., 1979) 419-425

J. Coleman, *Ancient and medieval memories: studies in the reconstruction of the past* (Cambridge: Cambridge University Press, 1992)

P. Courcelle, *Les Confessions de saint Augustin dans la tradition littéraire: antécédents et postérité* (Paris: Etudes Augustiniennes, 1963)

B. Croquette, *Pascal et Montaigne* (Geneva: Droz, 1974)

F. de Dainville, *L'Education des Jésuites*, ed. M. -M. Compère (Paris: Editions de Minuit, 1978)

F. Delforge, *Les Petites Ecoles de Port-Royal 1637-1660* (Paris: Editions du Cerf, 1985)

F. Delforge, 'Le Ministère pédagogique de Jacqueline', *Chroniques de Port-Royal* 31 (1982) 107-119

D. Denis, *La Muse galante* (Paris: Honoré Champion, 1997)

D. Donetzkoff, 'Les Sentiments et les Remarques de Martin de Barcos sur l'Oraison Mentale', *Chroniques de Port-Royal* 46 (1997) 257-351

J. Dubu, 'A propos de l'*Abrégé de l'histoire de Port-Royal* de Jean Racine', *Chroniques de Port-Royal* 48 (1999) 277-300

P. Ernst, L*es Pensées de Pascal: géologie et stratigraphie* (Paris: The Voltaire Foundation, 1996)

P. Fara and K. Patterson, *Memory* (Cambridge: Cambridge University Press, 1998)

P. Force, *Le Problème herméneutique chez Pascal* (Paris: J. Vrin, 1989)

P. Force, 'Invention, disposition et mémoire dans les *Pensées* de Pascal', *XVIIe siècle* 181 (oct-dec 1993) 757-772

H. Frankfurt, 'Memory and the Cartesian Circle', *The Philosphical Review* LXXI (1962) 504-511

M. Fumaroli, *La Diplomatie de l'esprit, de Montaigne à La Fontaine* (Paris: Hermann, 1998)

S. Gaukroger, *Descartes: an intellectual biography* (Oxford: Oxford University Press, 1995)

L. Giard, ed., *Les Jésuites à la Renaissance: système éducatif et production du savoir* (Paris: P.U.F., 1995)

L. Giard, L. de Vaucelles, eds, *Jésuites à l'âge baroque (1540-1640)* (Grenoble: Jérôme Millon, 1996)

A. Goodden, *The Backward Look: memory and the writing self in France 1580-1920* (Oxford: Legenda, 2000)

H. Gouhier, *Blaise Pascal: Commentaires* (Paris: J. Vrin, 1966)

H. Gouhier, *Cartésianisme et Augustinisme au XVIIᵉ siècle* (Paris: J. Vrin, 1978)

J. Grimm, '*Esther, Athalie* et le double échec de l'éducation théâtrale', *Autour de Françoise d'Aubigné Marquise de Maintenon*, ed. A. Niderst (Niort: Cahiers d'Aubigné, 1999) 2 volumes, vol. 2, 447-455

N. Hammond, *Playing with truth: language and the human condition in Pascal's Pensées* (Oxford: Oxford University Press, 1994)

N. Hammond, ed., *The Cambridge Companion to Pascal* (Cambridge: Cambridge University Press, 2003)

N. Hammond, 'Racine et la mémoire', in *Les Lieux de la mémoire et la fabrique de l'œuvre*, ed. V. Kapp (Paris-Seattle-Tübingen: Biblio 17, 80, 1993) 307-19

N. Hammond, 'Educating Joas: the power of memory in *Athalie*', *Seventeenth-Century French Studies* 22 (2000) 107-114

N. Hammond, 'Pascal, Port-Royal and the *Recueil de choses diverses*', *Romance Quarterly* 50 n° 2 (Spring 2003) 131-148

M. Hawcroft, *Word as Action: Racine, Rhetoric and theatrical language* (Oxford: Oxford University Press, 1992)

R. Heyndels, '*Camera obscura* de la mémoire: Descartes', in *Les lieux de mémoire et la fabrique de l'œuvre*, ed. V. Kapp (Paris-Seattle-Tübingen: Biblio 17, 80, 1993) 259-266

K. Hoffmann, *Society of Pleasures: interdisciplinary readings in pleasure and power during the reign of Louis XIV* (New York: St Martin's Press, 1997)

J. Holyoake, 'Montaigne's attitude towards memory', *French Studies* XXV n° 3 (July 1971) 257-270

F. Jaouen, '*Esther/Athalie*: histoire sacrée, histoire exemplaire', *Seventeenth-Century French Studies* 21 (1999) 123-131

M. T. Jones-Davies, *Mémoire et Oubli au temps de la Renaissance* (Paris: Honoré Champion, 2002)

C. Jouhaud, *Les Pouvoirs de la Littérature: histoire d'un paradoxe* (Paris: Gallimard, 2000)

R. C. La Charité, *The Concept of Judgment in Montaigne* (The Hague: M. Nijhoff, 1968)

J. Lacouture, *Jésuites: une multibiographie* (Paris: Seuil, 1991 and 1992) 2 vols

C. Larmore, 'Scepticism', *The Cambridge History of Seventeenth-Century Philosophy*, ed. D. Garber and M. Ayers, (Cambridge, 1998) 2 vols, vol. 2, 1145-1192

J. Lesaulnier, 'Les manuscrits port-royalistes et jansénistes', in *XVIIe Siècle* 192 (1996) 461-476

J. Lesaulnier, *'La Vie de saint Bernard, premier abbé de Clairvaux et père de l'Eglise*, d'Antoine le Maistre', *Chroniques de Port-Royal* 48 (1999) 249-276

J. Lesaulnier, *Images de Port-Royal* (Paris: Nolin, 2002)

E. Lesne, *La Poétique des Mémoires (1650-1685)* (Paris: Champion, 1996)

E. Lesne, 'Les Mémoires et leurs destinataires', in *Le Genre des Mémoires, essai de définition*, ed. M. Bertrand and F. -X. Cuche (Paris: Klincksieck, 1995) 27-44

J. Lhermet, *Pascal et la Bible* (Paris: J. Vrin, 1930)

R. Lockwood, *The Reader's Figure: epideictic rhetoric in Plato, Aristotle, Bossuet, Racine and Pascal* (Geneva: Droz, 1996)

D. Lopez, 'Discours pour le prince: Bossuet et l'histoire', in *L'Histoire au XVIIe siècle*, *Littératures Classiques* 30 (1997) 173-186

G. Magniont, *Traces de la voix pascalienne: examen des marques de l'énonciation dans les Pensées* (Lyon: Presses Universitaires de Lyon, 2003)

C. Maire, *De la Cause de Dieu à la cause de la nation: le jansénisme au XVIIIe siècle* (Paris: Gallimard, 1998)

F. Mariner, *Histoires et autobiographies spirituelles: les Mémoires de Fontaine, Lancelot et Du Fossé* (Tubingen: Biblio 17, 109, 1998)

R. McBride, 'Mme de Maintenon - pédagogue chrétienne et raisonnable', *Autour de Françoise d'Aubigné Marquise de Maintenon*, ed. A. Niderst (Niort: Cahiers d'Aubigné, 1999) 2 volumes, vol. 2, 411-424

W. McC. Stewart, 'L'Education de Racine', *Cahiers de l'Association internationale des études françaises*, 3 (1953) 55-71

A. McKenna, *De Pascal à Voltaire* (Oxford: Voltaire Foundation, 1990) 2 vols

A. McKenna, 'Les petites écoles de Port-Royal', *Chroniques de Port-Royal* 24 (1975) 13-40

L. Marin, *Le Portrait du Roi* (Paris: Minuit, 1981)

L. Marin, *Pascal et Port-Royal* (Paris: Presses Universitaires de France, 1997)

D. Ménager, 'Improvisation et mémoire dans les *Essais*', *Bulletin de la Société des amis de Montaigne* VII n° 1-2 (July-December 1985) 101-110

P. Mengotti-Thouvenin, 'Port-Royal, laboratoire de mémoires', *Chroniques de Port-Royal* 48 (1999) 15-55

J. Mesnard, *Pascal et les Roannez* (Paris: Desclée de Brouwer, 1965)

J. Mesnard, 'De la "Diversion" au "Divertissement"', *Mémorial du premier congrès international des études montaignistes* (Bordeaux: Taffard, 1964) 123-128

J. Mesnard, 'Les Mémoires comme genre', *Le Genre des Mémoires: essai de définition*, ed. M. Bertaud and F-X. Cuche (Paris: Klincksieck, 1995) 361-371

C. Meurillon, 'Mémoire et vérité: itinéraire pascalien', in *Revue des sciences humaines* 244 (1996) 139-157

C. Meurillon, 'Oubli de soi, oubli de Dieu: écriture et oubli chez Pascal', *Revue des sciences humaines* 252/4 (oct-dec 1998) 23-36

J. Miel, *Pascal and Theology* (Baltimore: Johns Hopkins University Press, 1969)

B. Neveu, *Un Historien à l'Ecole de Port-Royal: Sébastien le Nain de Tillemont 1637-1698* (The Hague: M. Nijhoff, 1966)

P. Nora, 'Les Mémoires d'Etat', in *Les Lieux de Mémoire. II. La Nation* (Paris: Gallimard, 1986)

B. Norman, *Portraits of thought* (Columbus: Ohio State University Press, 1988)

O'Malley, J., *The First Jesuits* (Harvard: Harvard University Press, 1993)

J. Orcibal, *La genèse d'Esther et d'Athalie* (Paris: J. Vrin, 1950)

R. Picard, *Nouveau Corpus Racianum* (Paris: Centre National de la Recherche Scientifique, 1976)

A. Piéjus, *Le Théâtre des Demoiselles: tragédie et musique à Saint-Cyr à la fin du grand siècle* (Paris: Société Française de Musicologie, 2000)

J-L. Quantin, 'Port-Royal et l'histoire', *L'Histoire au XVIIe siècle, Littératures Classiques* 30 (1997) 21-32

S. Rendall, *Distinguo: Reading Montaigne differently* (Oxford: Oxford University Press, 1992)

P. Ricœur, *La Mémoire, l'histoire, l'oubli* (Paris: Seuil, 2000)

J. Rohou *Jean Racine* (Paris: Fayard, 1992)

P. -J. Salazar, *Le Culte de la voix au XVIIe siècle: formes esthétiques de la parole à l'âge de l'imprimé* (Paris: Honoré Champion, 1995)

V. Schröder, *La Tragédie du sang d'Auguste: politique et intertextualité dans Britannicus* (Tübingen: Narr, Biblio 17, 119, 1999)

P. Sellier, *Pascal et saint Augustin* (Paris: A. Colin, 1970)

P. Sellier, *Pascal et la liturgie* (Paris: P.U.F., 1966)

P. Sellier, 'Des *Confessions* aux *Pensées*: les seuils platoniciens', *Transversalités* 60 (octobre-décembre 1996) 21-30

P. Sellier, 'Imaginaire et rhétorique dans les *Pensées*', in *Pascal thématique des Pensées*, ed. L. M. Heller and I. M. Richmond (Paris: J. Vrin, 1988) 115-135

Q. Skinner, *Reason and Rhetoric in the philosophy of Hobbes* (Cambridge: Cambridge University Press, 1996)

G. Snyders, *La Pédagogie en France aux XVIIe et XVIIIe siècles* (Paris: P.U.F., 1965)

J. Sojcher, 'Portrait de l'oublieux', *Europe* 597-8 (1979) 14-29

R. Sorabji, *Aristotle on Memory* (London: Duckworth, 1972)

J. Spence, *The Memory Palace of Matteo Ricci* (New York: Viking, 1984)

H. Stone, 'Marking time: memorializing history in *Athalie*', *L'Esprit Créateur* 38/2 (1998) 95-104

F. Strowski, *Pascal et son temps* (Paris: Plon, Nourrit et Cie, 1907-8) 3 volumes

C. Strosetzki, *Rhétorique de la Conversation* (Tübingen: Biblio 17, 20, 1987)

C. Strosetzki, 'Madame de Maintenon et la tradition humaniste dans l'éducation des demoiselles de Saint-Cyr', *Autour de Françoise d'Aubigné Marquise de*

Maintenon, ed. A. Niderst (Niort: Cahiers d'Aubigné, 1999) 2 volumes, vol. 2, 425-446

J. -Y. and M. Tadié, *Le Sens de la Mémoire* (Paris: Gallimard, 1999)

R. Taveneaux, *La Vie quotidienne des Jansénistes* (Paris: Hachette, 1973)

C. Taylor, *Sources of the Self* (Cambridge: Cambridge University Press, 1994)

L. Thirouin, *Le Hasard et les Règles: le modèle du jeu dans la pensée de Pascal* (Paris: J. Vrin, 1991)

L. Thirouin, 'Pascal et *L'Art de conférer*', *Cahiers internationaux d'étude française* 48 (1988) 199-218

A. Viala, *Racine: la stratégie du caméléon* (Paris: Seghers, 1990)

A. Villard, 'Les *Mémoires du Sieur de Pontis* (1676) au plus près de la parole', in *Chroniques de Port-Royal* 48 (1999) 57-77

H. Weinrich, *Léthé: art et critique de l'oubli*, trans. D. Meur (Paris: Fayard, 1999)

D. Wetsel, *L'Ecriture et le Reste* (Ohio: Ohio State University Press, 1981)

V. Worth-Stylianou, *Confidential Strategies: the confident in French Tragic Drama* (Geneva: Droz, 1999)

F. Yates, *The Art of Memory* (London: Pimlico, 1994, first published 1966)

INDEX